The Apple
Bites Back

by

Gerald Ayres

a memoir
the early years

for Guy

Contents

Visiting Gertie

Mama drives like a wild woman. She has to. She is being chased.

Gunning the Chevy coupe into the deep dark that comes on after all the movement stops, it's scary. It is for me. I am five. But not for my brother. Nothing ever frightens him. He is seven.

Mama leans over the wheel trying to find her way through all the flashings out there, a pint of Four Roses between her knees, desperate to see Gertie. Gertie is her special friend. Gertie can always make her laugh, make her feel safe, keep the demons a mile behind. They are too close at the moment.

Mama has had one of her blue days. She can't get her head on straight, not these last days, not since the news came on the radio. The dirty Japs (as they were familiarly called) had bombed a place called Pearl Harbor which is more or less part of America. Mama whirled around from her ironing and the hot iron clattered to the floor.

"The Japs will be coming up the beach down there," she yelled to her sister.

Auntie was sent out the door for Mama's medicine. Mama spent days recuperating, medicating herself, warding off the demons that could jolt her body with a seizure.

With Papa still at sea, Mama needs Gertie. Once locked together in talk they are inseparable. They follow each other into the toilet so that none of their thoughts would be lost. One sits on the lip of the tub as the other tends to business. Mama always carries the beers, motioning Gertie on before her, saying,

"I got the ammunition."

Auntie Gladys sits quiet in the speeding car. She has her hat on as she always does when going out, a small hat with odd peaks that looks like crumpled blotter paper. Auntie watches the road, barely glancing as Mama lifts the bottle for a little slice of courage.

"Are we going to sleep at Gertie's?" I ask. I need to know.

Gertie lives in a bungalow near Balboa Park in San Diego. On a steep hill where the small houses cling together for support. Behind her the yard falls off into a gully so deep that at night you can't see all the way to the bottom. She calls it "the arroyo." It sounds like something from a fairy tale but in daylight, abandoned tires and scraps of things make it seem less so.

"Sure you'll sleep," Mama says, none too certain. "You boys, both of you."

Auntie Gladys turns to give us a mild frown. We are making Mama nervous.

We reach Gertie's at last. Mama brakes by the trellis with its surviving roses. She yells so Gertie can hear us.

"Kids, cats, dogs and rats!" It is her favorite way to announce our little group.

Gertie appears. She's large and doesn't leave much space for light in the open door. Everything is large, her lips are full and red as a stop sign. Her breasts, large as upholstery, bounce inside her silky robe. Even though it is billowy, it isn't enough to get around Gertie. A thigh shows at its flap as she races to embrace Mama.

Gertie can tell Mama is weak by the way she gets out of the car. Mama dramatically accepts her help. We all head in to the small living room kitchen room. The radio is ranting on about the Japs.

"Please," says Mama and Gertie turns it off.

Gertie fills a glass from the tap in her small corner of a kitchen that is Jewel Tea in all its parts.

"Go help Auntie, boys," Mama says and pours from the pint that has ridden over between her knees. The cheap booze tinctures the water like a chemistry set experiment. She sees we boys haven't moved and gives us a look over her glass. We get out of there.

At the Chevy coup, Auntie opens a door and Burr and she struggle to pry loose the front seat. Gertie comes out to add some muscle to the job. With a coordinated breath the two women yank it from its moorings.

We boys walk alongside the seat as the women carry it around the house and into the dark back yard. Burr and I each put a hand on it which doesn't help the carrying but we're anxious to help.

Mama appears at the door. She is holding blankets which Auntie rushes to take from her. The two women look for a space for the car seat.

"It's so warm tonight, you boys will - it's like camping out."

I try not to cry but she hears something teary in my voice. I say, "Mama.."

"Go to sleep, Baby," she says and takes her drink back inside.

Gertie is running water. More help for Mama's medicine. I hear Mama say, "I so needed to talk to him but I don't know, how do you call a big Navy base and ask?"

"Poor baby, what're you gonna do?"

"I want to die."

"Shush that."

Burr says not a word as the car seat is positioned on a strip of struggling grass in the small backyard. Auntie arranges the blankets for us, assures us she'll be sleeping on the couch if we needed anything. Mama of course will be sharing Gertie's bed. They may well talk to each other in their sleep.

Auntie kisses us. She's the only one who seems to think of it. She climbs the back steps, looks back with concern at us. There's a bit of a breeze and she tucks a bit of hair back under her crumpled hat. She goes in.

Burr and I both take a perch on the seat. He pulls a cover up to his shoulder. He gives me a hip shove and I tumble onto the grass.

I don't mind. I lean back against the seat. I can hear the women inside. They are pouring drinks and getting more weepy about life, their voices dipping when they get too close to certain subjects.

"Didn't they let Bickings call?" asks Gertie.

"You know there's troops moving and things going, there's a war."

"Is he talking to you again?"

"Stop that, Gertie." Mama lowers her voice. "The boys could be listening."

Mama appears at the kitchen window. It's a struggle, but she gets it to slide down into place.

I can see the harbor, an impossible distance below, the lights of the ships where the sailors live their dangerous lives and perhaps right at this moment are having bare knuckle fights below decks. Or maybe they are sleeping, though they probably sleep best when the ships are at sea and their cots are rocked by the waves.

Sometime in the night after the voices inside slur off to sleep, Gerry's eyes open. He isn't certain where he is. Maybe in Coca Sola in the jungle where his father slides like a snake through the dark foliage.

No, it's Gertie's, that's where he is. The kitchen light is off and the small patch of yard is black. Out in the dark he knows is the edge where things drop off, the arroyo where now you couldn't see the bottom even if you were brave enough to crawl over and take a look.

Gerry stares into the black. Spots move in front of his eyes, like tricks your eyes can play on you, like the early warnings Mama receives when a spell is coming on.

These are more than spots. They are figures rising to the lip of the arroyo. Small gummy bear men who seem also to sway in the slight breeze. They are the color of shadow and grey. They peer at him. Their eyes are ash.

Gerry cries, trying not to.

"Shut up, will you?" his brother says behind him.

Gerry stops all sound. He watches. The transparent figures jostle with each other, trying to get a look at him. They needn't struggle so hard. They will all have a chance.

They will be back.

Hanging Laundry

Papa was still at sea. Actually, not quite sea but someplace exotic called Coca Sola in the Canal Zone. He had not asked the Navy to transfer his dependents even though he was there for a long time.

Mama and Auntie and brother Burr and I remained in the wood shingled house that memory makes huge on a hill somewhere in San Diego. I was four.

Mama is hanging her wash on the line out back. She is thin and lovely, long flowing hair and an aristocratic air that made even this homely act seem right for painting. Like Madam Bovary before her, she was always in the mood for art, not knowing how to achieve it, but seeming to have the need for some lift out of the mundane.

I remember a patterned apron, full body, a ruffled collar, tied at her slim waist. Too slim, she would say. But that is her familiar shame speaking.

Her middle name was Olive though she would redden if anyone were to discover it because they would immediately say, "Olive Oyl!" which distressed her because she imagined herself as skinny as Popeye's girlfriend. Besides, she was married to a sailor herself.

Oh but her sailor was more beautiful than the squinty-eyed Popeye. His hair, as the poets would say, was raven and his eyes green and full of danger. He was from South Carolina where men were hard and laughed at a buddy who accidentally lost a foot in the sawmill because such things were laughable, being only a foot.

Madeline clamps the sheets to a line out back, pulling clothes pins out of the pockets sewn into the front of her apron. Gerry is in the kitchen, holding onto a table leg from the white enameled kitchen set that mom had not finished paying for. He watches through the screen door as mama hangs the sheets, the wind lifting them around her slim and pretty body, billowing them like rising loaves.

Mama screams. She drops her clothes pin.

"Gladys!" she screams.

She turns from her sheets and races up the back steps, shoving the screen door ahead of her. "Gladys!" she screams again and shakes her hands which desperately beat the air like trapped birds. She races past us boys through the kitchen.

Aunt Gladys, my auntie, races into the living room in time to see her sister run up the sofa, screaming.

"It's okay, baby," Gladys assures her, running, too late to catch mama as she pitches over the back of the sofa and falls out of view.

It is one of mama's seizures which she never calls seizures but spells, that making them somehow less shameful. Her legs appear around the end of the couch, spasming, her heels rattling against the floor as she rides out the storm, the inner lightning that jolts her body.

Auntie was a small woman, under five feet. She was in the most generous of terms, not an attractive woman. As her sister was tall and beautiful, she was misshapen and small. But by God's grace she is able to get her sister, half-conscious after the racking of her body, to her feet and into her room.

The room where my mother spent so much time was a dark and private place, a place she went to lie still as death, a damp cloth over her eyes to slowly recover from her spells. My brother Burr and I peer in at this motionless woman. She was aware of our stares, for my mother was magical and could see all things without looking.

"Go away, boys. Mama is resting."

My Auntie came in a run from a rapid errand she had just taken. She brushes past us boys into her sister's room. Mama lifts up on an elbow. She is eager for her medicine. It came in a brown paper bag. Mama grabs it from her sister, unscrews the top, takes a swig, holds it in her mouth without swallowing. She hums an urgent command, waving her finger in the direction of her empty water glass. Auntie hurries into the bathroom to fill the glass. Mama's urgent humming becomes more urgent. The liquid is sharp in her mouth and her eyes fill with tears. Auntie rushes back. Mama grabs the glass and chases down her medicine.

Mama catches sight of me at the door.

"It's okay now, Gerry, let mama be. Go away now." She rests her head back on the pillow, pulls the damp cloth back in place. "Mama will be okay tomorrow. We'll go to the matinee."

"We don't have to," I assure her.

"Of course we have to. We have to occupy ourselves with your daddy gone. Of course we will. Go away now. Let Mama rest."

Those Eyes

My mother turned to me, her breasts spilling out of the familiar pink nightgown. She seems unaware of the exposure, flesh and nipple, white flesh and pink satin.

Frightening to me. But she is drunk and doesn't notice. She tilts my head up to get a full view. She claims my eyes with hers.

"Let me see those eyes."

She is in her safe place, the acreage of her bed, furrowed round with rumpled covers and pillows. Somewhere in the folds are the pads on which she writes her plans since she can't actually get up and do any of them, but they are her dreams and when she has taken enough medicine from the paper-wrapped bottle at her hip and chased it down with water, she then can speak of them, her eyes straight up as though these dreams are played out on the ceiling, enough to make her croon and sometimes to cry.

"Let me see those eyes," she says to her second born.

She takes my chin to hold me in her gaze. Like a puppy I try to twist away.

"Yes, I see it, son. I can see it there."

"What, Mama?" I ask not wanting to know.

"Just like Mama. With her spells."

"What Mama?"

"You will have Mama's spells."

That seemed to comfort her. She needed me to be if not her, then part of her. I was terrified but comforted too. She was inviting me. At last.

I was let in.

The Home Front

The Second World War was a blessing for our family. It split us up. The fighting on the home front stopped. No longer could my parents blame the other for not showing enough love.

Consider there was no television then. The radio was background to all that happened and happened quickly. Papa was off to Jacksonville, Florida to join his squadron before deployment to the South Pacific. We were to join him but only briefly.

Mama packed quickly while on the radio the pure incisive trumpet of Harry James carried on about stardust, whatever that was. When the tragedy of her own feelings came up, she'd sit by the open suitcase and weep with the singing girl about her man with green eyes since her Bick had green eyes too. She was up and moving, keeping beat as the music turned to boogie woogie and that sister group was wailing on about their bugle boy. Once packed, we were hustled down to the train station with a mob of folks called "dependents" to get on a train to Jacksonville. I asked Mama if this was the Chattanooga Choo Choo. She thought this funny because it made me sound stupid so she repeated it to the other passengers aboard.

Papa was something called a warrant officer now which was a big deal and he and Mom were smiling. These were happy days, a string of them, as Mama put a gardenia in her hair and she and Papa went to the Navy base club to dance and came back late and the laughter that reached my room seemed happy. The laughter stopped. There was a shushing to be quiet that came from their bedroom. Then noises, small ones, and Mama sounded like a kitten being stroked.

Dad went off to the New Hebrides and we were sent to Fresno,

California, where my Uncle Burr had become a successful agricultural real estate man. The plan was that he keep an eye on his sister while Bick was off to war.

Mama hated to be so near her brother. She feared his sarcasm and equally feared his Nina Foch wife who was so tightly organized even her hair was pulled straight back without the relief of a single curl.

Mama dreaded the lectures from her sister-in-law - she should get up, be healthy and find a job. She should stop drinking beer. Aunt Van had no clue about the pint bottles of Four Roses that were mother's milk to mother.

Auntie answered the call to work. She sold Avon products door to door. I have in a case where I store Mama's lockets and things, a medallion given Auntie for being the best Avon salesperson in the area of Fresno, California in the year 1943.

Brother Burr and I collected empty coffee jars and turned them in at the local movie house and got to see the matinee free. We were all part of the war.

On occasion Mama would take us out for a drive. She especially liked the Mexican part of town because there was a corner where a woman sold her homemade tacos from a bucket. It was eating out, in a way, since as Auntie reminded us, restaurants made Mama nervous.

It was heaven to me. As I unwrapped its paper the taco sent up a cloud of corn that to this day thrills me. The taste of fresh corn flour and lettuce and meat and the burn of the hot sauce that I worried would be too much for my tongue but never was.

Mama made it out to a movie too. It was one with Judy Canova, a goofy actress, ugly as an old skillet. She was playing a WAC in this movie. She had won a medal. The officer, holding the medal in hand, was stymied. He didn't know how to pin it on Judy without, ah, touching her breasts. It was hilarious. We all laughed.

Mama suddenly got to her feet. She said, "Gladys!" and brushed past people to get to the aisle. Auntie and Burr and I were right behind.

Mama made it to the sidewalk and collapsed. She had a grand mal seizure under the marquee of the theatre. These were the days before

911 so no one was called but a crowd gathered round as Auntie held Mama's hand and stroked her face with a hanky as her sister rode out the storm.

A soldier boy stooped next to Mama. In retrospect I realize he was only ten years older than I, since I was then eight. But to me he was a man.

"You have a car here, ma'am?" he asked Auntie. He seemed so calm I felt suddenly safe.

"We do, yes, but.. I don't drive, not yet." Auntie never learned to drive.

Mama's eyes opened as the soldier boy lifted her in his arms and carried her, following Auntie, to the Chevy coupe. He drove us home.

He helped Mama to her room as she staggered, holding onto the soldier. He placed her on her bed, leaving her to Auntie.

He came to the kitchen where Burr and I sat at the table. He sat. He talked to us. He spoke for some time, asked us about what we were up to and where we were in school and stuff like that.

I don't want to criticize my Papa but he was a higher rank than this soldier and he gave orders and gave them loud and if you questioned them and you were a small boy he'd knock you flat. This soldier boy didn't seem to be that type. Maybe because he wasn't in the Navy.

The windows dimmed as night came on and Auntie had made coffee for the soldier, eyeing him with suspicion since it was her habit to be protective.

Finally the soldier stood. He gave Burr a friendly punch in the arm. He put his hand on my head, ruffled my hair. He smiled, that man, he smiled and left.

I often prayed he might return. He did in a way. He came back to that busy movie of my dreams and I longed to join him wherever he was even if it was war and bullets were all around.

I knew he'd still have that smile.

The Great Crossing

Word came in 1944 that Dad was coming back from the South Pacific. My mother rose like Lazarus from her sheets and pulled back the blinds and light flooded the house along with a joy that only my mother could create when that was the mood of the day.

It soon dimmed. Further communication told us Dad was ordered to go directly to the Pentagon. He instructed his wife to pack up Auntie and the boys in the two-door Chevy coupe and drive across country to join him.

I wonder in retrospect how well he knew his wife.

It took a week of sorting and packing and throwing out and repacking before we shoved off. The 3,000 miles with all aboard – "kids, cats, dog and rats" as Mom liked to say though we were without cats, dogs or rats – was nerve- wracking for Mom. It was afternoon, perhaps near four when we finally squeezed into place and Mama, with the familiar bottle propped between her knees and turning to check once more whether there was any on-coming traffic finally pulled out into our residential B Street where there was never any traffic and we headed off for the grand adventure, the great crossing.

Mom was on the up-swing of her medicine and sang a little of "Tangerine" the song my Dad loved most. She whistled impressing us again with what a terrific whistler she was. She told us we were soon to be going up into the high mountains. Like the mountains she had camped in with her own papa and mama.

"You can't get anywhere in life without climbing a mountain or two," Mama let us know.

She laughed to herself, said "Oh Lordy" and squinted to concentrate on traffic. She was having trouble with her rimless glasses whose tiny screws were loosening and she had repaired with daubs of red nail polish.

We reached the outskirts of Fresno. Mom was squinting more, telling her sister not to miss the turn off to the highway that would take us up to the mountains. Auntie took out a bobby pin to scratch her head and stared at the long trip log the triple-A had stapled together for us. She wasn't certain there was a turnoff.

Mom was having trouble with the road. The center line kept coming up under her left wheel. She swerved back into her lane. Honking behind us.

"Close your ears boys," she said and then screamed out the window, "Sonzabitches!"

We sensed the car was slowing. "Just a minute, kids," Mom said. She glided off the two-lane black top into a county park. She jammed the brake and we jerked to a stop by a picnic table. Mom opened her door.

"Just a minute, kids," she repeated.

Auntie rushed around the front of the car to help her. Mom shook off her hand. She went to a stretch of grass next to the table and sat slowly. And then, like a glacial cliff that finally gives up its shape, folded to the ground.

She slept. Auntie and Burr and I took out some of the snacks and sat in a circle around my sleeping Mom, silently munching and watching her. Was she even breathing, I wondered. Having seen it done in movies, I leaned over and put a finger under her nose to feel for breath.

I looked up and noticed Auntie was closely watching. Apparently she was concerned. I had never known her to show fear for her sister, as though it would be disloyal. I nodded to Auntie. Mom was breathing.

We made 35 miles that first day.

The next night stays with me. We were crossing a mountain range, a sign said we were over 4,000 feet up. Our motel was a cluster of small white-washed cabins among the trees. Each cabin was a place apart. There was a small wooden house for just my brother and me with a narrow sitting porch. Some paces off, the adults had a cabin of their own. I had an inexplicable sense I had entered paradise, but I wouldn't have known to form that thought at the time.

The conifers and pines at that elevation seem magical to me, rising like cathedral ceilings over us. I sat outside our cabin and breathed deeply, feeling what later I could identify as tripping. Decades later.

There is a ground cover that native Americans, the Miwok Indians to be specific, call kit-kit-dizze and the pioneers who were forced to cross these heights called "mountain misery." The pungent sap of these ground shrubs clung to their boots and could only be washed off by time. It gives off an aroma that is sweet and sour and increased my sense these mountains were magic. I breathed in these aromas and my heart raced without reason but it delighted me.

I go into the Sierras even today and am cast under its spell. I am again the eight year-old who looks up and sees his brother on the narrow porch of what is our house, our house apart, our house in the woods. He nods at me. What is that? Even today I wonder. I imagine how perfect it would be to escape to this place, my brother and I, the two of us, and breathe out the rest of our lives under the spell of the kit-kit-dizze, in the cathedral whose arches God had caused.

There, there is nothing else but grace and measure, richness, quietness, and pleasure.

I could not have known that almost thirty years later, on a gay commune in the Mother lode country, on the site of what was once a Miwok village, I was to realize this dream. With a new brother, brother related not so much by blood as love.

Coming off the mountain and with many stops to refuel both car and mother, we finally rolled into Salt Lake City. It was there that Mom decided she couldn't go on without a few days recuperation. We checked into a motel.

She sent her sister out for Mommie's Medicine and again my teetotaler Auntie went in search of a bottle. There was a problem. In order to purchase booze in this Mormon desert, you had somehow to register with the state and get a card saying it was okay for you to unscrew a cap.

Auntie did this, taking us boys out to a nearby diner where, I later reflected, the waitress could have been Ann Sheridan and the guy down the counter in the leather jacket, Humphrey Bogart.

Mom was slow to get her legs back. She had Auntie post an item in the personals in the paper. "Driver needed to share trip to D.C."

The ad was answered by a soldier boy. In memory he has the same face as the boy who came to our rescue under the movie marquee where Mama was riding out one of her seizures.

Auntie squeezed in back between my brother and me which my mother often pointed out was a relief because it stopped the boys' continual fighting over whether one or us had crossed the invisible boundary on the seat between us.

The soldier boy was Southern and said "Yes, ma'am" when Mom offered him an occasional nip of her medicine. Other than that, he was a serious driver, eyes on the road, miles rushing beneath us.

When we reached our housing in Arlington my dad came out in his uniform, now with sleeve stripes indicating he was lieutenant. The soldier boy popped out from behind the wheel and gave my Dad a smart salute. Dad returned it. The soldier boy shouldered his gear and went off.

"Who's that?" Dad asked Mom.

"Oh Bick, I missed you, baby."

Mom lay her head on his chest and let go tears of joy. I think they were joy.

Yankee Go Home

Dad is again stationed in Jacksonville and we are in a rural suburb. I didn't know what was waiting for me in the deep south. I had been sort of south in Virginia but that was really more D.C. than south. After the move to Jacksonville I got deep into it. Stepped into it.

I would say the kids on the block but out in the emerging suburbs where my folks rented a small house on cinder block stilts and asbestos tile siding, there were no blocks. Not so's you could tell. There was two lane black top roads with hand-dug gullies to either side and some distance back beyond the crab grass, the house itself. The gullies were runoff for the afternoon down pours: after a half day of leaden humidity even the skies couldn't take it and burst into a relief of rain.

The boys down the road all seemed to come from Georgia or Alabama Mississippi, not having occurred to any of their parents to hatch a brood in Jacksonville. They came to Jacksonville to work at that Naval Air Station and not being kindly disposed to cities found a cheap suburb that looked like open country. Scrub fields and pine groves.

The boys down the road spoke a funny slurry language that I grew not only to understand but carefully to imitate. I done done it in no time. I was told first day that I was a Yankee, something I had never considered and they knew that because I talked Yankee and soon learned that wasn't a good thing to be when Jon Barber cracked my shin with a pipe.

My mother, whom I was later to read about in college when I

discovered <u>Madame Bovary</u>, had a longing for culture and class, not something she brought with her from Reedley High School in central California, having received her diploma only because her father owned the farm equipment store and was a big man in town.

She did understand, however, that her younger son was soon running out the door bare chested and bare foot and speaking in some atrocious red neck manner. Since she hadn't a copy of Flaubert's novel around about a woman in the sticks longing to put a silk slipper on the next rung up, she turned to her movie magazines. The kings and princesses of Hollywood were her aristocracy. They didn't speak red neck. Only supporting actors like Jack Okie. Not Gable and Garbo & Co. I embarrassed her. Dad lived by his hands, having made it from seaman to Lt.Cdr. because he knew planes and knew them hands-on, proving invaluable in the war by keeping the Graumans in the air off the island of Santo Espirito when there were few supplies available. He might have tied them together with palm fronds for all I knew. What I did learn, and then only at his funeral since he never found reason to tell his sons anything, is he was flying over Guam one afternoon looking down at the massive junk yard of broken planes and came up with an idea. He carted off enough of those parts to put together a workable plane and it was added to his squadron. Given a challenge, he met it with fierce determination, kicking aside anyone who got in his way. Mom who craved some gentility down among the hicks, wanted a white picket fence out back. Marion Davies had one. She saw it in <u>Silver Screen</u>. Dad went to work, sawing and digging post holes and nailing slats and putting my brother and me to work painting it white, something we did not do quickly enough so he'd give us an instructional kick as he passed by, nails sticking out of his mouth so he couldn't follow up with a salty word or two.

Next to come from Dad's smoking saw blades was a picnic table. Now Madame Madeline could sit out back and pierce the top of a Schlitz with an opener and after the foam stopped spouting, could sip of an afternoon and admire the flowers. Not our flowers, the flowers of the flower farm just beyond the back fence. It was cultivated by an old black man in a large straw hat. I wondered if he did that all on his own. Mom, who was by then going occasionally to the Southern Baptist Church, explained the colored man didn't do it alone, he had God's help.

I was ten years-old. I didn't know about races. I didn't know what it meant that my father was raised on a tobacco farm in South Carolina. I didn't know what thoughts he grew up with.

I came in one day from the cross-roads store up the road where I had bought an RC Cola and pedaled back home bare-headed, bare-chested and bare-foot, like all us kids did in 1946. I told my folks that a colored lady at the store had told me that RC was better than Pepsi.

"No such thing as a colored lady," my dad let me know.

I was confused. In a dark voice he spelled out his truth. There can be colored women but no colored ladies. Only white women can be ladies.

My barefoot buddies who now grudgingly accepted me as I continued my assault on spoken English, were just goofing around one afternoon and decided to have a Klu Klux Klan meeting, just a pretend one. One of the guys had an uncle who was in the Klan and told him about the torch lights and the speeches. So he jumped up on the picnic table and waved his arms in the air and said how all the N-word folks should be shipped on back to Africa. The other guys laughed and applauded.

I glanced over at the flower farm. Some distance off the old black man was hoeing a row. Minding his business. I wondered whether he could hear.

I was told to hop up on the table and add a few words. I didn't know how, I said. Jon Barber hit me across the head and two others shoved me up on the table. I tried to get into it. I waved my hands in the air.

"Yeah, back to Africa. All them.." and I sneaked a glance over my shoulder. The old man with his hoe was nearby.

I jumped down off the table. Someone more skilled at this language took my place. I jumped on my bike.

"Come on, Jinx," I said to my mongrel terrier and left the yard. My buddies followed, going for their bikes.

They had run out of hate words for the moment.

Auntie My Auntie

My compulsively efficient Aunt Van arrived in Jacksonville, hair locked in place, airline tickets in hand, schedules to meet. Van informed Mama it was time, time for her to get up, she had to get on an airplane.

"I don't fly."

"Of course you don't. The airplanes fly."

My wealthy uncle Burr had arranged an extended visit, as it was described, to a psychiatric hospital in San Francisco, the Langley Porter Clinic. Quite famous.

For Mama it was an invitation to hell. She of course would like her fainting spells to go away but she wasn't ready to give up her paper bag medications that had worked so well so long.

Fortunately Aunt Van had come with enough pills to turn my mother into petrified wood. I remember Mama being moved along by Van as she made her way up the ladder to the plane. She did not look back at her husband and boys on the tarmac. She was concentrating on where she was going to plant her next step on the ladder.

Auntie Gladys took over the house but had no defense against the harsh regimen of my father. Mama at least had a rapier tongue that sliced him to size, but that was not Auntie.

Dad came in and out the door with new orders of the day, such as, no comic books left in the living room. Should you err, he'd suddenly appear in your room and start kicking you without explanation. The game was to race about the house with his foot propelling you until you discovered the forgotten comic book and could stow it in your locker. Of course this was not a ship and we did not have lockers.

Papa was a Lt.Commander by this time, the recent war pushing him into officer ranks without him having attended the Academy. He was what was called a "mustang" and as such felt the need to be fiercer having more to prove.

I lived in awe of my brother Burr. He stood up to my dad, lifted his fists. He paid a price for it, falling back breaking a dining chair but he jumped back, fists ready.

Burr ran off. He was gone for two days. Dad was on the phone. I could see Dad was frightened for his boy. A sheriff discovered my 13 year-old brother in a bus station in Macon, Georgia.

Where was he going?

North, he replied.

It never occurred to me he might be gone in search of his mother.

The sheriff sent him home. Dad was surprisingly soft on him. He took Burr out back and sat at the picnic table and leaned forward to speak in low tones. Burr's jaw remained fixed but he nodded. That satisfied the commander enough that he slapped his son on the shoulder and said,

"We'll do all right, son."

Having discovered the way to my father's love, I did as Burr did and ran off. With my Georgia-bred buddy Joe Pete. We took our 22s to hunt our food, we told ourselves, and ran off as far as the local woods.

We lasted one night. Joe Pete had managed to shoot a small bird from its branch and dinner was its burnt remains. The ground was hard to sleep on, only fit for the bugs who appropriately lived there.

The stars through the pine tops seemed spooky rather than winking and familiar.

We went home the next day. Auntie threw her hands up and said "I have to call your daddy."

While she called, I took a long bath. As Dorothy said coming back from Oz, "Oh Aunt Emm, there's no place like home."

These warm thoughts were erased as Dad raged into the bathroom, grabbed one of my thin arms and lifted me dripping from the water.

His belt was out. He whacked and then whacked some more while I screamed for mercy. He dragged me dripping into the hallway where he could get a wider swing. The whacking seemed to go on for a while.

Satisfied his point had been made, he slid his belt back in place. He looked down at my sobbing small self on the floor.

"You worried the goddam hell out of us," he said. He returned to the naval air station, his world of real men. His younger son had at last gotten a taste of his father's love.

Mama lasted less than half a year at the Langley Porter clinic. Five months proved her limit. I heard later she had a shaky beginning with the Freudians. On her first session she told the therapist she was willing to cooperate but the ONE THING she will never discuss is her personal relationship with her husband.

I know these guys are trained not to laugh but it must have been a struggle.

Papa put Auntie and us two boys in the Chevy coup and drove like an escaped prisoner across the country, stopping little and then with much grumbling about time lost.

The Mama we picked up at the clinic was surprisingly cheery. Had her hair done pageboy like a movie star. She was smiling and hugging her sister inmates who had come to wish her well. They gave her an autograph book signed like a high school year book. I got a look at it later. The women praised her for being such a good time, the life of the party if indeed that was what they were having in there. Maybe she'd bring some of that party spirit home.

We drove down from San Francisco to Fresno to visit my Uncle Burr and Aunt Van before our return across country. My brother Burr and I had a chance to see our cousins, Bernie and Tom, who had changed since the war years when we knew them. They had passed into puberty and the conversations out of ear shot had become technicolor.

The adults themselves spoke in whispers behind closed doors. Something was going on. I caught a fragment from my listening post under the kitchen window. Aunt Van had my mother trapped in a one-exit breakfast banquette.

"You have duties to Bick too. You're his wife and there are things a man expects."

I sort of got the idea but I'm not sure Mama did. She didn't say a word. She had a phobia about snakes and things, and wasn't about to talk sex with my proper Aunt Van.

We left the next day, the car packed as we pulled out of the circular drive of Uncle Burr's big house. Kisses all around. Mom and Dad got into the front. Auntie leaned through the back window and gave Burr and me a kiss.

"Get in, Auntie," we hollered.

She stepped back, taking a place between Uncle Burr and Aunt Van. Papa drove forward.

Burr and I yelled. Where's Auntie?

"She's not coming," my dad said.

My mother looked down at her hands and dropped a tear. "The doctor said it would be better."

Burr and I got up on our knees to see out the back.

"I'm never gonna get well if I don't learn to stand on my own two feet," Mama went on. "The doctors said so."

The hell with her own two feet. This was our Auntie. We watched through the back window as she receded in the distance. Auntie had her hands crossed in front of her, watching us watch her.

I slumped in my seat ready for the 3,000 miles. I stared at the back of my tormentors up front. I hit my brother's hand. He had let it stray across the invisible border between us. He slugged me. Dad yelled at us. Mama told him to be sweet.

They were warming up to old arguments.

Auntie at Mid-Century

"You take the key so I won't have to get up to let you in," Auntie says.

"Okay," I answer.

Locking the door behind me I head down the narrow walk that separates the whitewashed cottages of the modest motel that is, as it turns out, only a block away from where we are now living in Pacific Beach.

Letting the motel door close behind me, I walk swiftly past the Mexican youth clipping the lawn to the well-swept sidewalk and putting the bright morning sun behind me set out briskly.

Deep breath. Fresh deep breath of air. Fresh salt air. Through the skull cavity and into the lungs cooling and invigorating the mind. I have learned this from my coach, yes, skinny Gerry, he's on the track team. He's a distance runner, though he didn't know it. I ran the mile though hampered by saving too much of my juice for the end kick. I was afraid if I didn't I would, as Madeline's child, collapse early. To excel or God forbid even be successful would make a target of you and God would gun you down. Problem with that is if Madeline were to go down I would have to follow. We had a Siamese connection. The blood that came from her wounds would be my blood.

This was indeed a new age, or half of one.

1950. Mid-century.

Again we are in a flat rented house but this is Southern California and banana trees bend past our jalousie slats. Jasmine bushes bloom with their harsh intoxications and fill my room with an intensity that frightens me.

Auntie was sick now though seemed as matter-of-fact and calm as she had been all the years she raised my brother and me, fraught years when my mother's terrors landed around us like trajectories.

Auntie had been operated on for colon cancer. A colostomy had been installed, something that in her calm and matter-of-fact way my Auntie lifted her blouse to show me. A plastic sack, hanging down from a red oval mouth bolted into her abdomen. She illustrated how it worked: she squeezed her abdomen and a little pencil of excrement appeared and fell into the sack.

I took off jogging, pumping breath, varsity-ready. I went to scout a way for Auntie to make it down to the beach. I remembered somewhere along the cliff top an abandoned cement bunker, empty except for shadows and wind through its empty windows. There were stairs going down from there to the beach. This would be slow but safe for Auntie.

Before taking the stairs, I paused. My eye fell on the bunker, the abandoned cement structure at cliff top. It was a fortification built during the nightmare war of my childhood when the Japanese were only an interrupted radio bulletin away.

I had been told that a teenage boy had hanged himself in the bunker. Years back. Maybe more than a few.

No one knew more than he was a teenager and there was definitely a hanging.

A boy died in there. A dead boy.

I felt a strange joy akin to that sudden breath I took as I broke the surface after a roller had roared over me. What was it, this joy in knowing a boy had died, that once he had life and he had taken that life and now he had learned to sleep. I wasn't alone. I wasn't the only boy who knew there was always the liberty to die.

There was a way out. That is, of course, if I needed one.

By afternoon, I had Auntie sitting on the sand, a blanket over her legs, fretting about me as I body surfed. I went too far out, Auntie felt. I disappeared under breakers. She called weakly for me and I came back and sat by her on the sand. Without words, we skimmed over the years we had shared.

I heard laughter. A barge was bobbing out beyond the breakers. Kids were climbing up on it and pushing each other off.

"Where you going?" Auntie asked.

"Be right back."

I ran across a mat of dried kelp, rust colored, that crunched under my feet. I waded against the current until a breaker bore down on me and I took the soft route of surrender and dove beneath it. I popped to the surface and saw Auntie on the beach, waving me back. I returned the wave.

The barge was farther out than I had thought. I stroked toward it, arms aching, trying to avoid panic. By the time I pulled myself up on the barge I had it to myself. All the kids were gone.

I waved at Auntie, not certain that her eyes could see this far.

Ah Auntie, my Auntie, she gave me the good stuff. As I slipped as a child into her room, the only light coming from her Zenith radio on its small table with her Bible and her glasses. We listened to radio. I realize how much of the goodness that may be in me came from my Auntie.

She had spent the years since she was dropped off in Fresno in a boarding house paid for by my uncle. She often wrote to us with what seemed a stub pencil to say she was going to church and keeping busy with the ladies in the house and hadn't seen much of her brother or his family since there hasn't really been that much time. There was no rancor in her.

I learned about narrative from those radio shows in Auntie's room after Mama somewhere off passed out and the entire house relaxed, took a breath, its joists and joints seeming to relax. Those radio shows were all narrative, spared the visuals of film.

I later made a living as a screenwriter and I so favored narrative over effects that I was criticized (I think it was criticism) for being too novelistic. Truth is, the pioneers of film, the giants like Griffiths, like Capra and Ford and Keaton and Hawks and Houston never went to film school for there were none to go to. They didn't sit in dark screening rooms and feed off the corpses of past bodies of work. Their narrative instincts came direct from Dickens and Twain and Kipling, maybe the Hardy Boys. Or - and this is a real nut-cracker - from their own hard time experiences.

On my barge I looked north up the broad beach. No sign of man or his structures, just God's creativity. In that pre-historic age before condos, the broad sands led north without interruption to the village of La Jolla.

I went to La Jolla High School.

My brother was also enrolled but didn't show up at many classes. He haunted the Museum of Natural History in Balboa Park. He was the protégé of an old herpetologist, a snake man in short.

His failure to show up at school forced them to put him back, first one year and then a second until both of us ended up sophomores. Burr smirked through this as he did most things.

After one last fist fight with the Lt.Cdr. over the dinner table, he weaseled my Mom into signing a document that lied about his age so he could join the Marines. My father detested the Marines. Of course.

Burr was soon in Korea. On the front lines. For eighteen months.

I sat out on the barge, Auntie back on the beach, seriously sick thinking of my brother off crisping giant Chinese with his flame thrower. He had to come back. He was the hero who would someday help me break out of the manic castle of my childhood.

Shortly after the century circled to its second half I had a birthday. I was fourteen. My parents bought me a portable typewriter. I don't want to whine about how seldom gifts came from them; enough of that. The typewriter became my sanctuary. Hunched over it, relishing words as they struck one after the other on the paper, I was able to live outside Gerry.

Typewriter and an English lit book were the twin blessings of this new age. I remember the book where I first met Wordsworth and Dickenson and other off-the-path dreamers. Especially Whitman, the wanderer of dunes on the other coast. I looked up, imagined him taking the wind into his lungs top of the cliff.

I slipped from the barge and swam for shore. Auntie was waiting her blanket now pulled up around her shoulders. She came for this week to sit on the sands and pull a blanket over her legs and listen to the old voice of the sea. And in a month, it would all be silent.

She would be dead.

Slugging Jeanie

Jeanie made a terrible mistake being nice to me. I didn't know how to deal with it. I was sixteen, dedicated to Jesus and still I wasn't happy.

With my brother gone off to Korea, the ragtag family now made up of two mutually hating adults called Mom and Dad with their miserable son moved up to Glendale, more accurately, had been moved by BuPers of the Navy up to Glendale where I would endure my last year of high school.

Then I met Jeanie.

Because of my membership in an evangelical church, I was put on a list for a Sunday morning TV show, teen-only and evangelical. It was black and white as all things were in 1952. It was a local station and had little to lose turning on their generators that early on Sunday. Not much else was happening.

I quickly got the idea. We kids, none of whom I knew, sang gospel songs with the purity of our believing hearts and then testified how Jesus had turned us around on the path of life even though we had barely stepped onto it.

Jeanie was among those kids. From Van Nuys. Blonde, oh my God was she blonde. Tall. Too beautiful to look at without danger of straying from that path Jesus had laid out for me. Too beautiful to look at without worrying that my shame at being Gerry might show, my cheeks redden and my eyes cast down. It was no easy job being Gerry. He was a slug.

She had breasts. Jeanie above all had breasts. Jeanie wore sweaters. Those sweaters gave evidence of the breasts of Jeanie. I was tormented

28

with worry. Did she notice when I sneaked a glance at those two most perfect breasts? Would she consider it presumption from such a slug as I? Would she tell Jesus?

Jeanie did a frightening thing. She put her face dangerously near to mine, smiled and spoke what I believed were words but I had trouble deciphering them. But I found an answer. I recall myself saying, "Glendale. Herbert Hoover High School."

She smiled and I began to think nicer thoughts about Hoover High.

"Class of '53," I explained.

"You mean you're a senior."

God, what a dumb ass I am. No one says "class of '53" unless you're an old grad but I couldn't have been that because no one in my class had graduated yet. You see the logic.

"I like the way you sing," Jeanie said.

So other than knowing that I wasn't good looking like my brother (words of my mother) and that I was bucktoothed (photos say it wasn't true) I sensed some danger now that I was growing over six feet. I might draw attention to myself. Things got only worse when I was told by Jeanie that I sang well.

I went home to my puberty cave and instead of reaching into my J.C.Penny briefs and working my ever growing handle to a Jeanie-fed conclusion, I instead sang. I listened as out came, "Jesus is a wonderful savior, He will carry you through.."

I listened again. This is what Jeanie thought was good singing? Mother opened the door since it was her privilege never to knock. She inquired sharply,

"Are you okay."

"Sure, Mom."

"Well, all right." She gave the room a quick surveillance. She was none too convinced.

Having been so frightened by Jeanie's kind words, I did the only sensible thing. The next Sunday morning I avoided her. I sang lustily as the camera moved in, trying to prove Jeanie not wrong about my talents but above all not wanting her to terrify me again.

After our half hour on the air, Jeanie crossed directly in front of me.

She smiled with a beam that would have melted the tundra and most damaging, winked at me.

"Hi," she said, given greater eloquence than I. I only nodded.

I ran home and shoved a chair under the knob of my door and pulled down my jockeys and slowly and in deepest terror, gave myself to Jeanie. Oh, Jeanie.

The next week I got even with her. Before she could speak to me, I said, "Hi" and slugged her on the arm. She seemed not to care for that. She opened her hymnal. The tiny camera light went red and she sang. It took me a beat to join in.

After our final prayer and Jesus at last was given a rest, we had cokes and cookies, the whole group of us young believers. Jeanie looked at me over the rim of her paper cup. I tried not to read too much into it.

"Do you like poetry?" she asked.

"Sure. I mean, some of it. I'm just getting into it. At Hoover. I got a great teacher who really has really.."

Where did I suddenly find all these stupid words? "Miss Shade, she's an old woman but poetry, she knows all about her poetry." I spoke the truth. Helena J.Shade was more iconic than cliché, a maiden lady in black crepe dress marked with chalk dust. She introduced me to my mates, mates for a lifetime. Starting with Whitman.

Jeanie put down her cup, came in close in that way that terrified me and said, or was it a whisper, I remember the words, "You don't have to hit me."

It might have seemed impossible for me to hate myself more but at that moment I did.

She handed me a small book and walked off. I looked at the book in my hand. It was called "The Prophet." Written by someone called Kahil Gibran. I read it through twice the first night. I forgot this was someone named Kahil Gibran. For me, the words were Jeanie's.

My folks owned a green Studebaker with a needle nose that resembled a target, one chrome ring inside another. I had a license now and since my folks were taken by roller derby and Gorgeous George wrestling and didn't like going out except for Wednesday night at church, they let me drive the car over to Van Nuys.

Jeanie's mother didn't seem like a mother. She was sparky and pretty and sexy and genuinely happy to see me. What's more, she beat it out the door soon after my arrival leaving me alone in the Van Nuys ranch house with her daughter. There was no father around. There had been a divorce.

Where and what went on in that living room in the ensuing months, dear reader, I confess I can't recall. There are only images. Kahil Gibran was soon joined by Omar Khayam. A fire was lit – that is the gas burner in the fire place was lit. The weather was not cool enough to warrant but poetry required it. We discovered, one of us did, James Joyce and took deep pride in reading <u>Ulysses</u> aloud to each other, imagining we were so sophisticated we understood what was being said.

Memory serves up images of the throw rug in front of the fire place. Images of the tentative, tense wrestle with love, two Christian and chaste teenagers invading each other's mouths and impressing their tensing bodies on each other. They nodded so earnestly together that like a double exposure in film, their heads magically occupied a single space. Two heads merging into one.

My mother became aware of the long hours I spent with my door closed. She burst into the room to discover me staring fixedly at a photo of Jeanie propped up in my civics book. She had the goods on me now.

"You ought to spend as much time thinking of Jesus." It was the first spiritual advice my mother had ever given me.

The revered maiden lady, Helena Shade, had wrangled me a scholarship to Yale. Jeanie and I shed tears as she stayed behind to attend Occidental in Pasadena. We had remained chaste but even though we took our Jesus seriously, we had been orgiastic in our hearts.

I bought Jeanie a red angora sweater before I left. If there was one thing I could imagine improving on the breasts of Jeanie, it would be that red angora sweater. Perfect met pluperfect.

Because my mother heard it was cold in the east, she sent me off to Yale with a blanket. It was vibrant red and called a Hudson Bay with a broad band of black at either end. And again because of the anticipated cold, she bought me a sweater on Brand Boulevard, the main street of Glendale. It was nubby and heavy and gave my mother the impression of protection against the cold of a real winter. She had never experienced one.

When I arrived at Yale I discovered everyone was wearing khakis called "chinos" and tweed sport jackets. I had enough pocket money for the chinos. The jacket would have to wait.

"Where is this place?" my father had asked. He was sitting in whatever chair had followed him from our last move. He never seemed to settle enough in any of our houses to have a special chair.

"New Haven. That's in Connecticut."

My father was grazing the morning paper. While not behind the paper, he spent hours studying his Bible. He had gone from a warrior for Uncle Sam fighting the Japs to being a warrior for Christ and a menace to any sinner who crossed his sights.

"You could go to Bible school. There's a good one out here in Pasadena."

"Now, Bickings," my mother said from her dark room down the hall. "The boy doesn't want to be near us, leave him be. He knows what he wants."

Her girlfriend Thelma had a son who married a local girl who loved to shop with her mother-in-law. This guy worked up to become manager of the tire department at Sears which kept him near his mother and away from uppity attitudes, both virtues my mother admired.

My parents assumed that if Yale wanted me enough to give me a scholarship they would be generous enough to send a ticket. They were not.

I caught up with the last guy to receive a scholarship to Yale from my high school (always one a year) and for eighty bucks bought into a ride with him and two other Yalies. It was the first time I heard they called themselves "Yalies." The drive took three days and two nights.

The car rarely stopped. I rarely slept. My gums bled from exhaustion when we arrived in New Haven.

Before I left, I had walked up the hill above school and knelt in a scrub-oak thicket and reached for God in prayer. Behind closed eyes where I so often had seen Jesus appear now came Jeanie whose breast I had enshrined in red angora. I considered it a holy act, the way she pulled her sweater off and then as a miracle the way she managed to reach behind her and unhook her bra so it fell down her arms. Her nipples, the taste of them was still fresh on my tongue. On prom night I licked them while we scrunched about in the front seat of the family's needle-nosed Studebaker and here again these nipples took center vision just as I was trying to get a bead on Jesus.

I knew I would have to ask forgiveness for that. Perhaps Yale would help.

My Posture Photo

The reason I walked out of Yale my senior year a few months short of a diploma had to do with my posture. It started me off with me failing my posture photo.

I would like to say it had to do with my mother but she never came within 3,000 miles of the place. Still I had inherited from her a congenital spine of irregular curve and twist, not enough to tempt children to rub my back for luck but enough to be picked up on the posture photos which were obligatory for Yale freshmen.

Within a week of the matriculation of the class of '57, all of us lined up naked as birth at the gym complex to be photographed, side view and front. Small sticks had been glued down our spines, their angles of repose measuring how far off the norm our posture was. If deviation was found, you were ordered back to a number of posture classes in the expectation that twisting and bending would line up your spine.

I was the last man standing, though imperfectly, in that class. Rather than kick me out of Yale, which they didn't have the power to do, they turned their heads and suggested I not bother to come back to class.

All good men of Yale, including the legendary Dink Stover of the previous century, known for sitting on an old Yale fence until he got dents (or so a song suggested), Dink and all the men of Yale stood tall with spines straight and, of course, good families to give them fortitude for the life coming up.

This was 1953. Eisenhower was president. The country was in a long yawn, having just wakened from the war. Yale was all male at the time, mostly the sons of Wall Street. Then there was Gerry, innocent of his future, making his way across the campus lugging his synthetic suitcase with its few items called personal and its Hudson Bay blanket.

He arrived a day before school was to start. He had access to his room in Bingham Hall on the Old Campus (all freshmen) but not to the massive freshman dining hall which wasn't to open until the next day. He would be dependent on the three squares a day he'd take in that noisy hall. His NROTC navy scholarship paid all tuition and threw in fifty bucks a month for expenses but even in the 50s that didn't feed a 17 year-old.

Gerry walked beneath Harkness Tower which was called Gothic though he wasn't sure why and into the vast green of the freshman campus, a commons enclosed by buildings older than any he had seen in the various sailor towns his father had moved them to. He stepped cautiously.

He couldn't deny a little thrill, as though a photographer might be lurking and his picture in these brochure-surroundings might appear in Holiday magazine. It was in Holiday he first saw Harkness Tower, shot through a leaded casement window with a pair of shoes resting on the sill, white shoes which the caption told him were called "bucks."

A little butterfly migration of a thrill, yes, he felt that but mostly he felt terror. Not just unease but formidable terror, the strong meat of suffering his mother taught him to offer up daily to placate their demons.

He found his way to the fourth floor of Bingham Hall. There was no one in sight. He slid his suitcase under the bed, a single creaking spring and a rolled up mattress. It sat parallel to another which told him he was to sleep for the coming year next to someone he had never met.

He dug out his genuine leather billfold and discovered he had five dollars and thirty-four cents. Yale would feed him, but not tonight.

He hustled down stairs. On the ground floor a door was open. Inside was the upper classman who was to monitor the entry's freshmen in some unspecified manner.

Gerry rapped lightly.

"I was wondering – you in the middle of something?"

The slim young gentleman looked up and a practiced smile took over his face.

"No, no, not yet you're not interrupting, you just go on ahead tell me what's on your mind."

The monitor was Southern and seemed soft of bone. He tended to list to one side as he spoke, his hands in the air leading the rich chorale of his words, which, being Southern, were sweetly flavored.

I told him I was looking for someplace open to get a meal.

"You go out through the gate there, see that arch? There's a gate there then just up the right there's a couple of really nice little café restaurants. Just up the right but across the street on the left side, you hear?"

The diner was Greek. That is, it said in chalky lettering on the window that the food it served was Greek. Gerry had never eaten Greek before but it was a sure bet that the Greeks knew hunger as well as any of the rest of us. He slid onto a counter stool and checked the menu. He gave it careful study for it spoke of things he had never heard of before.

The daily special. $3.50. Breast of lamb. He had not had lamb. He had had breast of chicken, he knew what that was, so he decided this being a new city and certainly a new life, he'd give the lamb a try.

It was disaster. This breast was not at all like the breast of a chicken. It was more like the breast of his mother. It was literally the lamb's breast and though protected from detection by a covering of olives and peppers and spices unknown in Jacksonville or Corpus Christi or other towns familiar to him, it was unmistakably the spongy substance of an animal's breast. Once he got it into his mouth he couldn't swallow. He slipped it into his paper napkin.

"You not finishing this?" asked the big counter man with the hair foresting his arms.

"I'm not hungry, not really."

"At your age? I was always hungry." He lowered his voice.

"Couldn't keep my pecker down."

Gerry wondered whether that was something Jesus wanted him to hear but this was his new life so he nodded.

"I've been driving for three days. My gums bled."

He shoved the plate from under him to clear the air of all the spices. He put his meager fiver on the counter and waited for the even more meager change. He was made uncomfortable wondering what kind of pecker that man with the enormous belly must have and whether all that hair grew down to greet it.

That first night at Yale he slept in the room alone. He was in a strange bed in a strange city, seemingly at the far edge of what was safe and familiar. He fought for sleep, trying to ignore his heart's knocking.

The next day three roommates arrived. They were all from something called a prep school. It was called Taft. They were all wrestlers. They had attentive fathers who dropped them off and presented them with porcelain Yale mugs that were placed on the mantel but were seldom used because the boys preferred drinking from quart bottles, especially after a wrestling match, to let their tensions out and when the tensions were at last replaced by good times they broke the bottles on the floor which made creeping out to the john in the night precarious. They belched a lot.

The only problem was my knowledge I was sent to Yale to convert the campus. Sent by Jesus, I was told by an underground evangelical group I had joined, spiritual commandoes who did the follow-up work with recent converts at the Billy Graham rallies. In Southern California where such groups grow as rapidly as bacteria in a dish, my group was called the Navigators. They were depending on me.

Sometime in the first week the boys across the hall gave a cocktail party. They were boys, surely, but seemed more like grown men with grown men's ways of standing and holding their glasses and talking what seemed like man talk. They wore blazers with prep school emblems sewn on the pockets and regimental ties that I learned should only come from J.Press not Brooks Bros. and certainly not the Yale Co-op.

I watched with fascination as one of the young gentlemen poured liquor into a silver shaker and gave it, as its name would suggest, a shake. Martinis. So that's where they came from.

I stepped back to let one of this superior breed step by and in so doing accidentally jostled the host behind me. His martini spilled down his pedigree tie. He gave me a tired look which I took for disapproval.

"You shouldn't drink if you can't hold your liquor, old sport," he said to me.

Within minutes I was back in my room. The roommates had stayed on to make new friends and compare prep schools. I sat in the window seat and looked out at the intimidating campus, at the colonial brick building with a bronze statue of Patrick Henry just below. He had his hands tied behind him. He was looking up, perhaps at eternity where he was about to go for having preferred liberty to life. Such men as that had been on this campus and here I was, not even able to hold my liquor which of course I hadn't drunk but how were they to know?

There was laughter from the party across the hall. I dug into my bag and took out my Bible. I had underlined so much of it. It was time I reviewed things.

The three roommates slammed back into the room. I barely had a chance to slip my Bible behind me in the window seat.

Cecil, Hero

Dad was wrong. Yale was not a godless place. It was a place of different gods and to my surprise, I was eager to embrace at least one of them.

The arts.

Which didn't particularly please the US Navy.

I entered Yale with a major of Electrical Engineering. My freshman courses included calculus, physics, economics and a particularly tiresome course in military history. Not only was I defeated by the text, a phonebook-sized manic ramblings of a war-crazed Prussian by the name of Clausewitz but it was the only course that kept up the pretense that we were actually members of the military. We stood to attention as the instructor entered. Before prying open the Clausewitz, he'd suggest "At ease" which wasn't necessary since the Yale undergraduates never got far enough above ease to actually require an order to settle back into it.

Since Yale was a liberal arts institution we were required to take a freshman survey course of English Literature. Enter Cecil. My instructor, Cecil Y. Lang.

This narrow slip of an academic with refined English features was the first grown man I had met who was openly proud of poetry. Not my father, none of my uncles, they were not on the poetry road. They would sneer at those who were, the message being that such were not real men. I got the message.

My uncle Bill, for instance, Navy like my father, would turn from his perch at the bar and deck the guy next to him. "Why you do that?" Dad would ask. Uncle Bill shrugged. He didn't like his looks. Not much Swinburne in that.

But not to worry, Cecil Lang seemed to have his hormones in order. He had wife and child and, most impressive, had returned from duty in the same South Pacific where my own head-thumping father had served.

Here was a poetry fanatic, a man of small bones, who said while in basic training a top sergeant had barked that he was going to own his ass and take his soul while he was at it.

Cecil laughed not so much in scorn as disbelief. What a bizarre idea. His soul would surely bring a higher price than the threats of a sergeant.

It never occurred to me before Cecil entered my freshman classroom that grown men read poetry, not only without apology, but with apparent relish.

Starting with the simple fable of Hemingway's <u>Old Man and the Sea</u>, Cecil introduced me to another notion: read each word for what it says; read each word for what it doesn't say.

There's a lot going on in literature and it takes a little looking. Metaphor and simile and that double-speak called irony, then allusions that if strung like Christmas bulbs light up when passed through the charged field of literature.

I preferred poetry to prose. For one, my buzzing neurotic skull kept me from reading too long (God save me from Hardy) at one sitting, for another, poetry seemed magical.

I thought of words on paper as dry chemicals which when mixed with the solvent of my passing eye, caused catalytic sparks to fly. John Donne, Andrew Marvel and all those sexy bad boys of the past, they came alive in me and changed the way I saw.

If I hadn't started Yale with the image of Cecil the Fearless laughing at the burly sergeant, I might not have changed. I would have lived a different life.

Cecil started each class with a ten minute quiz. Early along, he wrote on the board, "How does Hemingway's <u>The Killers</u> speak to the question of being your brother's keeper."

Next class, Mr.Lang stood before us and said he was prepared to tell us his thoughts on the matter but decided not to. "Instead, I'm going to read you what Mr.Ayres has written. He has said all that I could."

He read my exam paper aloud to the class. I slid back in my chair, studied my crossed hands and prayed that Madeline wasn't listening or Jesus either. Stepping out in life was stepping into danger.

Lang spoke to us of a story we were reading by James Joyce, titled <u>Clay</u>. It focused on a bird-like older woman who reminded me of my own Auntie. Her family tried not to notice her foibles: how her accidental choice of clay among the Christmas favors was a warning of death. How it portended the sweet lady's own death.

I was stunned. Pieces of my life were showing up in ways that Calusewitz never got around to.

Mr.Lang looked at his watch and announced the class was over. He was fibbing. What he meant was he was now at liberty to light up a smoke. He pushed open the window to blow the smoke out and told us we were free to leave but that he was about to discuss next week's exam.

None of us left.

Following Cecil reading aloud my exam, I changed my major to English Lit. The Navy couldn't stand in my way, but they weren't happy. I felt a sudden daring, something dangerous was being done.

Seventeen and already I was finding my heroes, modest ones perhaps like my Auntie, those sure to inherit the earth: Helena Shade at Herbert Hoover High School who warbled through Wordsworth till fields of daffodils danced in my head. And now it was Cecil the Fearless, returned from war to take on the academy.

Let me quote W.H.Auden on the returning veterans:

> Instructors with sarcastic tongue
> Shepherd the battle-weary young
> Through basic courses..
>
> And nerves that never flinched at slaughter
> Are shot to pieces by the shorter
> Poems of Donne.

Mr.Lang was 32 when he was my mentor. I note he was 82 when he died in Virginia in 2002. He had become an honored professor of English at the University of Virginia. He edited the <u>Letters of Swinburne</u> in six volumes and wrote other learned tomes. I note that Harold Bloom, the popularly recognized brain of literature, had a lively correspondence with Lang. Now that I would like to read

I wonder if he would have found it amusing that I ended up in Hollywood yet still fueled by the high octane of poetry.

A gift from my hero, Cecil.

A Girl Named Mercer

I had never met a girl named Mercer but I did my freshman year.

It was I think a tradition (but then how many repetitions does it take to make a tradition?) that freshman girls from Smith come one day a year to visit the freshmen boys at Yale. Yale was not co-ed in those ancient of days.

I noted one such visitor milling among the sunny crowds on the freshman quad, a brunette with Grace Kelley reserve and no shortage of beauty.

I came up to her as she stood among a small group of girls and I acted the goof as was to be expected of a boy of the west and offered to give her a tour of the freshman campus. In fact, I could make it simple: look in all four directions and you have seen it all without taking a step. Apparently these girls liked goofy because Mercer fell into step with me. We had a polite and proper lunch in the cacophonous freshman dining hall.

Mercer was a well-bred girl from Smith which meant no sex, of course. Fine by me. Between my twin commitments to Jeanie and Jesus and my general terror of thinking myself acceptable in sight of either Jesus or girls, I was just as happy to be walking with such a beauty.

My entry-mate Jim Herlan, as penniless as I, had landed a weekend job in the Italian suburbs delivering groceries for a ma-and-pa store. He was a pal. He got me to stand in for him a few times. Spending my Saturdays in a pickup carting provisions to smiling old ladies who tipped a nickel or two was no big sacrifice. Why not? You think I wanted to be singing boola-boola down at the Yale bowl with the swells in camel hair coats? I had done that once, minus the coat, of course. I had a little boola in me but couldn't muster enough to make it stick. Besides, it was expensive.

I spent my last nickel to visit Mercer in Northampton, snagging a ride with a Yalie who seemed so overtly pleased with how he charmed the girls that he couldn't wait to drop me on campus and forgot about me. He disappeared.

Mercer took me to lunch in the village where we ate, my God, raw clams. Mercer of good manners insisted that she was the hostess up here in Massachusetts so she covered the check. My protests were feeble.

After a polite walk back to her house and a tentative buss on her cheek, I walked through the dark campus aware of two simple truths: Smith girls don't kiss and I had no ride back to New Haven.

I dug out my last few bucks to rent a room in what looked like a boarding house, flaking wall paper, a Police Gazette on the table next to the creaky spring bed. It rained all night. I heard every drop, unable to sleep, in terror at being so utterly alone, belonging to no one, certainly not to the girl who had permitted me only a brushing kiss on the cheek.

In the morning there was a gathering in a local tavern and jazz was played while the proper young in sweaters and ties nodded their serious heads to the beat. I was introduced to Brandy Alexanders again quietly paid for by Mercer then found myself heading back to New Haven with some loud Yalies I didn't bother to know. I slept.

I was puzzled why Mercer invited me down to Georgetown (was it Baltimore?) to meet her parents or why they were looking at me over their tea cups in that townhouse parlor, or rather, how I perceived they were looking at me – cold judgment, polite curiosity? Polite, certainly. What were they thinking? In Georgetown they don't clue you in.

I felt out of place in this genteel parlor, this boy from the south, from asbestos-siding houses on cinder block stilts, this boy with the booze-crazed mother and phallic-armed father, here, sipping tea.

It never occurred to me they might have been sizing me up, that having invited me for the weekend they might have considered me in some way worthy of their daughter. It was never a thought I'd have, even though Mercer sent me a pair of argyle socks for Christmas, perhaps knitted by herself.

Above all, I never saw what they might have: a good looking young guy (forgive me, Mother, this is heresy) with an eager and not baseless wit, ingratiating to a fault perhaps but at least cut with a redeeming cynicism.

And how did I come by that? Okay, I guess I just described Madeline.

My friend Jim and I went to a way-off-campus art house before they knew to call them that, a converted Quonset hut that showed such oldies as <u>All About Eve</u> and <u>Laura</u>.

We were both thrilled by Clifton Webb's character in <u>Laura</u>, the imperious and deliciously cruel Waldo Leidecker. He had a tongue like a scythe. We tried to model ourselves on Waldo. And then when George Sanders appeared in <u>All About Eve</u> here was another paradigm to fit our freshman selves into: the equally imperious and cruel Addison Dewitt.

When these two men drew their tongues from their sheaths, the world assumed a protective stance.

We nurtured the notion that our heroism would come from words launched with appropriate hauteur. We two un-pedigreed mutts, the meek ready to inherit the earth as promised, sharpening our tongues for life ahead.

Looking back through the wrong end of the telescope, I realize that quipping to Mercer that I was her appointed guide was pretty much what my white-hat father had said to the frail girl from Fresno, my mother, when she paid a quarter to take a launch out to visit the <u>Saratoga</u>.

In my case, that's as far as the comparison went. Mercer and I faded apart. She scared me.

Too much beauty.

The USS Missouri

I was 18 the summer of 1954. I was in an ill-fitted midshipman khaki uniform. I had taken a train from New Haven down to Norfolk, Virginia to go aboard ship for my first summer cruise, part of my NROTC obligation to the Navy that was paying my way through Yale.

I walked down the pier where the battleship was tied up. Over my shoulder was slung my heavy canvas sea bag with my gear. I looked up at this giant ship and felt as small as Jimminy Cricket.

This was the battleship USS Missouri.

Actually I felt terror. No reason for that. I was a healthy kid, six foot two weighing a sliver-thin 154 pounds and even though I had pretty-boy looks I never thought them good enough since my mother had awarded me something second-prized called "personality." The handsome honors went to my brother.

Under the weight of the sea bag, I shambled up the steep plank. I had the impression that all of the 2,000 plus crew dropped what they were doing and turned to catch the pathetic sight of me. I saluted the duty officer and found enough voice to ask "Permission to come aboard, sir." He waved me on, not knowing the peril this involved.

I was assigned a bunk – rack as it was called – and told the cabin number but not where to find it. I asked a white hat and he jerked a thumb in the direction of starboard forward. A few jerked thumbs later I was in a deck-level large compartment that seemed like a barracks though its walls were metal and grey and the racks were five tiers high hung from the wall, or as I quickly learned to call it, bulkhead. My rack was fourth up, meaning I had about five inches clearance to the midshipman above.

The place was noisy with metal locker doors being slammed as the Academy guys (the chosen race from Annapolis) stowed their gear with the neat cornered-off precision of bricklayers. I prayed for invisibility.

I looked about for my locker. I approached a buffed-out Academy guy standing by his locker in baggy boxer shorts, standard issue, tied with a cotton string since buttons would gum up the shipboard laundry. I asked him if he knew where locker number so-and-so was. Without spoiling his perfect record of contemptuous superiority he said without a look up, "Message to Garcia." I was stammering a further question when he was generous enough to look at me and said in an even sterner voice, "Message to Garcia."

After I located my locker behind racks in a deservedly humble corner I was told by another "rot-cee" (as in ROTC) midshipman that the Academy guys were all familiar with this Garcia story going back perhaps to the Spanish-American war. An American hero was asked to take a message to a sympathetic dark-skinned collaborator named Garcia somewhere in the jungle. Was it Cuba? Without asking where or how, the intrepid Yank took off into the jungle and did not look left at attacking animals or right at tempting fruit but walked until there were no steps left between him and the hidden Garcia.

As things turned out, he found his Garcia and I found my locker. As I stowed my gear I was terrified that some of these fearless sea jockeys would note that I was in fact an impostor so I acted as if I were invisible, kept a grim face to cover the roiling panic within and went about my duties as best I could. Above all, not reveal I was a mutant: boy on the outside, inside a sick panic-consumed middle-aged woman who should be behind drawn blinds with a pint at her side being kept afloat by her abused but enchained younger son. His battle station should by rights have been his mother's mattress side not the loading room of a sixteen-inch gun.

We stood at quarters the following morning for an hour. The deck hummed with internal life as the massive ship pulled away from the pier. With the first motion of the ship I tightened as if going over the top of a roller coaster, readying for the descent. A strong compulsion to break ranks and jump to the pier passed quickly. We were off Virginia Beach, moving independent of land. It was a new sensation of both captivity and freedom. The buildings on the beach faded from view as the battleship took the center of the formation joined by its sister ship, the USS New Jersey (a rare event) plus a light cruiser. These larger ships were soon circled by a screen of destroyers. They became my new points of reference, dotting the horizon on every quarter. Fear passed and a satisfaction, serene as the surrounding water, took its place.

I was at sea.

As a lowly third-class midshipman, I rose at 0515, thirty minutes before the crew, and bare-foot, trousers rolled, joined my mates to scrub the starboard forecastle – that is, fo'c'sle. The decks were washed down with sea water pumped through thick canvas hoses. Then sand was thrown by a boatswain, much as a planter sows his seeds. We third-class lined up twelve-abreast with stiff brushes to work the sand into the teak wood decks. We progressed horizontally on the deck until the end man, squeezed against turret or life-line screamed, "Shift!" and we started the slow work in the other direction. After the sand scrubbing the decks were again washed down with sea water and the line of youngsters, now armed with broom-handled squeegees, scraped the decks dry.

Occasionally they produced coarse bricks called "holy stones" with a center socket worn into them and we were expected to apply enough pressure with a broom handle into the brick to go at scraping the teak wood – thus, holy stoning.

After the deck work I hurried to my locker to change for chow, that is, breakfast. Because of my deck crew job and due to the fact that first-class were privileged to step in where they pleased, I was usually one of the last to go through the chow lines. I wasn't sure whether the white-hat cooks were hostile to me or to midshipmen in general, but their crisp-burned spam was thrown at the tray with vehemence. At times there was a wait while a disgruntled cook wiped the sweat from his brow on his skivvy shirt arm, took a drag from the cigarette hanging from his lips and returned to serving.

I was privileged, I think it was a privilege, to be given brass polish and rag and to daily shine the plaque implanted in the teak wood quarter deck. The plaque, you could learn from reading the legend, marked the spot where the Japanese imperial government signed surrender papers while Gen.McArthur and top Navy brass looked on. This had happened many years before I got aboard, at the end of World War II. Years before, I thought. I stop now and consider: this was 1954. The war ended nine years before. But when you're 18, nine years is half your life.

My 30-year Navy father hated McArthur for setting the dress code of the day for the surrender in Tokyo Bay: undressed khaki. It was meant as a humiliation to the Japanese who arrived in top hats and morning coats to find their conquerors in open collars and casual khaki. For my father, it was a humiliation to Bull Halsey and the other Navy men who delivered the victory in the Pacific. Perhaps McArthur, who lived for publicity, realized that the Admirals in their gleaming Navy dress whites would outshine the General in his unimpressive Army regalia.

My battle station – general quarters it was called – was in the port gun room of the most forward gun turret. There were three 16 inch gun turrets aboard, two forward, one aft. When they fired, as they did during training down at Gitmo Bay (the now famous Guantanamo) the crew went below decks if they could and stuffed cotton in their ears. It was a hell of a bellow when these guns went off.

I couldn't tell. I was screwed into my gun room watching the breach block, the size of a Buick, come recoiling back to what seemed a nose hair away. I was standing on a small dish attached to the bulkhead; next to my face was a red arc painted on the bulkhead to describe the limit of the massive gun's recoil. I was to stand back of it. They needn't ask twice.

I was the primer man. That is, loading the gun required a crew above my head to ram the six-foot missile into the breach followed by six canvas bags of gun powder. Meanwhile the massive breach block lowered over my head. I reached up to insert the primer in its face: the primer resembled a rifle bullet. As the block hydraulically closed above me the primer was locked into place. Gunnery control took over from somewhere else on the ship, pointing the gun, having factored in distance to target, wind speed, current speed, the up and down roll of the ship – all this before computers. An electric impulse fired the primer which ignited the powder bags and the man-sized missile went off to do damage some miles off. Exciting.

Except when, during practice, I failed to insert the primer all the way. As the block went up, the breach jammed. It could go no further because the small plate that was to move in behind the primer instead hit the primer, splitting it. Bells went off. The 3rd class gunnery mate crawled down and removed the split primer. He held it up to me.

"If we'd been in combat, this would've gone off and ignited the bags with the block open. You know where we'd be.." He wiggled the bent primer at me. "Dead."

I responded as I did so often with a gulp and widened eyes. I noticed when in fact we had the opportunity to shoot the monster gun, the gunnery mate stood outside the gun room and observed our performance through a shatter-proof port.

Aboard ship was a classmate, Peter Andes, whom I was meeting for the first time. He wore an even sloppier uniform than I: he didn't take any of this seriously. A sort of round guy, with a slumping walk, he had a quiet cynicism and spoke out of the corner of his mouth. My kind of guy.

We would stand together in the long, long chow lines (big ship, big mess hall) and watch the sunset over the spectacular Atlantic, marvel at the silver-flashing flying fish that broke the surface like sparklers, and gossip about the pomposity of the Academy midshipmen.

"What's under your jumper?" he asked. It was a book, stuffed down the top of my whites. He reached under my jumper and pulled it out. It was <u>Madame Bovary</u>. He wondered how many of the crew were reading Flaubert. It hadn't occurred to me to wonder. I was reading it because it was about a neurotic woman with romantic delusions. In other words, a nut like my mother. Seems I couldn't escape her, even in literature.

After a few sessions screwed into the gun room I felt the panics of unknown origin return and rise to crippling levels. I looked for a place to lie down. I knew from my mother that when panics fall on you best lie flat and be as invisible as possible until the angel of death flies over. We were "dogging the watch" which means in practice that every few days I was getting two hours sleep, rising at midnight to stand watch, and then theoretically was given an hour more to sleep before reveille. Which in practice meant almost no sleep.

This was dangerous for me, though I'd never admit it to anyone. Dangerous because I had been told early along that I was to become epileptic like my mother. Who told me? My mother.

In those days before campus clinics and free therapy and pharmacopeias of pills being pushed on you, you had no choice but to tough it out. There was certainly no one to complain to. Beside, like the heroine in I Never Promised you a Rose Garden, I was forbidden by my demons to tell anyone they existed. For such treachery I would die. So I toughed it out in a defensive crouch, waiting for the seizures my mother had promised me for my desertion.

It wasn't easy to find a place to hide and perchance to sleep aboard this massive (three football fields long) ship but when the desire is all answers appear. Somewhere below decks was a passageway where, overhead, they stored the long telephone-pole-size rammers used to clean the sixteen inch guns. They came in ten foot wood segments with threads on the end to screw them together to reach down the craw of the guns. They were stored on racks over the passageway.

If no one was approaching, I could step on a few eye hooks to hoist myself and squeeze onto the corrugated platform of ramrods above. I was thin, and besides that, desperate. I had only a foot of space above. I felt safe. Invisible at last on the USS Missouri.

Sleep came.

I had no notion of homosexuality at the time. None. Nor did I look around me and find any of the nude men, their dicks dangling, a turn-on. I was still in love with Jeanie back in Van Nuys, California. Far from finding these guys appealing, they scared me. They were like cartoon men, too masculine by my standards. Like the guy who came back from liberty in Lisbon and sat naked on the compartment's shit can (read: trash can) and picked away the crabs exploring his pubic jungle. "Got one," he'd say and snap it between thumb nails. No one seemed to care. It seemed like, what? Too much flesh, too proud, too shame-free. Too masculine.

I was unprepared for my watch in the boiler room. The crews who run the engine spaces below decks are called "snipes." They wore dungarees and didn't come topside much where, because this was a formality-ruled flagship, you had to change into whites. It was said that some of the snipes went a little mental spending their time in the 100 plus degree rooms, either with steam boilers or turbine roaring engines, where standing under overhead blowers was small relief. Some never went on liberty when we came into port. What I wasn't prepared for, some of these snipes seemed to be messing with each other. I didn't know how else to describe it: please remember this was the early 50s.

I came down to report for my watch and there were two gobs, one sitting on the other's lap, on a metal chair perched on the open grid deck that revealed menacing equipment roaring below.

"I'm Midshipman Ayres, reporting for watch," I said, trying to ignore the fact that the one sitting on the non-com's lap was chewing on his ear.

"Well, Miss Ayres, go watch that gauge." I reddened. No one had called me "Miss" before.

He walked me over to a water gauge attached to a boiler. The water level was dead center on the gauge.

"Holler out if the level goes down."

"What happens if it goes down?"

"The ship blows up."

God, what a responsibility I had on my hands.

"Has it ever gone down?"

"Nope, not yet. But holler if it does."

I turned earnestly to watch it while the white hat went back to his buddies who were all laughing about something. I stood in front of that gauge for four hours. It didn't even tremble. Over my head a blower kept my heat down to a manageable ninety.

Later the white hat showed me the designs for a rocket he was working on. It would take him to the moon. I heard from another rotcee midshipman that these two snipes were married. I couldn't imagine what that meant.

At night, in my all but one from the top rack, I was exposed to more masculine rituals. Lights were out in the cabin. There were red "running lights" at deck level that suffused the cabin with a sort of nightclub glow. The men around dropped into sleep and farted audibly which I could understand given their diet of fried baloney and eggs for breakfast and creamed beef on toast for dinner which was called "shit on a shingle." I could also understand the camaraderie of the others who in response would call out, "Shit, Hollingsworth, I'm gonna sleep on the fucking deck you lay down any more gas attacks."

"I saved it all for you, honey," Hollingsworth replied in the dark to which others screamed "shut up."

Silence. Then movement.

First in the rack across the passageway. Movement under the thin blanket. The blanket is tossed aside. The guy is stroking has private member: it is not small and he doesn't seem embarrassed. Above me, just over my nose, there's some frantic jiggling followed by an unmistakable "ah!" and through the red-lit night fall glistening trajectories of sperm. This display prompts another: across the aisle, the guy who was stroking turns to his side so that his contribution can fly off into the space between racks.

There were more, but you get the idea. All I knew is that no one seemed hampered by embarrassment. Men. When I found it necessary to conjure up Jeanie lowering her strapless prom dress and frankly offering her breasts, I reached relief by keeping what is mine inside my cotton boxers and letting the results dry in the red night air and hoped no one would notice. Or judge.

Years later when I discovered my gay aspect, I thought back on those nights of flying cum, thought on those sculpted men with tapered waists I showered with and thanked whatever Gods may control such matters that I wasn't turned on. Not at that time. I had enough self-loathing to filter on a daily basis (after all, I had abandoned my mother!) that I didn't need to pile on more.

So maybe I had to scrub a few decks, put my back into holy-stoning the quarter deck but I got to visit Lisbon and Paris. Not bad for a boy from Glendale.

Lisbon was a crowded city of unfamiliar architecture and the chatter of strange language, but most important, it was bullfighting. In Portugal they don't kill the bull which was a bit of a disappointment but I was able to buy souvenirs of two long stickers, sticks with knife points on the end, decorated with many colored paper bits. It was difficult to stow them in my sea bag and carry them back to Glendale and present to my bewildered mother. But I did.

My friend Peter Andes, the Yalie who comforted me with the music of cynicism, had an uncle in Paris. The big ship docked in Le Havre and we took a train into the dream city that was hard for a boy to believe existed even while in it. Peter casually dropped that his uncle was a gangster, but by that time we were entering the man's apartment on the Champs Elysees that had a balcony looking out on that most famous of boulevards.

What could be more Paris than Fifi Lamour (that's how I remember her, surely a joke memory plays on me) the uncle's French mistress whose waist was so pinched it forced flesh up to her bodice and caused a deep cleavage which she would put before our noses, the noses of my buddy and me, as she was supposedly leaning over to kiss her gangster's bald head and mew something in French.

I could not fail to note that her deep crevice had been doused in some eternal spring of cologne, piquant I think the French would call it, terrifying to a young man who jerked off inside his baggy boxers wondering if Fifi in the gross arms of the gangster uncle knew the poetic American boy was sliding at that moment down her scented cleavage in search of release which never failed, it always gushed, leaving me fearful that stiff patches of dried semen on my Navy-issue shorts might be spied by my buddy but he never mentioned it if he did since he had always the same reaction to all things, a smirk, which is the one thing I really liked about him.

Strangely, when we returned to school I never saw Peter. We were friends for a season.

In 2011 I noted in the Yale Alumni magazine that Peter Andes had died in Manhattan. No further information. Made sense. He didn't reveal much behind that cynical smirk. Not even why he described his uncle as a gangster. He laughed at the ludicrous military and helped me stay sane that frightening summer.

I will always love him for that.

Driving Dr.Rose

The day I met Dr.Rose was the same day, this is why I remember it, I ran my head into the wall to shut out my mother.

She was ranting from down the hall of the small bungalow in Burbank she had rented for the summer. My father had been ordered on to Honolulu for his next duty and she stayed behind to adore my brother some more (as if he needed it) and he, this is also why I remember that day, was lounging in the tub as he whiled away the hours waiting for life to arrive.

He was out of the Marines. He had come back from eighteen months of combat in Korea, though not directly. He had detoured, driven perhaps by a rage to prove he was tougher than my father. The Marines had sent his unit to Japan for R&R before their return stateside. Burr was curious about Japan.

Only weeks away from discharge, he went AWOL.

He headed for the mountains, Japanese mountains of course which must have looked as though they were painted on scrolls, something exotic, I'm certain. He settled among some villagers. I was told by my mother (the only one in whom he ever confided) that he entertained the children with tricks: he could let a stone drop from his head and kick it with his heel. Mom made the AWOL sound sensible since it was so like her favorite son to love children and want to entertain them.

The Marines threw him in the brig for six months. Years later, involved with the famously avant garde <u>Living Theatre</u> in New York, I saw a play titled <u>The Brig</u> directed by Judith Malina. Set in a Marine brig, it was brutal, clamorous, terrifying.

My brother showed no damage from his time in the brig, the six months of brutal humiliation. He came back with a smirk and a shrug and that cock of an eyebrow that won all the girls.

It won me too. I loved my brother though he didn't seem to reciprocate. Perhaps I wasn't easy to love. I envied most his immunity to my parents. He had no fear. He put his fists up against my father. He wooed my mother, indifferent to her voodoo powers and how she could inflict her demons on you. He stared them down and smiled.

How I wanted to be him.

I should be grateful that Mom rented that cottage for the summer. It gave me a last chance to see my brother. I wasn't grateful that she and I compulsively tore at each other.

We were locked in a lifetime battle to drown out the other, so much so that on the day a car was coming to pick me up (a cheap ride-share I saw advertised in the paper) I lost myself to rage as mother screamed her worse from her dark room of sorrows and I rammed my head repeatedly into the wall of the narrow hall.

My brother called. I went into the bath where he was casually posed back in the water, his heel hooked over the edge of the tub, a smirk on his face. He had the cocky ease of a cowboy in a frontier saloon.

"What've you done now?" he asked.

"She's crazy."

"Shut the fuck up. She's your mom."

"She wants me to get her a bottle and lie about my age to the guys down at the corner 'cause they know her anyway. I wasn't about to, you know, I've become a Christian, you know that."

Yeah, he nods, he'd heard about it.

"You two are just alike." I hated when he said that.

"Don't antagonize her. Treat her like a date," he advised.

"Gerry!" this time she screeched. We heard her bare feet in the hall. She was suddenly at the door.

"Oh God," she said. She covered her eyes at the sight of her older son's nudity. She rushed back to her room for booze and some delusion of sanity.

There was honking outside. My ride was here, my share-the-expense ride back East.

"Got to go," I said to my brother. He gave me a wave that crossed in front of his face, palm turned towards me.

"Watch out for falling rocks," he said and smirked in that way that made me love him.

The car waiting at the curb was dented, old and I decided after seeing the two yahoos in front, meant for menace. I peered into the back. There sat a calm, soft-eyed black gentleman. He nodded graciously, leaned over, pushed open the door for me. He seemed courtly.

I thought if this guy can be in this car without being lynched, what do I have to worry about? I later learned that he had misunderstood what sort of drive he had signed on for. He was about to get out and seek other transport when the car stopped and in climbed an 18 year-old boy from Yale. He settled back in his seat.

I no more than climbed in than the parolees up front peeled rubber on the streets of Burbank and before they could make clear through the whistling of their missing teeth where we were going, we were heading east.

On Route 66.

Dr.Rose was in fact a dentist, just out of the Navy where he drilled the sailors' teeth in the Pacific. He was now heading back to what he claimed was the only real city, his city, the Big Apple.

He spoke to me in low musical tones, inquiring about my studies at Yale, painting an idyllic picture of his recent duty in Japan. Jamming this sonorous recitation was the screeching chatter up front. Like the country music they blasted from the radio, their words were a garbled lyric that disappeared along the landscape. "Shit, not in my fuckin' house, bitch, I said shiiit" and shiiit streamed out the window to join the hoe down coming from the radio.

Dr.Rose raised his eyebrows to accompany a deeply drawn breath. He turned to give me the sympathy of his dark eyes.

"You'll be studying a lot of great men up there, a lot of literature…"

I agreed, I think. That is, I nodded.

He studied the flashing scenery. He smiled.

"An open mind…" He savored the idea, his tongue moistening his upper lip. "You'll develop an open mind."

I nodded. I couldn't see anything wrong with an open mind. He leaned in close, his voice low. He told me the sad story of two Marines, officers he said, emphasizing the word "officers" who on the front lines of Korea after days of battle, one night in their bunker, had huddled together for comfort. That huddle had somehow heated up. Dr.Rose spared me details though his floating eyebrows did a lot of explaining. Suffering from the most unnecessary guilt, they turned themselves in to their superiors. They were both dishonorably discharged.

Dr.Rose shook his head sadly. "All for love."

Love? Maybe that was taking the huddle incident too far but I let it go.

When we got to the Pennsy Turnpike, I took over and drove the entire toll road in a night. Dr.Rose joined me up front. The good old boys fell deep into snoring sleep in the back, calling hogs in the next county. Dr.Rose got stern with me.

"You can't drive up to the Yale campus with these fellows," he told me. "You can't be seen with them."

"It'll be late, they're heading on to Boston."

"It would be a big mistake."

"I have a new room in Silliman College, that's part of Yale. I can just go there."

"You could stay a night with me, get some rest, look your best when you arrive on your campus."

I wasn't sure what he meant by my best since I always more or less looked like I did at that moment.

"I keep a place in Manhattan."

"Ah man, I love Manhattan."

"You've been there?"

"Once last summer when I had to change trains."

"The Big Apple is much, much more than changing trains."

"I guess, yeah, I know."

"What are your plans for Thanksgiving?"

"Eat a turkey, I guess, go to the chow hall, I mean dining hall, my brain is still aboard ship."

"Come visit."

"Visit you?"

"November is magic in New York."

Noon the next day the car pulled to a stop in front of a row of brownstones. As Dr.Rose took his suitcase from the trunk, he stooped to look at me in the back.

"Thanksgiving," he said and handed me his card. I looked down at it. "Dr.J.Everett Rose, DDS." The car roared off. I looked up and Dr.Rose was gone.

I examined the card, stuck it in my wallet. I didn't have that many plans for Thanksgiving.

Like, none.

George & Harry's

I had a roommate for the first week of my sophomore year who simply disappeared. No one could find him. I knew of course he had sensed some magical danger from me and ran off. Maybe he didn't like Silliman, the least popular of the residential colleges we had just moved into.

The second week proved just as bleak. A beaked monk of a Goethe scholar (actually a recent grad) who claimed I had converted him to Christianity the year before, a conversion that permitted this Tolkein creature to rub his hulking mass up against me in what he identified as Christian charity, he showed up. He was the only example I had to show for my crusade to convert the entire campus at Yale.

John appeared off a train in a sweat. He had been on his way to Boston but the demons that came at him soon after his surrender to Jesus were sitting on the train so he hopped off in New Haven to seek asylum with me.

I let him sleep on the missing roommate's bed. Twice in the night John rose up with a roar, batting the air against his tormentors. He left in the morning, after nuzzling my neck for Christian comforts.

Finding myself alone that night I noted John had left his demons behind. My heart rattled in me. I tried sleeping sitting up with the overhead light on. The demons were sometimes shy of light.

In the short gray afternoons I looked out my single window. Over a high stone wall below lay a cemetery where an old man who seemed painted in crooked jittery Van Gogh strokes raked leaves among the stones. He raked toward me until he was out of view behind the wall. Leaves fell. He would suddenly re-appear his head bobbing to the motions of his rake.

I watched for hours and slipped quietly into a dark so deep I could not even call on Jesus, friend of my youth.

I often wondered what became of the Goethe scholar. He wasn't poetic enough to be a Werther and kill himself. He may have chosen a slower death, the life academic, where he could be sighted by the occasional student, agog at this rare creature deep in the shadows of the library stacks.

He was a sweet friend.

The Secretary of Admissions, the man who conducted my initial interview in a hotel in Los Angeles, was a benign man with a soft smile. He was later to tell me how charmed he had been to see me stop at that hotel mirror and slick back my hair. He was still charmed when mid-terms came up and I was to be alone a week on the empty campus. He suggested I move into his suite in one of the fashionable colleges. He drove me out in the country where we had dinner at a colonial inn. When the food seemed not to agree with me he sent me off to bed. I went. He opened the door, looking in at me. He came in, sat on the bed next to me. He slipped his hand down my pajamas to rub my tummy. I froze. Moments passed. He left.

Leaving my demons to increase on their own, I joined a few new friends at George & Harry's, a coffee shop near campus. All was harmless chitchat until I was suddenly hit with a – what? A slug to my gut with no fist in sight. I felt a dizziness, a heart that sped out of control. I knew I was dying, then, at that moment. I was 18 years-old.

I stumbled to the john. I sat on the can and breathed and then breathed some more, waiting for the storm to pass. It didn't. It kept rolling in like those breakers on the Pacific I used to tame by diving under them. These intense rollers of panic I could not dive under.

After the attack in George & Harry's I went into safe mode, staying in my room for days, not able to focus on my books or calm the interior storms. For distraction, I pulled myself from my window seat and walked across campus to the street with the clothing stores and concentrated, fiercely so, on the swimming patterns of foulard and regimental ties in the windows.

I had come from the constant sunshine of Southern California, from the Ossie and Harriet naiveté of a public high school. I felt alien in these sunless winters among the well-heeled graduates from pedigree schools I hadn't even known existed until I arrived with my single bag on campus.

I knew the problem. I had gone east and left my mother behind. Like Pandar at the close of <u>Troilus and Cressida</u>, she had bequeathed me her diseases.

I would sweat and seek about for eases meanwhile among a few friends, not the flashy types but the meek, those common denominators who made me most comfortable.

There was Jim Herlan who was the only undergraduate on record who had permission to live off campus. He lived with his mother, a dentist who lost her license for spending more time leaning over a bar than her dental chair. She followed her son to New Haven. I escaped to their ragtag apartment when I felt the demons dancing in the cornices and since the Herlans had no extra bed, I slept on a row of table chairs set side to side.

On the cold rush back to class in the morning, I found enough focus to read, say, Machiavelli's <u>The Prince</u>. I was on safe ground, doing homework on a public street.

I had another friend, Ted Harrison, tall, patrician, a snob whose neurosis caused him incessantly to rub his forehead with a slim aristocratic finger. I felt he was my tormentor who granted me audience to expose my defects with lip curling sarcasm.

Early in sophomore year I sat in his barely-furnished room, one of the old ones with the tall bootless windows, while he quizzed me on my Christian belief. I knew I was swimming among sharks, but reluctantly, I told him the story of the redemptive blood of my Savior.

"You actually believe that?" he asked. I felt my last prop had been kicked from under me. By a sneer.

I looked down at the record turning on his portable player. It was Edith Piaf. Ted could actually recite the French lyrics along with that throbbing sparrow. You can see how I thought him superior.

It was a heavy walk back to my room. I felt ruined. I stayed in for a week, bargaining for sleep, running in place, dropping to my knees, praying for green pastures. Sometime during that dark night it occurred to me that if I didn't believe in Jesus the demons would consider their work done and disappear.

No Jesus, no demons.

I always felt Ted considered me an exotic curiosity back at Yale, a bumpkin from the west who spoke sometimes knowingly of the metaphysical poets and could make him laugh in way that left behind a lopsided smile. Laughs aside, I couldn't understand why he hung with me.

After Ted had nuked me that cold Yale night in 1954, I was a wreck. I decided it might be better to be in motion, get out of my Boris Karlof digs above the graveyard.

Maybe Dr.Rose and Thanksgiving in the Big Apple would be just the thing to take my mind off of, well, things.

A Bite of the Apple

I had only one wisdom tooth. That is, I had only one left.

The various others had been yanked by various dentists near various navy bases in the south. I mentioned this to Dr.Rose on our trip across country. I was concerned that I should get rid of this last one also, giving my other teeth more living space. I was still haunted by my brother's taunts that I was bucktoothed.

In the back seat of the speeding car, Dr.Rose tilted my chin up, had me pull back my lips and assured me I had the most minor of overbites. In fact, he claimed, it made me rather handsome, a concept new to me.

He poked a thumb inside my cheek.

"Not a problem," he assured me. "We can have that out in no time."

So it was settled. When I called Dr.Rose to say, yes, I would like to visit for Thanksgiving, he suggested I arrive a day early and come directly to his office. His office was in Harlem.

I followed his bewildering instructions from Grand Central to a subway that eventually came above ground and deposited me at 125th Street and Lenox Avenue. I blinked around at the surrounding buildings. This was one of those unusual days of harsh autumn light. I checked the instructions in hand and thought to stop someone and ask for a little help.

By this time my Yale metamorphosis was complete: I appeared on that Harlem street in baggy chinos, intentionally dirty white bucks. Oxford cloth button down shirt under a Shetland wool sweater, both from Brooks. My proudest achievement was the duffle coat with hood at the ready and wood peg buttons.

I had driven a lot of deliveries for ma and pa in the New Haven neighborhoods to achieve this look.

It certainly drew attention from those passing by. I wasn't keen enough to realize that on that fall day in 1954 I was the only white college boy on Lenox Avenue.

A large-bosomed lady took a look at the instructions and pointed nearby, telling me had it been a snake it would've bit me. We both laughed.

I climbed to the second floor of the four story building. Dr.Rose's name was on the frosted pane. I knocked. The door opened. Out came a patient holding a cold compress to his cheek. He glanced at me and hurried on. Behind him was Dr.Rose who insisted I call him Jay.

"Gerry, you made it, young man, kudos for you."

I wasn't quite sure what a kudo was but I took it as part of Big Apple lingo and stored it for further research.

"Here, give me your bag," Jay said. "It'll be safe here." He motioned to the floor next to his dental chair. I looked around. There was no one else in this small office, no nurse, no one answering the phone.

Jay reached into an overhead light fixture and pulled out a wad of cash, peeled some off and returned the rest. He saw me watching and gave me a rich laugh.

"My bank," he said.

In the bar below Jay ordered us both martinis. He quizzed me about Yale and my studies. I told him, you know, how I had changed to an English major now and he shook his head, not sure that was wise.

"But it's broadening me, you remember, open mind."

Dr.Rose found this hysterically funny, repeated "open mind" and ordered us both seconds.

It took no time at all for that tooth to be gone and a compact placed in the socket which I kept in place with clenched jaw.

He insisted I need rest and should be early to bed and certainly shouldn't be tossed about by a subway ride. He got us a taxi that went downtown at such speed that the tossing about was considerable. He told the cabbie to stop at a little eatery he knew, called something like The Wagon Wheel which was crowded by the most laugh-prone crowd of men, all of whom seemed to know Dr.Rose.

A entirely elegant and slim black man named Don Shirley threw his arms to the air and let them fall on Jay's shoulders. I noted that he wore white gloves.

"Don, this is Gerry, you must meet him, he's a young scholar from Yale."

"I don't doubt it for a moment," said Don and added the code word, "And comme ca?"

"Don't be stupid," Jay said with some heat. "He's in love with a girl in California."

"Darling, by last count, that's three thousand miles away." Don went off trailing laughter. Jay explained to me that Don was a famous pianist, both jazz and classical who actually lived in Carnegie Hall, in one of their guest apartments. The gloves? He wore them after having insured his hands for $10,000 each. They were his asset.

Though Jay had said this was an eatery there seemed to be more drink than eat but Jay did get them to hustle me up a burger and fries.

I realized I had at last reached the Big Apple. All around me was rich and strange and somehow glittery, though the fellow with the gloves did leave me wondering what he meant by "comme ca".

Jay got me to bed early. His studio apartment with a Pullman kitchen in one corner was, he told me, temporary until he built his practice back to previous levels. He shared his single bed with me.

He snapped on the radio. Out came the Everly Brothers, exhorting me to dream, dream, dream. I took their advice. I fell immediately to sleep.

That next day, Thanksgiving, Jay took me to a ball in Harlem. Well, not exactly a ball, not the kind in which people whirl each other round the floor. No, this was called Miss Black's Ball and was more like a fashion show.

It took place in a cavernous hall with a long model's runway down the middle. Above was a wrap-around balcony with balustrades. Jay took us up some back stairs he knew and pushed his way to a railing to give us a good look at the show below.

Down the runway came what seemed an endless parade of elegant models, in long gowns that exceed my vocabulary, one more beautiful than the next.

There was a sudden commotion behind me. I was not aware but a gentleman had come up and slipped his arm around my waist. Dr.Rose was aware and angrily shoved the guy, sending him sprawling.

"You ought to be ashamed," he barked at the man.

"Fuck you," he politely replied.

I didn't think I needed protection but Dr.Rose did. He let me know that this sort of show might draw unstable characters. What sort of show, I wanted to know.

"A drag show," Dr.Rose answered.

I think I understood but I wasn't about to believe it. "You mean all those girls.."

"All those girls are boys dressed up as girls."

"You're kidding me. They're too pretty."

He smiled and patted my cheek.

"Sweet boy."

Jay pulled me aside to shake hands with a sweet faced old man with a crown of white hair. A very old black man. As we moved to the door, Jay confided that this was W.C.Handy, the man who wrote "St.Louis Woman." Really? That seemed like an awful long time ago. I looked back and the elderly gent was smiling softly as he chatted with someone. He didn't seem too mindful of his fame.

"Where we going?" I asked the good doctor.

"The Village," he answered with what seemed exceptional relish. "Greenwich Village," he added just in case I wasn't keeping up.

The Village. Another bite of the apple.

Jay took me to a narrow townhouse on Van Dam Street, one in a row of matching houses. Unlike the others, this one was filled with music and people were crowding in.

Jay ran interference and we were soon in the narrow parlor floor crowded with partiers of all races and inclinations, I think you would call it. All had to shout to be heard.

Jay made a show of introducing me to our hostess, a stunning presence named Leontyne Price. Jay and she did some kissy-kissy. Next to her a mountain of a man with a mountainous voice protested, "And what do I get, no kisses for the working staff?" Jay gave the big man a hug and Leontyne told him not to bother, he hadn't lifted a finger to make all this happen. The man was Bill Warfield, Leontyne's husband.

Jay put his mouth to my ear to let me know that they were both famous singers who had just returned from a tour in Russia where they had starred in <u>Porgy and Bess</u>. The word was that Leontyne was destined for the Met, just you wait. Bill had sung "Old Man River" in the film of <u>Showboat</u>. I couldn't take my eyes off them. The pair seemed to glide among their guests in a dimension apart.

I found myself dancing (dance being an up and down jiggle) with a man who held one hand aloof with a smoking cigarette while his lithe little body, apparently without bones to encumber it, invented its own choreography. It was obvious he was black but his gender was beyond definition. While dancing with me he'd exchange words with others frugging past and then turn back to me with a smile like the week before Christmas.

His name was Roscoe Lee Browne. He was an actor and I was told, a one-time track star. We were photographed dancing together and we ended up in <u>Ebony</u> magazine. I was tempted to send the photo to my Dixiecrat father but it would upset my mother too much.

There were sudden shushing sounds and the crowd sat. Don Shirley, now without his white gloves, sat at the baby grand. Out came Gershwin. An enormous number of folks crowded into the small parlor room, others stacked up the narrow flight of stairs that led above. And something astonishing happened.

Bill sat on the piano bench beside Shirley. Leontyne sat at his feet, on the floor, rested her head on his knee. He looked down at her and sang a question, "What would you do if there was no Crown?" She looked up and replied, "I loves your Porgy." Soon he was telling Bess she was his woman. It was not only a fact that the power of their voices reverberated up and down the passages of the narrow house, but it was the conviction of the roles that they so suddenly slipped into that made believers, rapt devotees, of all us folks crowded around.

When the song ended, there was a silence so clear you could hear the scrape of Bill's knuckles as he moved a tear off his cheek. He looked down at her. She looked up at him. They kissed. And the folks stomped and applauded.

Like a real diva, Leontyne cast her eyes to the floor. Bill pulled back among crowd, pulled up his knees to rest his chin and looked at Leontyne. She folded her hands on her lap. She nodded to Don Shirley. He played music unfamiliar to me. It was an aria from opera, I later learned, about a lady who protests to the man who is about to rape her that she has sacrificed her life to art. That is, just before she does him in with a knife to the heart.

She sang "Vissi d'arte" from <u>Tosca</u>. Her voice filled the room and soared up the stairs and undoubtedly reverberated in rooms above. It was beauty, pure and powerful and I was sitting in the midst of it.

Vissi d'arte.. I lived for art.. vissi d'amore.. I lived for love..

This was the best Thanksgiving I ever had.

The Apple Bites Back

As the party thinned out, Bill Warfield nodded to Jay and we followed him down to a basement space. Also joining us was a young Puerto Rican boxer with complexion smooth as ivory, mocha as the oldest of ivory.

We sat in a circle on crates and chairs. Bill Warfield reached into his pocket, pulled out rolling papers, shook green leaf into it. He said to me in his rattling basso, "I don't know what the boys do up in New Haven these days but here, young man, we are about to break federal law."

I nodded eagerly. I wasn't a Fed. He licked the joint, sealed it, lit it, passed it around. It came to me. I hesitated. I had never even smoked.

"Suck air," said Bill. "That's a boy."

I sucked and got enough marijuana down my lungs to set off a bout of coughing. When the joint came my way again, I did a better job of it.

I felt I was swimming in the cold night air as we came out on the Village street, despairing of ever getting a cab. We went uptown on the subway. Jay was saying something to me. I was nodding with exhaustion and booze and the controlled substance. I didn't understand him at first.

"What did you think of the boxer boy?" Jay was asking.

"He didn't say much," I answered.

"Did you find him attractive?"

"Yeah, I guess," I answered.

"Bill does," Jay said.

"What do you mean?"

Jay shrugged and looked off down the rattling car. Let one draw his own conclusions.

As for getting the patient early to bed, this time it was early in the morning. I was groggy from art, marijuana and booze and creating stretch marks from an opening mind.

The radio at our heads was playing <u>Mr.Sandman,</u> send me a dream. Again music to fall to sleep with.

I woke in the morning next to Dr.Rose but strangely unable to see anything. Something was going on with my peter. I realized that Dr.Rose had draped a hand towel over my face to shield me against the harsh realities of what was going on below. He caused me to reach orgasm in his mouth and because he was mannerly, tiptoed into the bathroom to accomplish the same for himself.

I didn't think to question any of this, nor did we discuss it. He had been kind to me, opening his apartment to me, sharing his bed. I was his guest.

This was the Big Apple after all.

I told him I had a train later and he assured me we had time for an afternoon party in a townhouse in Harlem. It was a long and narrow parlor floor, crowded with folks yelling, dancing, drinking. And here was marijuana again.

I was delighted to see Roscoe Lee Browne. He smiled as before in that way that resembled Christmas lights. Jay didn't seem to take to him.

"Do you want a drink?" Jay asked Roscoe. Roscoe's smile reached back to both ears as he replied.

"You made that up."

Sensing he was being toyed with, Jay went off to get drinks. I found an edge of sofa to sit on and looked around at all the fabulous people. I was aware that Roscoe's eyes were on me. I turned to look.

"What?"

He smiled sweetly. "Ah bello, I know your type. You can sleep in the gutter all night and next day wake up looking innocent as a choir boy."

I had no idea why he talked to me like that. I thought he liked me. Jay came up with drinks.

"Grazie, darling," Roscoe said and put his down.

Drawn by the music, Roscoe jumped to his feet and took off with a hip swaying stride. Eyes were on him as he strode the entire length of the parlor floor apartment, his mouth open in a smile that greeted whatever house gods might be around. He reached the window seat at the far end, grabbed the hand of a beautiful lady bird named Abbey Lincoln. She fell into stride with him, laughing with her head back and chin up.

Guests cleared a space as the pair came the distance to the back wall. As they pivoted, they grabbed two others and headed back for the front window, now four abreast. I today can still experience it, music, laughter and some strange surrender.

The walk continued, picking up others at each pivot until the entire party was striding, arms linked, their combined energies seeming to liberate them, including the boy from Yale who at the last linked his arm and tried as best he could to sway his shy hips to the music.

At Grand Central I bought a ticket for New Haven. Here was Gerry, a disappointment to his parents, heading back to Yale when he should have been in Bible school in Pasadena.

A Man Among Men

Our NROTC training the next summer, 1955, took us not aboard ship but to Corpus Christi, Texas, for flight indoctrination. We midshipmen were crowded into the cockpit of a PBY, a giant sea plane, the patrol bomber that commanded the Pacific in the just passed war. We were waiting for our brief turns at the stick.

The craft had taken off on water doing a little wave bounce before getting in the air. Slow to gain altitude but once there we cruised with a faint hum, the sparkly glass of the Gulf of Mexico moving under us.

The pilot nodded over his shoulder. It was my turn. With fear or was it joy, somewhere rocky in between, I slid into the pilot's chair. With encouragement, I pulled back on the half-moon wheel and the nose tipped up. I pushed forward and the nose came down again even with the horizon.

An odd sensation, moving this air-born box car around with such ease.

I considered becoming a Navy pilot.

My new buddies (squadron as they called themselves) were nightly in the Quonset hut officers' club with lots of Budweiser from a can that bloated me but didn't give me much of a buzz. I shot pool with the boys, I mean men, not well but I clowned so that when I missed a shot I got them to laugh. I was the kind of guy that made the other guys laugh.

At last a man among men.

A dangerous thought. I dared to feel grown, not only grown but a grown man. I wore a crisp khaki uniform like my father's, drank beer with my squadron, all the things my father did. It was a time-out from the daily pummeling of anxieties. Young still but a man and it seemed to work.

Until it didn't.

On August 5, 1955, I got a weird message. Mid-afternoon, I was trying to log some z's in the barracks when a white hat came in and told me to go see the chaplain. Chaplain? I didn't know there was one. I came into the chaplain officer's quarters, saluted both him and God. He motioned for me to sit. He was studying a paper in his hand. He did not look up.

"Are you close to your brother?" he asked.

Where did that question come from?

I shrugged and admitted sure, we were close, I guess. He handed me a telegram. It said in its totality:

BROTHER BURR DEAD DAD

The telegram was woefully bare of detail.

Given emergency leave I managed to grab various hops on military cargo planes. After crisscrossing the west half of our continent, sleeping on large coffee table sized cable rolls, even dropping off for an eerie half night in Alamagordo where all this nuclear stuff had its beginnings, I finally reached Honolulu, Barber's Point, where my father had just been transferred and where my brother had been visiting.

When my brother died or killed himself (a thought I couldn't dismiss) I pieced together the facts. He had in mid-afternoon taken a high speed short cut home through the immense sugar cane fields. His car went off the road, landed on its rear and tumbled to a stop among giant boulders. The boulders were left road side when the fields were cleared for planting.

The boulders were in clear sight of the road. This was mid-afternoon. Burr had not been drinking.

Whatever were the motives for him driving his car off the road and to his death, little was said in the week that followed. Little was said of my brother Burr either. There were none of his mementoes dragged out and put on the mantel for reflection, no pictures to shed light on his short life, no words to praise this beautiful boy unless the words had to do with how much the loss of Madeline's beautiful boy was a problem for Madeline.

The week turned out to be about her.

Florentino, A Flower

The suspenseful run-up to the funeral was whether my mother would collapse or be able to get out of her magical bed. She didn't know. How could she anticipate such things?

One thing she had not anticipated was the arrival of Elizabeth Florentino. Nor had I.

This slim Filipino beauty flew in from California and knocked on my parent's door just one day before my own arrival. My mother hobbled to the door to let her in. She gave her name as Elizabeth Florentino. She was Burr's fiancée, she added. Mom staggered back which the girl took as an invitation to enter so she did.

Burr had dated this girl the first six months upon his return from Korea, a time he lived in Fresno with his Uncle Burr. With customary charm he persuaded the local community college that he had graduated high school and the certificates were in the mail. Meanwhile, he needed some college prep classes. These classes qualified him for the University of Hawaii where he was just about to matriculate. The high school records never arrived.

Elizabeth Florentino who preferred to be called Liz said she and Burr had loved each other very much. As soon as he started classes in University of Hawaii and got a job he was sending for her.

My mother sought support from a door jamb and said it seemed odd he had not mentioned her. Liz pulled out a pack of letters bound by ribbon and offered them. Mother couldn't bear to look.

Mom buried her face in her hands and with a sobbing voice through her fingers said they were sorry but couldn't put her up. Liz said she wasn't asking to be put up. She just wanted to get to the funeral home.

Mom went on speaking through her fingers, hearing only her side of the conversation. "Papa wouldn't be happy having you staying here, a colored girl. He's from the South."

She lowered her hands and gave the girl a top sergeant squint. "You're not pregnant, are you?"

Dad was at the opposite door. He walked in, put out a hand to this girl, "I'm Commander Ayres." Not only was it in his nature to give a pretty girl every benefit of doubt but he was offended by his wife once again characterizing him as a backwoods yahoo.

"I'm Liz Florentino," the girl replied. "Your son admired you so."

Dad shot an accusing glance at his teary wife and said to the girl, "You stay here for now."

Mom followed her groans back to her room.

"I don't want to be a bother. I just want to rent a place and get a job here, near the cemetery."

"What're you gonna do with yourself?" Dad asked.

"Visit him, your son. Visit him every day."

"Every day?"

"It's the only way I can live."

That confused my dad. "Well, put your stuff over there. That couch folds out."

Liz went quietly out and found a store, bought groceries, cooked dinner, cleaned the house. She carried a hot tray of food into my mother who lay back with a cloth over her eyes. From under the cloth Mom said, "Oh darling, that's not necessary. I won't eat."

"I'll just put it here."

Liz set the tray on the bedside table. When she picked the plates up later to wash, the food was gone.

It was this slim Filipino girl who answered the door when I arrived. She lurched towards me, putting her head in my chest.

"You're Gerry," she said and began to cry.

"Hey, hey, what's up? Who're you?"

She was embarrassed. She pulled back, wiped her tears away, managed to say, "Burr talked so much about you - "

"He did?"

"I think I know you already." She giggled in embarrassment and offered her still wet hand and said, "I'm Liz, Liz Florentino."

"Florentino, isn't that a flower?"

"Ah, I don't think so. Can I hug you one more time?"

"Sure. I mean I'd like that. Great."

She hugged me and said into my chest, "Burr and I were getting married."

Before I could respond to that, I heard a familiar voice from the back of the house.

"Gerry.."

I pulled away from Liz. "Mom," I said.

"Won't you even come and see your mother?" the voice said from the dark room.

"You better go see your mom," Liz said.

"Sure." I started off, stopped. "You sure that doesn't mean like little flower or something?"

"Go to your mom."

Liz was an angel. We never stopped talking that week. We drove the narrow asphalt road where Burr had died. She got out of the car and sat among the waving sugar cane and stared. By this time there was not much to see

I learned from Liz that Burr had that small book of poetry a Yalie undergraduate, Michael Smith, had put together. It included a few of my poems. He showed it to his marine buddies. She said he was proud. He never let me know he had received the little book I had sent him in Korea.

I'm sure we would be discussing such things if only he had waited two weeks, two weeks and I would have been there. Instead I am in the room that was his, sleeping in his bed which brings a certain terror. I look idly at the books he had bought for the semester coming up, left scattered on his table. One of them is an introduction to psychology. I grab it. Maybe there's help.

God knows I needed some, what with the Dark Queen up the hall foreseeing death to herself and all the house now that her sun's gone dark. As always I tended to let poetry be my feelings – Alas! what boots it with uncessant care to even write a fucking poem or strictly meditate the thankless Muse now that Lycidas is dead, at least that's what Milton wrote when his friend died young.

No, I didn't meditate any thankless muses but I struggled daily with a boiler of anxiety building within. Familiar anxiety, the same the gods let fly from their lazy feasts above that found its mark in me as I sat in George & Harry's. From that moment terror was my constant companion.

I took Burr's psychology book to the john and sat on the can and read and read the blurring pages, hoping for relief.

My only relief was Liz. I was able to tell her of my anxieties. She said she was beyond all emotion and wanted only to be at Burr's grave for the rest of her life.

I made a deal with her. I would fly back to San Francisco with her when the time came. If she still felt she needed to live near Burr's grave, I'd buy her a return ticket. Right there in the airport.

I hooked her by saying I needed her to give me courage to resume my life. It wasn't a lie, but in truth, the anxieties I felt after his death were not unique but deep and familiar.

She finally agreed. We both went on with our lives.

In the majestic Punch Bowl cemetery, a detail of Marines lift their rifles and fire into the air. They march my brother's coffin forward and put it in its place in this God-created bowl. He lies surrounded by mountains, Diamondhead at his feet.

In the car leaving, Dad turns in tears to Mom.

"Well, baby, we lost our boy."

I look out the window.

I hadn't. I hadn't lost him.

Falling Into Jeanie

I certainly didn't tell my grieving mother that Jeanie Meyers was flying up to San Francisco to meet me.

A plane took Liz and me to San Francisco. We held hands all the way. I got off. Liz got a connection on to Fresno. I always thought we had saved each other's lives.

How Jeanie got her mother's permission down in Van Nuys plus the cash, I can't remember. I do know it seemed the most adult thing I had ever done.

We considered renting two rooms at the St.Francis since we certainly couldn't share the same room. I had read in a detective novel that the ubiquitous house dicks could arrest you if your door were locked and you were performing in ways that were not pure.

Problem was we couldn't afford two rooms. So with fear and trembling, we shared a room in the St.Francis, that famous hotel in San Francisco.

We were careful to change out of sight of each other in the bathroom and spent whatever money we had left to venture down to the huge glittery showroom below. We had neither been to a nightclub show and nothing could seem more sophisticated and, admit it, adult than that.

Harry Belafonte was performing. I had never heard of him and was not prepared for the power of a real star. I also was not prepared for a man to seem so physically attractive, in some porcelain way even beautiful.

I knew men were not to be thought beautiful but what other word to describe this mocha smooth man with his white shirt in glaring contrast. Shirt open, chest glistening with sweat. His striped satin pants flowed snugly around his melons making even them seem somehow tropical. His voice was sweet as a bird in fog, voice and features suggesting nothing but peace and pleasure.

Jeanie and I held hands across the table. No one could object to that. We even allowed ourselves steady eye contact. It was then I sensed truly I was falling into Jeanie.

We were startled when Belafonte himself, mic in hand, strolled by our table, singing a song with a calypso beat. He lifted the card stating prices from our table, pretended to read it and sang, "Drink up the minimum." The audience roared. Belafonte smiled at us, showing teeth enough for many smiles.

After the excitement of the show we rode in solemn resolve to the room above. I for one was frightened to close the door entirely. Not wanting to break the law I left it ajar - a mere fraction - and wondered whether Jeanie thought this odd. She didn't say.

I somehow managed through fumbling and short breaths to lose my pants to the floor leaving them within easy reach in case the house dicks broke in flashing badges. I boldly unbuttoned my shirt front and lowered my naked chest onto Jeanie, onto her also tropical breasts. She locked her eyes in mine. My feet stayed rooted to the floor. We made love.

I fell into Jeanie and had the sensation that someone had covered my ears. There was an echoing silence in which I was no longer part of my surroundings, I was only within this forbidden beauty hoping Jesus wasn't watching, hoping breath would last and erection too though God knows I had never been without one since meeting her.

This was all. This was Jeanie. The universe lost its horizons.

Paradise lasted only two nights. I was to take a flight to Minneapolis where I'd hook up with my new Yale buddy, Alan McCarthur. He would drive us on to New Haven.

I remember lying in that lavish hotel next to my Jeanie when I was struck with an idea. Not a good one. I rose up on one elbow, my face an inch from hers, a distance at which the most sincere things could be said. I was scared she might be pregnant. She said she wouldn't be but she didn't sound convinced. She would know in a few days. She was due for her period

"Send me a telegram to Alan's in Minneapolis."

She seemed confused. I went on.

"If you've had your period, say 'My cup runneth over.' If you haven't, then say 'Thy rod and thy staff are no comfort to me.'"

We laughed. We were in love.

When I arrived in Minneapolis, there was a telegram waiting. It read,

"My cup runneth over. Love, Jeanie."

All seemed great.

Sea Changes

My junior year at Yale was a sea change. Now that Burr was dead I defied God and said, as I wrestled in my sheets at night, that nothing mattered any more. Not mother and her faults, not Dad and his.

I had the temerity to say to my God, go ahead, kill me, give me the fits. Don't think me rude but I'm going to roll over and get some sleep.

Some times it worked.

I was put into a two bedroom suite, one bedroom mine alone. There were two guys in the other bedroom, one an incipient businessman whom I did not relate to. He was a class ahead of me. By the end of the year, he went out and bought a Chesterfield coat and a Homburg hat and marched off to the Taft Hotel to be interviewed by reps of Proctor & Gamble. He graduated. I never heard more about Proctor & Gamble. Or about him. We seldom spoke.

That left me with the other roommate, Cort Bryan. He was a burst of sunshine. As a writer he signed himself C.D.B.Bryan. He planned to make a career of writing and succeeded, his most successful book turning out to be Friendly Fire.

His natural father was a writer. His stepfather, John O'Hara, certainly was a writer. O'Hara's Butterfield 8 won Liz Taylor an Oscar. A charming bean pole of a boy, Cort loped along with ease and laughed at his own jokes which was usually justified. A loving mensch, he seemed not too bothered to be sharing quarters with Gerry, the chatter box neurotic.

Cort had quietly declared himself a writer. I envied him. I wished I had his courage. Seeing how casually he slipped on his writer's habit, eased my panics. His laughter helped just as much.

Still I fought daily against head-swimming gut-wrenching paralyzing panic. It was difficult for me to read my texts.

I became aware of a clicking in my inner ear. It was, I believed, early warning of an approaching fit. I discovered if I were to stop, even if walking on campus, dead still on the walk as others went around me, the clicking would stop, my pulse would slow and I could cautiously go on.

In my junior year with the good natured Cort as a roommate, I began with some caution to feel normal. Some days. Parts of some days.

I allowed myself to write, not in the important way that Cort did. He was taking a course called Daily Themes in which they had to submit a page of writing a day. I could not take that course, it wouldn't be allowed in the Navy curriculum. But by walking the shady edge of things, not presuming myself to be a real writer, I wrote a short story titled This Little Tinley Stayed Home and dropped it in the mail to the Yale Literary Review.

To my astonishment (that is, fear) they published it. I wondered why. I knew no one on that prestigious centuries-old magazine. I reasoned it was late in the year, they had run out of the good stuff and this fell into their hands so why not run with it? Late in the year, who would read it?

I can tell you someone who didn't read it – Madeline. On my summer break I offered her a copy to read and told her how surprised I was to see myself in print. She didn't take the magazine. Instead she buried her face in her hands and moaned, "Don't show me. What if it's no good, I'd die of embarrassment."

.

In Gertie my mother had a girlfriend to whom she could spill in torrents. I had such a "girlfriend" in classmate Alan McArthur. A slim pale white boy from Minneapolis whose father was high up the flour chain at Pillsbury Mills, he had been his parents' social secretary and knew all about where people should stand at a wedding and what to wear and what to serve on all occasions.

Alan and I ran up a modest tab at Morley's, the famous undergraduate eatery where, it says in song, the Whiffenpoofs assemble. The bill may have been modest but still a strain on my fat free wallet. Alan most often grabbed the check, ignoring my protests. He felt elegant in these surroundings, as did I, pretending to enjoy the raw clams I was forcing down my throat.

My other buddie was Alan's roommate, Cade Ware. Cade was what I wanted to be but gave up trying. He was silent (I'm out of the running already), studious (ditto), had beautiful even features which he modestly kept behind horn-rimmed glasses that made him look like a young T.S.Eliot.

What placed him in a far off orb of celebrity was the news he was to spend his junior year in France, a year abroad at the Sorbonne. Speaking fluent French. Sipping small espressos at cafes. Smoking Gauloise. I was never destined to be Cade just as I was never destined to be Gary Cooper. I loved him.

Alan and Cade had a third roommate, one I was most distant from. Stanley Selzer, was a serious inward-peering scholar not destined to become one of my "girlfriends" to dish with. Stanley made me feel the continental divide between the separate coasts on which we were raised. It wasn't just that he was a brain and I felt myself an accident at Yale, a nitwit with occasional flashes of whatever flashes and impresses people. It wasn't that he was New York Jewish and I was California Lucy and Desi. It wasn't just that we grew up on different coasts — how about on different planets?

He favored silence. He breathed a melancholy atmosphere of his far off planet. Me, I never had a thought I didn't express and even though I suffered my share of melancholy, it was offered as a public event and you all had to hear about it and run to my side. I was too near the sun. Stanley came from the distant shadows of Pluto. On those occasions we spoke, he paused, went to his familiar inner space and tried to translate. He came back with a soft reply which I also attempted to translate

Stanley was dating a girl named Anne. A girl from Smith. Anne was equally as brainy as Stanley, a sociology major who chewed through massive books written by a man named Talcot Parsons, books with phone book covers printed on phone book paper and from my point of view totally unintelligible.

Anne and Stanley dated by going to the Yale library stacks to study together for the weekend. I understood from Cade and Alan that they had lots of sex not because they were knocking down the walls, no, but because Anne was the daughter of NY lefties of the 20s and 30s who believed in modern art and modern morals. She didn't particularly look like a sex vixen but more of a girl who would cloister in the stacks, chewing on her nails and running her hand through unbrushed hair.

But I had it on Alan and Cade's good authority that she was all in favor of free (as in "willing") love.

One Sunday afternoon Anne was in tears in the hallway. She and Stanley had had a big row and it was over.

I can't say my motive was about sex, nor did I consider myself a sex dog. Remember I dated one girl from Smith for over a year who permitted me to kiss her on the cheek and I was grateful. As for Jeanie, well, she existed out of time, not part of my tangible east cost history. Perhaps I mean, I wasn't worthy of her.

I saw Anne as a lost child and being the good son of Madeline I rushed to the rescue. I offered to take her to the station for her return to Smith. What this meant is hire a cab. What this meant is I had few if any bucks. But I was in automatic rescue mode so I got the two of us in a cab and on the way there, at a loss for words, kissed her instead in the back of the cab. It seemed very nice for the two of us.

I waved her off to Northampton. Without money I had to walk back to campus.

We started dating and sure enough, she did end up in my bed though neither of us seemed to launch into flight. A pretty factual encounter but, look at me, I was having sex with my Smith girlfriend. Cort Bryan, my roommate, was impressed. Only later did I realize our early lack of passion was not a moral failure. It was a symptom of wrecked interiors. We instinctively shared neuroses which is to say, were meant for each other.

I early along offended Anne by reading her a poem by my favorite,

W.H.Auden, in which he warns "never commit a social science or be on terms with guys in advertising firms." She felt she was being mocked. I resented that. People should appreciate my sarcasm. Admire the invention at least and ignore the welts.

I hitched a ride to Smith one weekend with some flush boys, I assumed flush since they owned a car. I spent the afternoon with Anne, meeting her friends, learning about brandy Alexanders. On the late drive back it occurred to me I wasn't ready for a relationship. But how could I communicate this to Anne? I loved her in my neurotic way – in both our neurotic ways – the sweet impish beauty of her face, her slim boyish body, her fierce dedication to matters smart and, not to be ignored, her crush on me.

The answer to my question was familiar: go nuts. Failing that, act nuts.

Somewhere between those extremes I had a vision, I later wrote to Anne. I was nodding off in the back seat of the rich boy's car and woke to see the heavens open out the window and the Almighty who looked like a very young and compelling Jesus told me to give up sex and be chaste and thereafter loyal to him. I wrote Anne about my vision. We would be unable to see each other.

Not too long in the thereafter time frame, I was at a party one Saturday night, though where and how I can't remember since parties were not something I recall doing. A call came for me. It was my roommate Cort. He had tracked me down to say Anne was at the door. Could I get back? It sounded urgent.

It was. Anne had run off from Smith with a group of Dartmouth boys and went to a chilling mountain cabin where it rained for the weekend which explained why she was wearing high hiking boots that were muddy and she herself was a mess.

The motive for her taking off seemed obvious, she said through tears she tried to make involuntary. It was? I asked. The letter I had sent her.

Cort beat it out the door.

She quickly grew weary of the beer-belching sons of Dartmouth and crashed thru the undergrowth down the mountain and arrived penniless at a train station where a civic minded traveling salesman was willing to spot this teenage girl to a train ticket. He even ordered drinks to help her knit up the ragged sleeve of care. She arrived muddied but resolved when Cort opened the door.

We hid Anne in the room for the night since it was against rules to have women in evidence after dark. The next day her parents drove up from Forest Hills to fetch her. Her papa, a Mr.Bartlett, I immediately took to. He was a Pickwickian character, short, generous of body, with a silent wit given to puns. And he seemed tender with his daughter. For that matter, with me too. He didn't demand to know how she ended up muddy in my room.

Her mother, Mrs.Bartlett, was a Swede through and through, which is to say, it wasn't easy to see what was inside. She was thin as a leaf about to give up to autumn. She seemed most often distracted by things just over head. She liked suddenly to laugh, a light jingling of bells and then lean forward to touch your arm for emphasis.

As we ate silently in Silliman's dining hall, no one wanted to discuss what had happened. Mr.Bartlett described how difficult it was to find parking and his daughter would have to walk several blocks.

"Do you have luggage?" Mrs.Bartlett asked.

Anne shook her head in silence and ate her lunch. Her mother sized her up, nodded and returned to her lunch.

These people were not Bick and Madeline. That much I knew. What I didn't know is that in a little more than a year, Anne and I would be married.

Somewhere in that same year I dared to think myself a writer.

Sea changes.

Cabbages and Kings

My buddy Alan McArthur, one of those poor creatures who had been bitten by the acting bug, had staged in the Silliman College common hall a performance of G.B.Shaw's <u>Saint Joan</u>. It was a dressed-down affair, a table and a few chairs served as a set. And we all had roles to play.

I remember I played Warwick the meanie and Cort Bryan with leering intensity played the executioner. The director was a dear small man who was a graduate student in the Drama School and Joan herself was played by his wife, a girl from Texas with an accent as thick as cactus syrup which made such readings as "light your fires!" come out more as an invitation to a barbecue than a defiant screech at the Holy Church.

Alan asked that I write a parody skit for the cast party that was to follow. I always jumped at a chance to delay homework, so I dashed out the parody. It seemed to go well.

The dean of the Yale Drama School was there as a courtesy to the young director, his graduate student. After seeing the skit, he approached glass in hand and asked whether I had written a play. I immediately lied and said I had. He said he'd like to read it.

I ran back to my typewriter and within a week had a copy of a one act play on his desk. It was called <u>Cabbages and Kings</u> and was a (I hoped) humorous re-telling of the Rumpeltstiltskin story. Coincidentally, years later my buddy Shelley Duvall asked me to write a script on Rumpelstiltskin for her Faerie Tale Theatre. I did so gladly. I was acquainted with this Rumpelstiltskin guy.

The Drama School dean read my script. I was too naïve to realize how unusual that was. Even more unusual, he asked if I'd like to join the beginning writing seminar in the Drama School. I said "Sure" or something perhaps more academic. I later learned no undergraduate had ever been offered this chance to take a course in the graduate division.

The playwriting seminar was taught by a grand old man named Esler or some such. I remember a visitor to the class, a faculty member perhaps. The instructor leaned in to whisper in the visitor's ear all the while glancing in my direction. The visitor turned to take a look at me.

What was that about? What had they heard? It certainly never occurred to me Mr.Esler might be saying something positive.

My priorities became clear. I stopped going to class. I wrote plays. Surely I could goad the Navy into booting me out of the NROTC scholarship for disciplinary reasons. If I were simply to quit, I'd owe them for all the tuition they'd paid already.

Problem was, the Navy was slow to be goaded even though I stopped going to my Navy classes. I even skipped the final exam. My pissed-off Navy advisor assured me I was on my way out.

I lay dramatically on my couch in New Haven waiting for my discharge papers from BuPers. They didn't come. And then they didn't come.

Instead I received in the mail orders to report for sea duty in Norfolk in June. If I failed to show I'd be considered AWOL and the shore patrol would come knocking at my door.

So, Ollie, it's this way: I wasn't actually in the Navy but the Navy was sending me to sea.

Either way, I was packing my sea bag.

Halfway to Elsinore

June 1955. I am once more on a train to Norfolk to report for duty. This time aboard a destroyer, the USS John Hood. My uniform is more crisply up to military standards than the one that hung from my skinny frame two years earlier as I went in dread to board the Missouri.

I walked up the plank to the USS John Hood, saluted the duty officer and asked permission to come aboard. He vaguely returned my salute.

I in fact loved being aboard the destroyer, to be in the "tin can navy." The vessel was small and swift and could nose its way through sixteen foot swells that washed over without seeming to slow it down.

In the words of Bessie Smith, that blues singing goddess, "I ain't good lookin', but I'm built for speed."

The crew was not more than 200 able bodied and they were close knit, knew their jobs and did them without being weighed down by formalities and regulations. Altogether a lot of laughing and ass slapping and hard work.

The USS Missouri, that historic battleship, was the flag ship when I sailed on it, which means the top command of the fleet, the admiral himself had his quarters there. It was against ship regs to come topside in your denim work clothes. Since going to chow meant getting in a long line on deck, you have first to change into whites.

On the destroyer they seemed to live in their blue denim work uniforms.

One of the surprises of the Hood was I got to know the Chief Corpsman, a man named Clem. Clem was an old timer, must have been in his 40s. He was mother hen to all these youngsters aboard. As corpsman he was head medic, an equivalent to what we call "nurse practitioner" today.

I saw him come down to the cabin where a sick 18 year- old was toughing out a flu or just old fashioned sea sickness and put a cool hand to the boy's brow and tell him something funny that seemed to help. Clem always seemed to help.

The rumor was that before his enlistment Clem had been a hoofer in vaudeville. The proof came in the North Sea as we steamed over the north extremity of Denmark heading down to port in Copenhagen. The swells were giving us a good roll. On deck, in a space between two deck-level cabins, the crew sat huddled in their pea coats and watched Clem. He stood on the pitching deck and went into a soft shoe routine. He didn't crack a smile as his foot slid one way and was overtaken by the other and he whirled and seemed grandly surprised to find us all there watching him. We roared and applauded and stomped on the heavy metal deck.

On the bridge, the CO looked down and didn't react so we assumed this was fine with him.

I seemed to forget the sword hanging over my head. Any day, it's true, orders could come through from BuPers booting me out but I didn't mention this to anyone. That would have made it real.

My only problem was the Hood's version of Captain Queeg, the nutty officer of the <u>Caine Mutiny</u> played in the film by Humphrey Bogart. This man wasn't the captain, but a step down, the executive officer.

On our voyage to Copenhagen I was put in charge of the midshipman navigation division. What that meant was a small group of us sat in the "navigation shack" – one of those deck-level cabins that Clem danced around – where we plotted the ship's course across the Atlantic. Not that the ship was dependent on us but we had better discover our location to be near to what they calculated.

We went out at sunset with our sextants – none of these exist anymore, I imagine, in this age of satellite locaters – and peer into the heavy contraption of prism and moving mirrors and cause the stars to meet the horizon and record the exact time of the sighting.

Our goal was to get three coordinates on our charts that crossed lines forming a triangle that could be no larger than a dime. Inside that dime, the Hood's location at sea. It was hoped.

The XO, executive officer, who was our supervisor, popped his head into the navigation shack and asked if all was shipshape and squared away. I jumped to attention and told him indeed it was. He glanced around, none too convinced and his head disappeared out the door.

In a few moments, the ship's intercom blasted out, "Midshipman Ayres report to the Executive Officer's quarters." I took off at a run, breathless as I stepped up to his door in officer's country, an off-limits area I hadn't seen yet. I knocked. No answer. I knocked again. The door jerked open and the XO motioned me in.

As I stood at attention, my hat off (we don't salute in the Navy with our hats off), he had a question.

"Mr. Ayres, why do you allow your division to throw orange peels around the deck?"

"I'm sorry, sir, I didn't notice. I'll get right on it."

"That's not the question, Midshipman. The question is, why do you allow it?"

"It won't happen again, sir."

"But why did you allow it?"

I stood rigid, unable to think of another answer. The XO walked around me, opened the door. It was my cue to leave obviously. As I walked out he had one last word.

"Why?"

I raced back to the navigation shack and told my guys what happened. The only orange peels we could find were a few pieces on the table where one of the midshipmen had worked on his chart. We quickly threw those incriminating bits over the side and went back to our navigation plotting.

The XO didn't bother to knock, nor did he stick his head in this time. He opened the door and walked quietly in. We all looked up at him. I called my guys to attention.

The XO gave them all a grave look.

"Mr.Ayres has brought to my attention that you men have been tossing orange peels around the deck in wanton fashion. Wanton."

I felt my heart fly out of my body.

"I'm grateful to him for bringing this to my attention. When we dock in Copenhagen, first day you will all go over the side to chip paint. Mr.Ayres will be granted liberty. Clear?"

He didn't wait for a reply. He walked out.

What could I say? They had heard my version. They were pissed and somehow weren't sure what to believe.

I told Chief Clem about this. He shook his head sadly and said we must understand the next guy. What's to understand? Seems the XO lost his wife and his hair all at about the same time. He was gobbling pills from Clem to control his ulcers.

I was too young for wisdom. The wise move would have been to say, fine, guys, I'm going over the side with you and spend first day in port chipping paint. I'm not sure it even occurred to me. I just wanted off this bucket with the crazy XO.

I needed a drink. Mama's medicine.

The guys barely looked at me as I put on my khaki uniform with its khaki billed hat. They ignored me as they went over the side and I walked down the ladder to Copenhagen.

I had noted on the slow crawl into port that the country leading up to Copenhagen had a sort of paint box beauty to it. There were carefully laid out plots of flowers and vegetables surrounding the colorful cottages. It looked like a fairy tale.

I saw a street car. It seemed to know where it was going. I jumped aboard. I spotted a tavern with small round tables on the walk and I jumped off the car.

I quaffed a few delicious Danish brews, maybe more than a few. I spotted another trolley clanging its way up the boulevard. I ran and jumped on it.

It may have taken three trolleys with a few stops for fortification before I reached the massive central Square of Copenhagen. It was crowded with bicycles, a flowing current of bicycles that never seemed to stop.

I spotted another café with outside tables. Sitting at it was one of the midshipmen from the Hood, not one of the disgruntled ones chipping paint. He waved at me and I sat down with him.

I had even more beer. I remember ordering a steak. Sailors always order fresh meat when they get to port so I sipped beer waiting for my steak. Moments passed.

I looked down and in front of me was a plate. On the plate was the bone of a steak. The steak had been eaten. There were a few fries left.

"What's going on?" I asked. "Who ate my steak?"

"You ate it," said my shipmate. "You nuts or something."

No, it was early in my drinking experience and I didn't know what a blackout was. All I could do now was regret the pleasure of eating my steak, though my stomach didn't seem to know the difference.

I looked up from the eaten steak. Across the table sat a Danish boy in uniform. He smiled and offered his hand. His name was Svend. He was a Danish midshipman.

He knew a U.S. ship had come to port and would send on liberty into the Copenhagen square midshipmen, college boys his age. He wanted to exercise his almost flawless English. He wanted to meet some American boys who would share his interest in Shakespeare.

Shakespeare?

I came alive over the steak I didn't remember eating and asked him what his interest was in Shakespeare.

"It has been too poorly translated into my Danish, thus far. Thus far is a good phrase. I want to translate it myself."

"While in the Navy?"

He smiled and turned to watch the bicyclists flashing past. "I will not be all my life in the Navy."

I made some lame joke about not expecting to be discussing Shakespeare in a square in Copenhagen and that like Horatio I had yet to learn there were more things twixt heaven and earth that I ever dreamt of. Thus far, that is. Yes that is a good phrase. Thus far.

It's said that clichés come from true and common experience. Maybe Horatio had figured that out himself twixt heaven and earth. This Danish midshipman, Svend, possessed a beauty so perfect you would expect him to be on a travel poster. Blond, strong even features, teeth that actors pay a fortune to achieve, blue eyes fit for scanning horizons and a manner so polite, even courtly, that it was obvious I was no longer either in Kansas or for that matter Glendale anymore.

I learned from a letter that Svend was to send me later that the café in which he appeared as I came out of a blackout was called the Giraf. There were now two of my shipmates at the table with us. They lost interest in Svend and me and started plotting their evening.

It was as if Svend and I fell into each other, comparing excitements about Shakespeare. The shipmates shoved off. Svend stood to shake hands with them and thank them for coming to Copenhagen. It wasn't our idea, quipped one of the boys, but it looks like a good one.

They all laughed. And left. Leaving Svend and me standing by the table. He motioned to a motor scooter parked a short distance off.

"Would you like to see some Copenhagen?"

"Oh yeah, certainly, but they would fry me if they caught me in uniform on the back of a scooter. Navy regulations."

Svend gave this small thought. "Maybe for a few blocks."

I agreed that I hadn't seen anyone from the ship who would be apt to report me.

"Thus far," he said.

"A good phrase," I assured him. "Very English."

He kicked his scooter into a roar. I jumped on and held onto his solid body as we scooted through traffic. It turned out to be more than a few blocks before we arrived at his parents' house in a residential area.

He called out for his parents as we entered. No reply. He motioned me to follow up stairs. In his room, in this ancient of days before rock stars, his walls were covered with nautical charts, a print of a sailing ship and, interestingly, a page ripped from a book that said, if you squinted close at its legend, it was a portrait of Christopher Marlowe. A competitor of Shakespeare in a sense but someone to whom Shakespeare owed some gratitude. It was Marlowe's invention to write his plays in iambic pentameter. Shakespeare followed. Marlowe also dealt with matters metaphysical while the gore flowed red among the iambic feet of his text. Ditto Shakespeare.

The great difference between the two men was, Svend pointed out, Shakespeare was an actor turned good businessman who knew how to manage a theatre while writing the most perfect plays in history. Marlowe, on the other hand, was an all-out bad boy and got himself killed in a tavern fight while still in his twenties. It was only some years later, when such things were talked about, that I learned Marlowe was a homosexual. But then, also later to be considered, what was Shakespeare? A married father and good businessman and inter-stellar talent who wrote endless sonnets in adoration of a young gentleman. What did that make him?

We didn't get into such matters back then. We were excited to share our own thoughts and, yes, even dreams of one day writing well and even loving the right girl well.

Svend suggested I not break Navy regs. He pulled clothes from his closet and tossed them on his bed.

"You're taller than I," he said. "It is 'than I' is it not?"

"Sounds right to me but I'm from a high school in California."

"California," he said and his eyes went off somewhere. "How forturnate."

That wasn't my point but I agreed.

Svend stripped to his jockey shorts, hung his uniform in the closet. It would have taken a man or woman insensitive to perfection not to note the smooth understated perfection of his body. I was surprised to find a heat rise in me. Embarrassed, I grabbed the clothes he offered. The trousers were a little high water but the shirt was fine and I was in heaven.

What heaven? Here was a brother of sorts who was helping me along, assuming I was worthy of his help and had knowledge to share. Thus far.

A young woman sat in the living room quietly reading when we came down. It turns out that Merete was his cousin. She had recently lost her father, a Danish poet of reputation. She had brought a book of his poetry to give to Svend.

But first she gave him a kiss which he leaned down to receive. It was not a cousin's kiss. It was a lover's kiss. These two were in love.

Svend told his Merete about running into an American midshipman who loves Shakespeare and, in fact, he wants this new friend to read aloud something for them to hear.

Svend pulled Shakespeare's sonnets off the shelf and I found myself reading about lust, what an expense of spirit it is, lust in action. Curious. I had often over-drawn my spirit account and knew how expensive it was, though my lust had not actually had that much action unless you include under the cover shaking in a nighttime dorm.

Merete said it was beautiful to hear and that I had a good voice, maybe I should become an actor. I took that as empty praise. I was more concerned about fighting off my daily demons.

I suggested she read one of her father's poems.

"But it is Danish," she said.

"I hear it. The way you read it, I'm sure I'll hear it."

In a small voice she began to read. As the emotions rose, so did the volume. Svend watched her with what I imagined was intense love or some such. It certainly was without a single eye blink.

Merete had to pause. Tears had formed. She picked up the tea napkin from the table and blotted her eyes. Svend exhaled a long steady exhale. She went on with her reading.

I was right in one thing. I didn't understand the Danish but I understood the beauty of this girl. Quiet, living for the moment in the grief over her father but, more strongly, in the love of Svend.

She closed the book. Svend slid onto the couch next to her. She put her head on his shoulder. He kissed her hair.

It was decided. They would take me to the Tivoli Gardens, that ancient public complex of parks that had been charmed by fountains and paths and ponds on which lovers paddled their craft.

We found a table under a huge dark tree that was lit intermittently by paper lanterns in its branches. I asked Svend if he knew an English poet, Andrew Marvell, who described a citrus grove in the Bermudas as having orange lanterns hung in a green night. This tree under which we ate dinner had the same effect.

He did know Marvell, especially the poem in which he was trying to get his coy mistress to bed. "Had we but world enough and time, this coyness lady were no crime." But time was running out, the poet protested, since at his back he always hears time's winged chariots drawing near and where does that lead but to death?

"The grave's a fine and private place, but none I think do there embrace," I quoted. We all drank to that.

Svend stopped Merete's laugh with a kiss. The kiss went on. She seemed embarrassed but could not deny herself his kiss. It occurred to me that I loved them both. If it were only possible I could be insubstantial as this heavy summer air and live somehow between them, loving them both. Could it happen? It hadn't. Thus far.

I changed back into uniform at Svend's. I had to get back aboard ship. I told him I had only one more day in port. I had mentioned to him I had been taking foil classes at Yale but gave it up because it was my style to give things up when I have a talent for them. Svend suggested if I were free the next day I could go with him to his class – saber. Saber took stronger arms than I had. I agreed to go.

On the way back to ship I stopped at a kiosk that had on display, alas, a slim Penguin edition of <u>Hamlet</u>. In English, of course. They also sold tickets to a performance of Hamlet to be performed the next night in the actual castle of Elsinore where the depressed Danish prince did in most of his family. On impulse, I bought a ticket for that. Bus ride leaving at such and such a time, a cheap theatre ticket in back. I didn't ask whether it would be translated into Danish. I sort of assumed all that would wait until Svend had time to sit down to the task.

In saber class the next morning my Danish best new friend didn't seem to realize how heroic he seemed. He was serious at his sport and his broad blade slashed at his opponent with surprising force but no anger. I suppose I was movie-marinated and assumed that a man with a wildly slashing blade was obviously pissed off, pissed off at the invader or the murderer of his father or, worse, at the love thief who took his lady from him.

Svend was just good and for that morning, unbeatable.

I showed him the <u>Hamlet</u> I had found in a public kiosk. We were back in his kitchen for pickled herring and dark bread, lunch by Danish standards but new to me. And beer, of course beer. I felt as though I was initiated into a secret fraternity of – what? Cool and European? A boy with a hero who was at last a loving brother too?

Was I aware of any of these things? Yes and of course no. It is the yes part that stays with me.

He picked up my book. "Where do we start?" he asked.

I laughed. Silly to think we were going to sit there and read the whole of <u>Hamlet</u>.

"I've been told the page numbers are there for the intellectuals," I said, "so why don't we start on page one?"

That made sense to him. He opened to the front.

"FRANCISCO at his post," he read aloud. "Enter to him BERNARDO."

"Doing good," I said. Svend laughed, read on.

"Who's there? says Bernardo and Francisco answers, 'Nay, answer me: stand and unfold yourself.'"

I put my hand out to his, stopping him. He looked up.

"What?"

"That's it."

"That's what?"

"The whole play." He looked down at the page, wondering whether he had missed something. "There's a problem always in Shakespeare – I have this great instructor at Yale a guy who lost a leg in Iwo Jima – the problem is about who is he and who am I. Ontological."

"I know the word ontological."

"So everybody stops for some long monologue that says either 'this is who I am' or 'this is not who I am' and then goes off in all sorts of directions doing whatever the hell they want which may or may not have much to do with the monologue. Then someone stands up in the end and says these were all actors and you know about actors, they don't know who the hell they are."

I took the book from Svend and read.

"Who's there? Nay, answer me: stand, and unfold yourself. Already they're down to the major question, who are you and who the hell am I?"

"What is this unfold?"

"It's like laying down your cards on the table."

He made a grunting noise as if to say he understood. Or maybe he didn't agree. I went on.

"You have all these ideas about you and then the other characters have ideas about you, they're like mirrors, they all give you different reflections."

He looked down at the book. "This will be lot of work in Danish."

"A lot of work in any language."

He stood. I looked up. "What're we doing?"

"Stand and unfold," he barked as if a military command. He went out the door. He kicked his scooter into a puttering roar. I climbed on back. His body after only a day seemed familiar in my arms.

We spoke no more of Shakespeare. Where did we go, curving up side streets and climbing small hills lined with fairy tale houses, what dream did we travel the streets of that day? Some may be real. Some may be real only in memory.

I sat on the bus in what I was told was early evening though that far north and middle of summer it is hard to determine what is evening. Night is a few hours of dark gray before the next day brightens things, as if the stop on a camera had slowly widened.

I was sad. I had talked myself into this once-in-a-lifetime experience to watch Hamlet killing his kin in the actual castle in which it happened.

Svend had told me he and Merete would be eating late at the same café in the Tivoli Gardens and they would wait in case I could make it back.

Small consolation. It would be too late. I sat on a bus with a pack of serious tourists watching the suburbs of Copenhagen dim in what was meant to be evening and hating that I wasn't in the Tivoli Gardens.

I stood. I walked up the aisle to the driver. As is universally true in

Scandinavia, everyone speaks English as opposed to my home country in which everyone speaks English and no other. Patriots don't speak foreign languages.

I asked the driver if I could get off. He asked if I were sick. I jumped at the idea. Of course I was sick. In a suburb that could have been anywhere I got off the bus. I stopped one of those multilingual pedestrians and asked how to get back to Copenhagen proper.

He pointed off at a trolley stop.

After a long wait, I took the first of what was to be many trolleys. Since I couldn't trust the light in the sky, I kept checking my watch. It was getting later. And after that, later.

I jumped from the last of the trolleys before it came to a full stop. I could see the entrance to the Tivoli Gardens down the boulevard. I sprinted towards it. There was no one at this hour in the ticket booth. I ran past familiar coordinates, a path here, a fountain there, a bench where we three sat only a day before.

The café where we ate in the open at a small round table, there it was, maybe forty yards off. I stopped. No one was sitting at the table. No one was sitting at any of the tables. The lanterns in the tree above went off one by one as if a stage manager were throwing switches.

There was dark.

It is custom when going out of port to stand at quarters. I stood in the white sailor jumper and bell bottoms that we midshipmen wore aboard ship. We were in formation on the starboard forecastle, more or less at attention. We watched the kingdom with its magic slide from view. Finally there came the piercing of the boatswain's whistle. We were dismissed from quarters.

I reached under my jumper where I had slipped Hamlet. I had torn out a page. The page included a note written by Hamlet to the girl he supposedly loved, Ophelia, a girl he had treated like mud since his major love affair was himself or his mother which was a form of self.

The note reads:

O dear Ophelia, I am ill at these numbers;
I have not art to reckon my groans: but that
I love thee best, O most best, believe it. Adieu.

I may have done no more than failed to show for dinner that last night but to me it was a major failure. If only I could have seen Svend and Merete one more time. I could have looked at them in a way that would have told them all. They would have read my thoughts, surely.

It was this same type of magical thinking that caused me to drop the torn page over the side and watch it taken by the tide. In this reasoning that has no reason I pictured them on the shore as they walked in Scandinavian silence, not needing to hold hands. They would pick up the page from the foam. It wasn't signed. It wasn't necessary.

They would know who sent it on its way.

Cade Rising from the Tube

After Copenhagen we sailed to the port of Chatham, England, down the river Thames from London. As with all sailor towns, there was a pub not far from our berth. To distinguish it from what we call a bar they draw warm beer from taps, even beer dark enough to make one wonder if the specimen shouldn't be sent on to the lab. When we got our extended shore leaves, we progressed tap to tap to even larger pubs in London.

Before we went ashore, the Chief Corpsman gathered us midshipmen on the fan tail (rear deck) of the destroyer to warn us of the perils of whores and gonorrhea and suggested condoms and thinking about mother instead. That filled our heads with thoughts, mother not one of them.

The hustle of London and its twisting side streets was bewildering to us green Yanks. We did find our way to Westminster and got a look at the poet's corner but mostly visited the pubs, disappointed to find them closed at the most unpredictable hours of the day.

A group of my mates and me (we don't say "mates and I" in the Navy) were headed for a pub through a sidewalk crowd when a voice rang out.

"Gerry!"

I turned to look at the entrance to the subway, what they call the tube, as passengers were disgorging. A hand was waving at me above their heads. It was Cade. My Cade, my buddy from Yale. What was he doing in London?

He gave me a wild American hug and told me he was headed home from Paris via London. I had forgotten about his junior year abroad. He had gone to the Sorbonne itself, something as unimaginable as riding your house in Kansas to a land far away.

He had something to say, eager enough to grab my arm and steer me into a pub. I barely had a chance to wave goodbye to my shipmates.

He seemed to be burning high octane. He was no longer the serious scholar of soft words I knew at school. He grabbed us both a mug of beer at the bar then slid into a booth. He had news. About Paris.

"You learned all the dirty words in French?"

He waved this off.

"No, no, more important than that."

"Oh yeah?" I leaned in to hear because the crowd was noisy in this pub. He whispered something. I couldn't follow. I said, "What?"

"I discovered I was homosexual," he shouted.

I know in fact that all Brits present didn't freeze at their stools and turn to look, but they might as well have. I assured him I could hear, he needn't shout.

He machine-gunned me with information about the first French boy who seduced him and took him into the underground of French gay bars and how for the first time he realized it wasn't Minneapolis that was his home but a more portable place called "gay."

This was grave information. I stared into my warm beer. "What are you going to do?" I asked.

He laughed. "What am I going to do?"

"Don't shout."

"Everything!"

"What about Nan?"

"I already wrote her, told her the engagement was off."

"Wow."

"That's the best you can do? I tell you the most earth shattering news of my life and you say 'wow'?"

"How'd she take it?"

"I haven't heard yet. But I got a letter from my mother."

"You told her?"

"She said she wanted to talk to me before Dad gets wind of it 'cause, as she said, she has to live with him."

"God, that's serious."

Cade frowned, trying to express his pity for me and my inability to cheer his raising his flag of freedom.

"I liked wow better."

"Okay, wow!"

It seems I knew two Cades. One was the aristocratic scholar with T.S.Eliot glasses and deep thoughtful eyes. He pursed his lips and carefully spoke his thoughts as though stepping his way on stones across stream. This often involved endless cups of coffee. I remember his spoon slowly stirring his cup and wondering whether he'd ever get to the point.

The Cade who returned after France had transformed him was movie-star handsome, with hair I think you call raven. His cheeks glowed apple red. After he discovered his gayness he developed a talent for drink and became stylishly flamboyant. How would this do at Yale?

He sang Noel Coward in the shower ("I'm world weary, so weary, everything is gray or brown.."), merry and loud he came to my room in tufted smoking jacket, a cigarette in ivory holder circling his head and with his other hand lifting a stemmed glass of sherry. This was Yale in the 50s where the undergraduate body was largely made up of the stuffed-shirt sons of Wall Street.

Yale was not co-ed at the time. Girls were not permitted except in daylight or else stay the night and sneak out at dawn. There were no homosexuals at Yale, I would have sworn to it. I do remember a slim pair of young men holding hands as they crossed the quad at Silliman College.

But that was in the dark and besides, I knew these two were drama majors.

Back to the Barn

The USS John Hood was a week out of Norfolk, "heading for the barn" as the old salts say, when the news finally came. I was on midnight watch in the CIC, the Combat Information Center, which could be mistaken today for the control room of a recording studio. Radar scopes with a sweeping green image like an arm that could detect another vessel in the water – a bogey, so called – and for an instant it would blip light green then fade back into the dark. It was the duty man's job to report all such bogey blips. The background was a music of static and radios.

As a midshipman I was sending practice messages on a radio system that apparently coded our words, ship to ship. We were to make up dummy messages.

My message was, "Is this the farce that launched a thousand ships?" No reply came.

At that same time, a signalman on one of our sister ships was sending a Morse code message by blinker light. A message for me. From the Bureau of Personnel, BuPers, informing that upon receipt I was to consider myself no longer a member of the armed forces of the United States but until our arrival in port, was to report to the duty officer of the Hood. I was his guest, so to speak.

It could not have remained a secret. Many hands aboard the Hood could read the message as it blinked across the dark waters. Scuttlebutt, the fine old Navy term for gossip, has only those at hand to scuttlebutt about. I was certainly at hand.

A good thing I had made a friend in Chief Corpsman Clem. He assured me the world had not just ended and even allowed me to use his typewriter in the sick bay (his little clinic). No one else on the ship spoke to me. I was sent to Coventry.

I took the time to write a poem to Anne and a letter to Svend. For Anne I did a rewrite of Solomon's famous song:

My beloved spake, and said unto me, Come rest, my fair one, and settle this while with me. For, lo, the summer is past, the rain is upon us and rages; the flowers have folded in their beds; the time of the singing of the winds is come, and the voice of thunder is heard in our land; the fig tree drops forth her wrinkled fruit, and the vines with the withered grapes give up their life for a season's spell. Come, my love, my fair one, and settle this while with me.

A little grim, you might say, for a love poem.

The letter to Svend told him what had just happened to his American friend. So quickly out of the Navy and free now to become a writer. This was most certainly freedom but looked at from the perspective of someone just in his twenties with no prospects it felt like a helluva load of freedom.

My dad at that point had been transferred back to Jacksonville, Florida. He surprised me by driving "his bride" (a little large at this point to imagine in a wedding dress, my mom) up to Norfolk to come aboard the Hood and welcome me home.

There was the Commander, in full uniform, coming over the ladder and asking permission to come aboard. My heart did something: sinking was the least of it.

We went to a local coffee shop, the Commander and his bride. I hesitated and mumbled and finally got it out. I cannot go back with them to Jacksonville. I have been ordered back to the empty summer campus of Yale.

Why?

To turn in my uniforms and any books the Navy had purchased for me. I was discharged.

This fell heavy among the grits and gravy. Dad looked off. Mom reached for one of her many tissues to mop up the drama forming in her eyes. Dad looked squarely at me.

"What do you want us to do?"

That was my dad, asking to help, being the can-do man others had known him to be. On my behalf! I reasoned he had already lost one son maybe he could do a salvage job on the remaining one.

"I'm gonna have to come up with tuition."

"How much is that?"

"The first semester, twenty-five hundred."

"Dollars?" asked my Mom and did a mop up on her eyes. Dad took a deep family sigh and said, "Go on back to Yale. I'll see what we're gonna do."

"Papa," said his bride, "we don't - "

Dad put a hand on her's and said, "Never mind now, Madge."

What do you know. A new father. Giving me a fresh opportunity to disappoint. Or so my thoughts ran as the train click-clacked me north.

By the time I got off in New Haven, I grabbed a pay phone in the station and called home to say I had arrived. Mom was still being dramatic and tearful about my future until Dad grabbed the phone from her.

"You doing okay, buddy? I went down to my little bank and we got the tuition covered." He handed the phone back to his bride. "You coming home now?" she asked in a pitiful whine. I told her I only had a few weeks before the new semester began. I'll prepare for that. "Love you, ma," and I hung up.

I stood in the booth, ashamed to have doubted him, my Dad, the can-do guy. I don't know whether he robbed the local bank or asked for a loan.

All I knew is he came through.

Yale Station

There was mail in my box at Yale Station, as the post office was called. To my surprise there was letter for me, a letter from Svend.

Dear Jerry,

It was wonderful to get your letter, so it was proved that you are a living person, and not a dream of a person with human feelings and thoughts, and who were not afraid of opening himself, so that another human being could get a taste of those thoughts and feelings. Most people hide themselves behind a mask. I have one and you possibly have one too, maybe it was therefore I felt so relaxed when I started talking to you in the Giraf, and I felt I don't give a damn about the mask. It is very rare, so I wondered if it was true, but when I got your letter I knew it was.

As for Merete she sent me a letter the day after you had left in which she said that I was not enough interested in her, so we had better stop. She was so very right about that, we could never have made it.

Well Jerry the time is up and so is this small piece of paper, so I will stop with a thank you for the days we talked.

I give you my best wishes to you and your girl – you know it is a good thing to love and to be loved.

Sincerely yours,
Svend

I had quickly opened the single-sheet airmail letter and tried to read it as I hurried back to my digs in Silliman. As I reached the entry, my steps slowed. I made it up a single flight then sat on the stairs and read the letter for a second time.

I shared Svend's astonishment that those few days were not a dream, not just notes from a floating world that are hazed over by wish and desire.

Merete had left him the day after I left. Was it somehow my fault? I was raised by magic Mom who knew that life was the inevitable consequence of her own thoughts. I had the same curse, or do I mean gift?

In Magic Mom's defense, she was a romantic. Her dreams came in swoons and she spoke them from her bed, on her back with hands lifted to draw them in the air. Her fantasies became my own. Without her dreams, how stale, flat and weary all the uses of this world would have been. And yet.. Svend seemed to find me real and worthy.

But what had I done to Merete? That first night when she read her father's poetry aloud and I listened, hearing feelings but not understanding the Danish, Svend would whisper to me the sense of what she was reading and she would look up suddenly. Was she irritated? She went on.

In the conversation that followed as I enthused about the poets who had become my portable family, he tried for a while to translate to her what was being said. As his excitement mounted, he forgot the whispered translations. Merete settled back and read silently in her father's book.

The next day, the lunch of herring and Hamlet, Merete was to have joined us. But she called to say that she would be a disruption to the flow of conversation and she knew how much Svend had wanted to meet an English speaking boy.

Do I look back and think of that as jealousy? Who knows? All I do know is I clutched onto Svend from the back of his scooter, stopping at various sights where apparently both of us were busy lifting our masks. I remember looking across the water at a rock where the seated bronze figure of Hans Christian Anderson's little mermaid sat.

Beautiful in her modesty, not modesty of expression but of body. A slim boy-like body with pears for breasts. Her expression, I imagined since I was too far off to tell, seemed sad as she stared down at the water. She had the same body as Anne. I always disappointed these girls. Even those of bronze.

I tucked Svend's letter into my shirt pocket and continued the climb up to my room.

I was sailing in uncharted seas where there be dragons. I had lost my coordinates. I was reading with rising heat a letter from a man. Not any man. A man of strength, beauty and above all, a fondness for me.

Why the mysterious heat that rose in me?

I was dating Anne, the girl from Smith, a real brain and she loved me. And I her.

End of question.

The Barge She Sat On

In this first semester of senior year I went deep under water. Sea change was still decomposing the old Gerry. Those are pearls that once were my eyes.

I now knew I was to be a writer. A playwright. The how and where weren't settled. I stopped attending classes. I couldn't make sense of the books that lost focus on my lap. I wrote plays instead and when I felt too afloat on a crazy cloud, read poetry aloud to my dark room.

I went out and bought How Not to Write a Play by Walter Kerr. It cost $3.50 as books sensibly did in the 50s. The book liberated me. It said write what I hear and hope the actors hear the same: above all don't prompt them with instructions in parentheses. The words should steer the emotions if well written.

Worked for Shakespeare.

Cade initiated a weekly sherry/tea in my room for the three of us, Alan McArthur being largely our gleeful audience. Cade strolled around the room, cigarette holder and sherry glass cutting the air for emphasis and related stories of how the French had corrupted him. His roommate Alan sipped his sherry and bent his slim body over his knees so convulsed was he by Cade's stories.

Until he no longer found them funny.

Alan came in tears to my room one afternoon. He threw himself on my couch. The image of Oscar Wilde's Dorian Gray which I had just read came to mind. With much handkerchief wiping he got out his story.

Some jocks or hooligans (he used the words interchangeably), perhaps sparked by the newly flamboyant Cade, had broken into their room when they were gone. They rummaged into Alan's desk where they discovered magazines in his bottom drawer. They were male posing magazines. The intruders ripped up a few magazines and left the rest on Alan's desk for all to see.

In those modest days, these risqué magazine showed muscled men in g-strings looking down in admiration at their curling biceps while below, the avid reader was looking down at the bulging package in the G-string.

Alan was a pale and sensitive boy who craved to be artistic. He knew it was perhaps hopeless to be an actor but he rather imagined he looked like William Holden, especially the bare-chested Holden in Picnic.

Unfortunately, in tone he more resembled the Roz Russell on the porch drooling over Holden half-naked sweating in her yard.

I suggested he ignore those idiots. His two roommates agreed. It will all be soon forgotten. Sadly, his hysteria mounted over the weeks that followed. He left Yale in shame, returned to Minneapolis where he earned a degree at a community college. He continued to be a part of my life, sporadically, importantly.

I got a letter from Alan saying he was heading on to San Francisco. Not perhaps with a flower in his hair, but in hope of a freer life there. He said he had grown a pony tail. I wanted to see that.

Unfortunately, Alan missed my first produced play. The Yale Dramat (an undergraduate group) put on an evening of one act plays. They included a play of mine, The Barge She Sat On. It was my first experience of hearing my words spoken by actors and set up such a terror in me I had trouble sitting through rehearsals. During the performance itself, I stood near the door.

The play concerned a girl named Madeline (what else?) who lived in fantasy on her family's Long Island estate. Her fantasies were fed by things she found rummaging in her attic, particularly a picture book of Cleopatra on her barge. She imagined herself to be Cleopatra.

In the spirit of the French plays that were at that point turning my mind to gelatin, namely those of Giradoux and Anouilh, this was a contrivance about what happens to the young girl when an escaped lunatic wanders into her garden. He, inevitably, imagines himself to be Julius Caesar.

The undergraduate who played the escaped lunatic was a stunningly handsome young guy named Ron Moore. If fate is the word for inevitable, Ron turned out to be a mentally unstable piece of business himself.

He soon disappeared from campus. He moved to Manhattan. I heard he was living with a wealthy man. A man who not only loved Ron but loved the arts.

The man's name was Sam Wagstaff. This story-book prince charming, from old New York aristocracy, was closeted at the time. In order to reach Ron I had to ring Sam's number twice, hang up and call back. The fifties.

My Drama School instructor, Mr. Eisler, passed on to his class a one act play I wrote. It was adapted from a short story by Prosper Merimee, the man who wrote the story for perhaps the most perfect opera of all time, <u>Carmen</u>.

The story I adapted was <u>Mateo Falcone</u>.

Given my taste for gloom and foreboding, this play concerned itself with Sicilian peasants and their harsh code of honor – especially as applies to the killing of snitches. Young Mateo Falcone is beguiled into informing on a runaway countryman hiding under a mound of hay. Upon discovering this betrayal, his father who was as rocky as the terrain had the harshest of decisions to make. But he makes it. He takes his son off and shoots him.

Whether Bickings yanking me dripping out of a bathtub to taste his belt had anything to do with this choice of story never occurred to me. Young men are morose by instinct; old men by choice.

A group of Drama School actors came to me and said they were putting on a performance of my play. Did I want to be a part of it? What did they need? Well, for one, they hadn't been able to track down a bale of hay, central to the action.

"I'll get you one," I said. This effectively gave me reason not to attend the performance itself. If you think of it, where do you find a bale of hay in New Haven? And where come up with the money? Pride spoke in this case and I spent days worrying where to find the hay. Knowing I had failed them and perhaps fearing again the fiery baptism of hearing my words spoken on a stage, I stayed away.

Within a year, I ran into the baby-faced Latin guy who had played Mateo, ran into him on the streets of Manhattan. He asked what happened? I was mightily embarrassed. I wasn't well I told him using an excuse that always worked for my mother.

"How was it?" I mustered the courage to ask.

"Sensational. We didn't know where to reach you. Your phone was off."

"Yeah, I turned everything off up there."

"A group of us, we're here in the city now, we wondered if you had any more plays."

"I'm thinking about one," I mumbled, took his number and got out of there though for an instant it was rather nice to hear him say the play had been sensational.

Dangerous but nice.

Magic Realism

In those last few weeks of winding down at Yale, I was taken by someone now lost in the mix of memory to meet his painter friend who lived off campus. Not a Yalie. An older guy, this painter. Maybe even thirty. I was excited to meet someone living the life artistic which was my barely permissible dream.

I walked the few blocks from trim campus quads to rows of real houses, weathered bungalows not kept as clean as those in Glendale but then Glendale never had snow and winter grit to tend with.

I was thrilled as I entered the painter's small house though I was careful not to reveal anything as gauche as an emotion. He had an easel set up in his living room, a place of clutter that smacked of the real thing, a working painter. His name was Wynn Chamberlain and he did something called "magic realism" which rang no bells.

His paintings seemed to favor everyday figures done with almost cartoon precision as they walked into dreamscapes or unlikely situations. Bafflement and contradiction, I realized immediately, were the trade marks of this magic realism. Maybe of all art.

At the gathering was an exotic dame of many years, slim as a letter opener, with theatrical makeup and the held gestures of a silent movie star. Turned out that's what she was: a silent movie star. Her name was Aileen Pringle. Though I had never seen one of her films (how would you back then?) I was deeply impressed and realized how impressed my star-addicted mother would be.

This bird, perched on the edge of her chair, black dress but more in my memory, black feathers trembling from a hat, she was unlike anyone I had met. All elegance, but she was sweet to me and emphasized her talk by tapping her lacquered nails on my shoulder and giving me a look that said what she was imparting was not only privileged but important. I was impressed.

Whoever was that friend of Wynn's who took me there, told Miss Pringle that I had just had a play produced by the Dramat. I tried humbly to add I was about to have another done by the graduate Drama School, though I fear my humility failed to come through.

Aileen insisted I send her a copy of my play. She'd add it to her papers. Her papers? The New York Public Library kept an archive of her memorabilia. I of course sent the play to the exotic lady though I don't know if my undergraduate play is resting in the back shelves of the library with photos of all those others, like Valentino, turned ochre with age as though cured by decades of nostalgic dreams.

Also in the painter's house was an elderly gentleman, tall and stooped, whose eyebrows hung over his face like an awning. He had protruding teeth spaced oddly, a white muff of ruffled hair and an eye that squinted to hold you as he spoke while the other went large and watery.

His name was Carl Van Vechten and I was told I should be impressed. I was. He was one of those older men used to power, it surrounded him as a force field that drew you in. I felt both flattered and threatened as he leaned in close. I felt his shadow slip over me though there was no shadow. He suggested I call when I next got down to the city. I assumed he meant New York.

I learned that he was an old time compatriot of Gertrude Stein and was in fact the executor of her estate. He was also part of the Harlem Renaissance which meant he not only encouraged such protégés as Langston Hughes but was important in getting society white folk to go to Harlem in ermine and pearls (that's poetry again, Lorenz Hart this time).

As I later got down to Manhattan to visit Carlo, as Carl Van Vechten liked to be called, he took a photograph of me. I wasn't aware that he was famous for his photographs, mostly of celebrities in the arts and more often than not of black artists. I was twenty-one. The boy in the misty photograph (Carlo had something against clarity) set against a backdrop of patterned cloth, is someone angelic.

Beautiful, in fact. Me, Gerry. Though I didn't see it at the time.

No wonder that queen of the silent screen tapped me with affection with her lacquered nails, no wonder Carlo brought his force in close to my face and insist I call him when I was in town. I kept his card.

Wynn the magic realist asked I come later that week, he wanted to paint me. I realized his motive might not be entirely artistic. He was a part-time homosexual (my forgotten friend had said) and maybe Wynn was up to something.

It is true that my friend Dr.Rose proved himself a sort of homosexual. At least, he approached me in such a way but it didn't necessarily mean that I – you can fill in the blanks.

Above all I had a craving to be considered avant garde, part of the arts. Maybe in that world toying with homosexuality was considered hot. Posing for a picture wasn't compromising though it did seem embarrassing.

The passably handsome Mr.Chamberlain had me sit an afternoon to be painted but soon after lowered me onto his day bed for some hasty tugging and disrobing and before my initiation into art was done I found myself being mauled in the name of, what? Sex? Love? Not a joyous experience but I figured I was at last avant garde.

I later heard the painting was included in Wynn's New York show and that it sold. That seemed creepy. My face on a stranger's wall.

It became obvious that I couldn't go on being a struggling artist in this college room, and not wanting to get my Dad on hook for more tuition, I made my move.

"I'm thinking of dropping out," I said to the dean of something or other.

He dropped the file he was reading with dramatic indifference and replied, "Oh yeah, why's that?"

"Unless I can get a scholarship for another year. I haven't done much with the last one."

For some dim reason, he found that amusing. He laughed, picked up another file. "Why don't you join the army?"

"I just got kicked out of the navy."

"Oh yeah," he said and read the file in hand.

"They read much poetry in the army?" I asked.

"Sure, lots."

He didn't look up.

On my twenty-first birthday, February of 1957, when the rest of my Yale class were preparing to graduate, clay pipes and mortar boards under the expensive smiles of their parents, I was tossing clothes and books into a suitcase.

I was taken that night by Wynn to the outskirts of New Haven. He led me through the menacing streets, well, at least they were dark and the shadows seemed menacing, to a jazz club. A Negro jazz club. He told the musicians that this was my twenty-first birthday and they served me my first legal drink and then sang "Happy Birthday" with a bebop beat.

This sealed it. I was bohemian at last.

Well, sort of.

As I packed for the last time, never to see Yale again, I took down a book of Auden's I had bought with money I didn't have. I tore out a poem, In Praise of Limestone and folded it into my wallet. It was my journey cake for the trip I was about to take in life.

It praised the pliant, water-yielding landscape of limestone and encouraged us, the inconstant ones, to be just as pliant in our ways. Long before Timothy Leary and Ram Das and the Harvard acid-droppers suggested we drop out and tune in, here was Auden, with a great deal more wit, suggesting something similar. It was he who fed my errant heart.

In another poem I took with me, Under Which Lyre, he advised me "never make love to those who wash too much" and then closes with a commandment:

> Thou shalt not live within thy means
> Nor on plain water and raw greens.

> If thou must choose
> Between the chances, choose the odd,
> Read The New Yorker, trust in God,
> And take short views.

Advice I took to heart.

It was much later that I bought Andy Warhol's book, <u>Popism</u>. I was put off by its tone of a gushy high school girl, the type who draws unicorns in the back of her copy book but I was surprised by what Andy had to say about Wynn: "The people who entertained were the ones who really made the sixties, and Wynn Chamberlain entertained a lot, not only out in the country but also at his Bowery place."

Not me.

I was across town working in a zipper factory.

Wonderful Town

I am in Times Square. It is late summer, crushing humidity, still I'm in chinos, Oxford button-down shirt and regimental tie, a seersucker jacket with crinkly blue and white stripes. Standard dress for 1957.

From the honky-tonk turmoil of those giant signs whose lights tumble like waterfalls down around us and a gargantuan mouth blows Camel smoke rings over the traffic, I duck into an old building. Its stairs are wide. The elevator looks narrow and metal-lined. I don't trust it. I kangaroo up three flights of stairs to an employment agency I had found in the phone book.

A little barrel of a man in large black hat has his key in the lock. He is closing early for the Sabbath.

He believes me when I say I have just graduated high school in New Jersey. My speech isn't Jersey but I look appropriately young and I don't want to prejudice my chances by a mention of Yale.

"I need a job," I get out between breaths. "Just something temporary, just for, until I'm expecting to be drafted. Something. Soon."

He doesn't share my urgency. He reaches into a side pocket of his double-breasted, fumbles around as though his fingers could see and pulls out an index card.

"Show up first thing Monday. Don't be late."

I take the card. I read aloud.

"Barjo Manufacturing. What do they do?"

"Zippers."

Having spent enough time on a recent New Jersey graduate, he squares his hat, puts his hand to the worn wood railing and takes the stairs down.

"My God," I say. "How wonderful. Zippers!"

As I left the employment agency I let myself drift in the tide of pedestrians. Wonderful town. Of great help is the fact that the streets are numbered, crossed by avenues also numbered except for Sixth which was given another name which we as natives all ignored.

I calculate if I head east from Times Square I will hit Fifth Avenue where a left will take me north. I am to meet Anne at the Metropolitan Museum of Art. Some thirty blocks but I was young and six foot two and 154 pounds which translates into no body fat. In fact not much body at all.

I relish the shifting street scenes of the city, especially the walk up Fifth where the stylish never stroll but stride. My kind of people, I liked to think. Style and stride.

I stop and peer in at Tiffany's. Each window is a framed work of art with a priceless stone or two at its center. Wonderful town.

Anne had taken the subway in from the garden community of Forest Hills. She had dropped out of Smith within a week of me being booted (resigned, let's say) from Yale. She had the grades to graduate with honors in a few months. She asked her parents if I could stay with them while finding a place in Manhattan. For reasons obscure to me, she wanted to be there to help out. I guess. We loved each other, yes, in a rare neurotic way and she was graced with a talent not to point out that I was perhaps a little nuts. In return, I didn't dwell on her eccentricities. Well, we didn't at first.

Her parents were old lefties and easily accepted their daughter's physical relationship with me in these Sylvia Plath 50s. I loved Anne, yes I did, but I loved her parents too. She inherited from them a devotion to art. It was their religion. It was to become mine.

Anne stands among the columns at the entrance to the Met, clutching reading material which she is careful never to be without. She spots me, waves. I climb the broad steps and feel I'm entering a church. God knows, I was in need of a new anchor now that my evangelical chains had been hacked and thrown over. Young believers lounged on these temple steps involved in what must have been important chat. I was a crasher. I averted my eyes, humble in my silence.

Looking back at a photo, one with serrated borders and the date stamped on the lower margin (Sept 1957) I realize those eyes were not humble. As I leaned toward camera on Anne's porch steps, my head tilted down while my eyes looked up at camera with promise. Some sort of promise. Large, brown, they showed a brush stroke of white beneath the pupils as did those exotic boys painted by Caravaggio and El Greco and Guido Reni whose portraits I was slowly meeting at the Met and other holy places.

Anne and I walk the massive halls with religious seriousness, reverently lifting our eyes up at the richly confusing masterpieces.

It was the Bronzino that nailed me into place that day. Anne wandered off as I stood in front of Bronzino's portrait of an aristocratic young man. The boy stands in a black ruffled short coat and crushed hat, tasty couture that suggests the family had money back in 16th century Florence.

One of the young man's hands is planted on a hip as if a challenge. The other rests on a small book, a finger inserted in the page he was reading when we arrived and caused him to look up in that superior way.

Superior in the best sense of the word. Not just assured but bred to it. There was a beautiful arrogance greatly enhanced by one eye that seemed to wander off to the opposite wall. The beauty of imperfection.

Perhaps he was aware of his power, his sexual power. I like to imagine it drove Bronzino as he bobbed and weaved before his canvas, he who had himself started his career with an intimacy with his teacher, code word for entangled bodies and a wet interaction of art.

Was his young subject interested in more than breeding young Florentines to please his titled family?

It didn't matter. Not the walleye, not the arrogance, not my fantasy he might have a revealing shadow life, he was above all the conqueror of his space, at home in the universe of this frame. He wrote the rules for that universe and lived them instinctively.

Through it all he was anchored by the book he was just reading and will again once we leave, or better, if I will sit with him in the late shadows where high emotions gather, he will read me a portion or two. Who knows how long it will take?

Bronzino's boy. I wanted to be him.

Why Did I Ever Leave Ohio?

On Monday I am in the garment district. I forget and jump into a rickety elevator with dented metal walls. It is crowded with Puerto Rican girls, chattering like Carmen's cigarette girls, setting up a sort of choral music of their own. They tell me Zabin Zippers is on the sixth floor. I panic, knowing we are running out of air. The elevator comes to a stop. The door takes an eternity to open. I push through the girls and out.

A Puerto Rican girl holds the door. She yells, "Coming up?"

"In a minute," I answer. The door closes. I take the stairs at a run, stop, gulp some air, race on.

Zabin Zippers occupies the entire sixth floor, a loft that is loud with zipper machinery. The workers are all Puerto Rican. They glance up curiously at what looks like a clean cut college kid and then go back to work. The factory manager, identified by his clip board and the fact he's the only one not working, is a handsome Latino, vigorous and bilingual. He flashes a smile and points me to the walled-off corner of the loft. It is the office.

Through its windowed door I see a large man at his desk. He waves me in. Fading graphics on the wall say this is <u>Zabin Zippers, Barton Zabin, Pres</u>. The windows in the century-old building rise to the ceiling. Across the street, 17th Street, a building with identical windows stares back at us.

The large man covers his phone to introduce himself. His girth keeps him from more than half standing as he shakes my hand. He is Mike, the bookkeeper. Once off the phone, he explains I am to work for him. I will have a title. Assistant Bookkeeper. I know nothing about bookkeeping. I know nothing about zippers. I look around. Twenty years younger than the others, I seem to be the only assistant in sight. I'll have to learn in a hurry.

A salesman in a well-traveled suit and a hat he shoves to the back of his head, slides to a seat at a long table and grabs one of the three phones. He gives me a glance and starts yelling into the phone in Yiddish. Two other salesmen wander in and also grab phones. They are jovial and loud and make some cracks about this goyisha kid – or was it shagitz? - and then helpfully explain what that means.

Beyond them is a door leading to the only other room in this suite. Its plaque reads: Barton Zabin, Pres.

I soon learn the boss has little to do with zippers. He mostly dabbles in the theatre, a Broadway investor. A player, they say. I can see what they mean when I finally meet him.

He is a flashy piece of business with a curling white mane, expensive tailoring. He walks in a cloud of cologne. He likes the ladies, you can sense this down to his gold cuff links which he shoots from his sleeves for effect. How better to entice the girls than promising them Broadway when you are a producer, even though you are still in the promising category yourself? Mr.Zabin had failed thus far in his investments; all closed in the first week.

His alliterative name went on those down-market zippers that were designed to get the buyer out the door before jamming or stripping their teeth, cheap goods but the bedrock of capitalism. He paid his laborers little though he did make a show of going into the factory at Thanksgiving and handing out frozen turkeys.

Mike, the bookkeeper, lifts himself with an expense of breath from his cushioned chair and shows me my station — an accounts receivable posting machine. It resembles a wheeled typing table with some weird machinery on top. I am to insert a bill needing to be paid into the machine, each client having a separate card I can locate in a standing file that is rolled next to me. I enter such data as quantity, length of zipper and color. Temptation Teal, Island Blue, Raspberry Delight, Black Diamond — all poetic names.

I push a button and the machine rattles out a printed invoice.

The actual punching of zipper tape to length and affixing bottom stops and sliders, all that is done out in the loft where voices can be heard rising above the clang of the machinery.

The hall door bangs open. It is Honey Bear, the secretary. She grasps the door jamb for dramatic effect. One of the salesmen looks up. "Here's trouble," the salesman mutters.

Honey Bear breathlessly starts in on a saga about a fire in the subway that caused her to be late. She is somewhat in the proportion of a stump or, kinder, like a honey bear. She is pale, without makeup, as though the terrors she has just witnessed gave her no time for fixing her face. Big Mike polishes off his biali.

"Was anybody killed?" he asks.

"Almost!" Honey Bear screeches.

Mike wads his napkin and tosses it across the room scoring a perfect hoop into the trash. The door to the inner office opens. The silver-haired Mr.Zabin steps out, absorbed in paper work. He is startled as Honey Bear comes at him, mouth busy with her woes. To his eternal regret he once slept with this girl and she thinks this gives her status. Mr.Zabin swears not to remember it.

"Okay, you're late," says Mr.Zabin. "Go put on your face."

She's forgiven. She scampers off. I look up at the giant wall clock. It clicks loudly as it jumps forward a minute. Honey Bear's makeover takes seven clicks.

She vamps softly back in. The contrast is startling. She now has Cleopatra eyes, penciled lines of Mediterranean colors tapering back almost to her hairline. The goal is to make her seductive. By default it makes her resemble a raccoon, seductive perhaps to other raccoons.

"Gonif," the salesman screams. He slams the phone down. He turns to me. "Gonif, that's thief, you understand?"

"Thief," I repeat.

"Kapish?" Mike asks.

"Yeah, yeah, I ah, kapish."

The salesman swivels in his chair. "So where you from?"

"South Carolina, I mean, that's where the family is from."

"Any Jews down there?"

This confuses me. I wasn't quite sure which ones were the Jews.

"We have colored folks," I answer. The salesman bats the air as though the issue is settled.

"They're Jews."

I loved the zipper factory and they seemed to love me. I was odd man out in a favorable way, a tall goy with boyish good looks and at 21 was about to marry. They were Jews as they kept reminding me. I can't recall we had any of those in the WASP communities of my childhood. But here was my first taste, taken in by a sudden family who plied me with all sorts of delicacies like lox and cream cheese and something extra-terrestrial called pastrami and dinner rolls that sounded like coughing if you called them correctly, chala.

In a few months when Anne and I married, child on its way, they were concerned and sent home large wholesale boxes of toilet tissue for our family use. Or two frozen turkeys. Or a three-decker sandwich to take to the "little lady." I began to learn something of the humorous wonderful language which said such things as put your ass on the plate and your mouth to God's ear and then mazeltov for luck. I struggled with the pronunciation and they delighted in my fuck up.

In the protestant world I grew up in, raging father and Tennessee Williams mother, there was little sense of family, certainly not a cohesive loving one. Everyone seemed too preoccupied watering his own neurotic garden. No one on my side, I truly felt. As a child you were dropped into a narcissist free-for-all and if you wanted needs met you had to be either louder or more pitiable. Rage and sickness were the family traits. All of it marinated in shame, that oppressive worry about what others, especially relatives, were thinking.

My many Jewish uncles in the zipper factory made lively humorous stories out of the assorted tragedies of their lives. Then laughter. I was included in the laughter. Family at last.

Fortunately they told me that if I didn't learn to laugh at myself I'd miss the biggest joke of my life.

Also fortunate was a sign I spotted the first week just a block down Sixth Avenue and around the corner on Sixteenth Street. It was propped in the window of Mama Baraldi's Italian Restaurant and it said Mama Baraldi had a room for rent.

It was $16.00 a week. I was to make $60.00 a week from Zabin Zippers. A four flight walkup with bath in the hall, an airshaft up from the kitchen that filled my room with garlic. A tall narrow window looked out at a terrain of tar covered roofs with awkward-angled pipes and chimneys. Looking out that window I knew I was a real New Yorker.

What I wanted most was the life of the artist, whatever that was. I instinctively knew it was not to network with Yale contacts and secure a job with a future. No, working in the zipper factory and living above Mama Baraldi's kitchen protected me. I could pass unnoticed off in my doggy corner of life, presuming to create art, unseen, certainly beneath the radar of Madeline's spies.

But not without a price. I was alone again with my demons, this time without a tree in sight, someplace to send my fancies off to perch. I had to arm wrestle my anxieties to gain a few patches of clear breathing during the day and finally hard-won permission to sleep two or three hours at a stretch during the night. A habit I developed at Yale.

My refuge was Forest Hills. It was all trees, a green so deep it had violet in it, not the yellow green of Southern California trees. I took the F train out sitting in sweat on the hard-woven wicker seats to visit Anne and her parents. Anne and I were falling in love by slow steps. Which steps? You don't keep score when you're 21 and you're a boy.

Not only did we rattle back into Manhattan on the F train to see the museums but we saw a revival of the musical, Wonderful Town and I finally discovered where the lyric about this town came from, the one that ran on a loop in my head about the Bronx being up which I never visited and people ride in a hole in a ground which I avoided as much as possible because of my creeping claustrophobia.

Wonderful Town was at the Civic Center, a large auditorium that wasn't exactly Broadway but staged Broadway revivals. With real Broadway stars.

The real Broadway star in this case was Nancy Walker. From the moment she walked on, faked a stumble and then looked over her shoulder at the imaginary log in her path, made a face and continued on, I knew I was in the presence of a star. Why did that face make me laugh? Why did her squaring her shoulders and striding on to whatever lay in store make me love her? My eyes never moved from her so long as she was on stage.

Mostly I stayed in my rented room and wondered who the others were who lived on my floor, or shared the shower. We passed in the hall and exchanged hesitant smiles. I wondered how long they had lived there. How long would I?

I had come to New York to write so that I did in the small room four flights above Mama Baraldi's kitchen. I started with a stage adaptation of <u>Bartleby, the Scrivener,</u> a short story by Herman Melville about a young man all alone in his chosen universe. He was a junior bookkeeper as emotionless as the figures he enters in his ledgers.

What was I at this point? A junior bookkeeper.

After a week or two my adaptation seemed to me skilled but uninspired. I put the lid back on my portable Olivetti and lay back on the day bed - which was my night bed as well.

The late summer sun had gone down but its heat still radiated from the tar roofs that were my view. This was my chosen universe. I had come here to live the life of the artist.

Was this it?

I reached into the space between my bed and the wall and put a choke on a half bottle of rye, a Manhattan brand with fake cut-glass patterns. I swigged down enough of it to return to my original thought. What was it? Oh yes, Nancy Walker.

She and the young girl who played her sister were sitting on their boarding house bed, circled by the blue tint of a spot, wondering when this town was going to hurry up and get wonderful. They sang about it.

"Why oh, why oh, why oh - why did I ever leave Ohio?"

Good question.

Howl from Howie

Morning. A pounding of someone running up the stairs then a banging at the door of my Mama Baraldi pad. It was Howie. A friend of Anne and of her one-time boyfriend, Stanley. Howie and I had met a few times when he visited Stanley at Yale and he somehow got in mind I was a Gatsby character. Howie was himself short and Jewish, frenetic, with hair that looked as though he got it that way by pulling at it. He adored me so of course I adored him.

He was impressed at Yale that I was writing an epic poem on Hitler. Yes, Hitler. I had just read Milton on Adam and the battles in heaven and as so often happens, if I love something I sit down and imitate it. The sincerest form of flattery.

I was reaching for iambic organ notes, full of Nazi rallies, riots and slaughter. I got about twenty pages in before losing interest. But I read it aloud to Howie. He loved my reading voice. Another gift from the dramatic Madeline.

Howie was just back from San Francisco, from the City Lights Book Store. He had bought a slim book of poems by a man named Allen Ginsberg. Its title was <u>Howl</u>. Howie had traveled this distance to hear me read it aloud.

I sat. I read aloud.

<u>I saw the best minds of my generation destroyed by
madness, starving hysterical naked,
dragging themselves through the negro streets at dawn
looking for an angry fix,</u>

<u>angelheaded hipsters burning for the ancient heavenly</u>
<u>connection to the starry dynamo in the machinery of night</u>

The nitro in my head was shaken. Nothing had prepared me for this. Not Andrew Marvell or the sonnets of Shakespeare. What moved me most was the scatter shot inclusion of all things crazy that seemed to come from my own mind. They zigzagged with the logic of a psycho. The voice was explosive in bitterness and crazed in self-pity. My kind of guy.

I had a new hero.

I called Anne and told her I had something she had to see. A book Howie brought me. She wanted to meet in Washington Square but I didn't think it was much of a park. You saw more people than trees. Too many guitars. Since I wasn't yet into Woodie Guthrie, I didn't enjoy sitting among the strummers.

We'd meet tomorrow, Sunday, at the Seagram building and go from there.

I was just learning of my claustrophobia. I needed space which is a challenge if you're going to live in Manhattan. I judged every elevator on whether it would give me room to breathe should it get stuck between floors.

Anne and I sometimes went to sit in the plaza of the newly-built Seagram Building. The architect was Mies van der Rohe who was for us children of the 50s a celebrity. It was a place of true proportion, its form simple and as satisfying as a haiku. The actual sitting in the plaza made us feel part of the vast creativity of the building. As a claustrophobe, I reveled in its openness. Though the dark building that rose above was lifeless as a mausoleum, we saw it as a mythic stele lifting us to some eternity above.

The garden at the Museum of Modern Art was another sitting place for Anne and me. Her parents were charter members and in her teen years Anne took drawing classes there on the weekends.

The art at MOMA was mostly new to me. A world opened and my eye raced to catch up. That gave us two fine places to sit in Manhattan.

The garden at MoMa and the Seagram Building.

We discovered teas in the Palm Court at the Plaza Hotel. Behind the potted palms a string quartet played. The silver settings laid out on the snow-blinding linen suggested nothing had changed here in a hundred years.

You would think we preferred silence, looking around these sites, Anne and I, that it was our way of coping with intimacy. To a degree, yes, but we had a set dialogue of cultural chitchat. It kept us glued together. Also allowed us to ignore how neurotic the other was. We were at least sounding sane.

We added the Russian Tea Room as our favorite indulgence. It was dream-like, red leather banquets, under-lit elegance with an occasional flare of a brazier being rushed to a table by waiters in loose Russian blouses. I wanted to believe I was in the company of Tolstoy, the man who gave me Levin, one of the first green idealist since Adam tended his garden. It made us feel rich, then privileged, even though to get there we may have had to root under the couch cushions for dropped coins.

Some evenings we wander the dimly lit streets to the Five Spot on the lower east side. There was a magnetic man wearing shades in this dim room and doing mystical things on his piano. Theolonious Monk. The cover in the small club included a few beers.

Within months there came a comet across the night skies, Ornette Coleman whose plastic sax blatted alarm among the stars. I was fixated by his bass player, Charlie Haden, a beautiful boy who seemed carved out of angel food. Anne and I were told these were revolutionaries and we were thrilled to sip beers in their company.

How many riches were available to the artistic poor in Manhattan. In the late 50s, let me hasten to add.

Those times never came back.

Flamenco from Brooklyn

I had a date, I guess you'd call it that, with Carl Van Vechten. What do you call going out for the evening with a 77 year-old man when you are fifty-six years younger? All I knew is he was a published novelist and a highly regarded photographer of artists and celebrities. I didn't question that he might chase me around the furniture trying to show me his nickel. It wasn't going to happen and it didn't. My naiveté was believing he liked me for my conversation. Who knows?

I had followed up when I got to Manhattan and called him. He said he had tickets for a dance concert, a flamenco dancer named Jose Greco.

As I showered in the hall getting ready I was struck with a poem, one I hoped would impress Mr. Van Vechten. It arrived in stanzas and I ran from the shower, dripping and wrapped in a towel, into my room to write down what had just popped into my head. It took some time to finish the shower and the poem.

I was running late as I sprinted from the subway to his building on Central Park West. He seemed grouchy. I was guilty and apologetic. His vast apartment seemed like a museum to me, one that needed more light and a little dusting. Paintings, Tiffany lamps, posters, books and learned magazines spread across the antique tables. I wanted to pick up all of the items and turn them in my hand and ask Van Vechten why they were important enough to be there.

I was struck by a large portrait of Carlo, as he liked to be called, that hung in his sitting room. Must have been done in the 20s. His chin was down, he fixed us with a wide-eyed stare. His mouth was opened enough to reveal prominent teeth. It struck me that he looked like me.

Not exactly so, but there was something in the posture, the teeth and the gaze that told us he needed an audience that made it seem like me.

Carlo hustled us out to a taxi, fussing that I was late. We saw Jose Greco do his stuff. Carlo took some pleasure telling me that Jose Greco was actually a Jewish boy from Brooklyn. Maybe. But boy did he know how to pound his heels and glance back over his shoulder at his ample rump. I enjoyed it.

Carlo took me to dinner after the theatre at an Italian restaurant, the Capri, next to Roseland dance hall. The Capri like many things chic was not to be judged by its cover. It had a back room which you reached by walking through the kitchen. That is where we ate, under a mural of the Amalfi coast. I didn't know at the time what it was but the mural and the obviously broken English of the waiters told me I was deep in Italy.

He asked me about my plans. I told him I had dropped out of Yale and was hoping to be a writer and was working in a zipper factory. He ordered manicotti and explained that that was Italian for hand muff and I will notice when it is served how it indeed resembles a hand muff. It also resembled an enchilada which as a boy from the southwest I knew all about.

The manicotti gave weight to the cliché that food can melt in your mouth. It did just that. He ordered pasta with white clam sauce. I had only had red sauce and meat balls up to that time. It was also delicious. I was stepping up.

Carlo launched into a long story about being in a seedy bar in Tijuana some years back. He made it seem dark and sinister and sensual, what with cheap guitars and heavy-lidded young men of who knows what price. He had to go to the john and was directed to a smelly room in back. It had only a long trough with tap water drizzling through it. Carlo was stopped short by the sight of a young guy lying in that trough, in full suit and tie. He said to Carlo, "Go ahead, I'm from Yale. Piss on me."

There was a moral in this, I think.

Did I have a girlfriend, he asked. Yes, a girl from Smith who inexplicably dropped out of Smith just after I left Yale. Carlo frowned and said that sounded serious. I assured him that Anne was a real brain and she could go elsewhere. He corrected me saying what sounded serious was Anne's affections. I suppose, I said.

I told him I had written a poem for him.

"When was that?" he asked. He seemed surprised.

This afternoon, running in and out of the shower. Carlo took it, saying gravely, "A naked poem."

"I was wrapped in a towel," I answered, too late to realize I was lacking humor. He read the poem carefully, glancing up at me occasionally.

"Who actually wrote this?" he asked.

I almost lost my manicotti.

"I did," I answered.

He saw I believed what I was saying. He frowned, read the poem again and looked up, nodded. I worried he might have seen one of the stanza as a flash shot of himself. It was, sort of.

> The bumpkin young in open shirts
> Have never known a glance that hurts,
> They have no troubles;
> It is the aged who worry some,
> Who, if invited, never come
> Without their doubles.

"May I keep this?" he asked.

"I'd like that," I said and the manicotti slid down my throat without a problem.

Carlo walked me to the subway. He invited me to come to brunch on Sunday. There will be some people there I should meet. Yes, I said, love to. He nodded good evening like a perfect gentleman, not even suggesting I go up to his apartment. I quickly stepped down the subway steps. I hesitated at the first landing, looked back up. Carlo was still standing, his penetrating stare on me. He gave me a small salute. He walked off. A perfect gentleman.

In preparation for seeing Carlo again, I hurried east to the Strand

Bookstore looking for one of his books. They had only one hardcover, not first edition but among the first printings. It was <u>Nigger Heaven</u>.

Truth is I only really enjoyed one of Van Vechten's books which I read sometime later: <u>Peter Whiffle</u>. It stands out as a case report of an empty but stylish young American of the 20s in France and of other fashionable drop outs in the D.H.Lawrence American west and so forth. Because of his beauty and style, everyone is attracted to Whiffle but no one knows how to read him. The book's real value is its catalogue of all things tasteful, clothes, furnishings, cultural events, the right but unexpected places to visit. It is a manual for snobbery, but a pleasant one. Like the shield of Achilles, it's an overview of the hero's society

Carlo wrote novels for only a decade, in the 20s. He had started as a music critic for a New York paper (long gone) and because of his friendship with Gertrude Stein and his travels to Europe, he was in part responsible for introducing the US to Stravinsky and Najinksy and others. Because of his attraction to Harlem (how much of that was sexual, I don't know) he made it chic for the upper class to travel north on the island for a dangerous taste of jazz and sin. In ermine and pearls, again poetic words, this time Lorenz Hart.

As usual I arrive late. The Sunday brunch is down to coffee and sweets. I bring with me <u>Nigger Heaven</u>. I ask Carlo to sign it for Anne. Her birthday is coming up soon, June 10. He takes out his Mont Blanc fat and expensive pen with its gold collar and inscribes the book to her. As he writes he says to me, "If you want to be one of my boys, don't be late."

What does that mean?

The apartment is full of highborn homosexuals, and if not highborn at least high achieving in the arts. I do catch a glimpse of Carlo's wife who lets herself into the vestibule. As she passes the proscenium opening of Carlo's study her fingers wiggle at us under the shadow of a large brimmed hat. I learn she is Fania Marinoff, an actress of another era. She makes a flashing first impression. Style and stride. And leaves the boys to their party.

In the kitchen the sweater-wearing homos are having drinks and chat. I feel awkward and turn to my familiar defense, sarcasm. I am told that the tall gent eating the éclair was until recently Tennessee Williams' lover. He's a writer. His name, Don Windham. He asks me politely what my game is? Game? What I came to New York for. I answer that I hope when I am his age I am a successful writer.

He gives me a look that tells me I am a rude little nipple and turns his back. I was humiliated.

Mr.Windham at that point was 37 years-old which on the gay calendar is about 27. Not because vanity causes all gay men to lie about their age (just some) but the greater truth is they naturally look younger than heterosexuals. They take better care of themselves. More creams.

I was invited back one more time to see Carlo. In the evening. He had his assistant with him for a photo shoot. They took pictures of me. Clueless as I was, I didn't know why he wanted to do that. Maybe his friend Donald Gallup had told him I had promise. He was a library expert from Yale whose class on bibliography I took, maybe he spoke to Carlo. Mr.Gallup liked me, even gave me a passing grade which I don't think I deserved. The class consisted of three people so if you start flunking people, the class might disappear altogether. Or so I reasoned.

I was mightily impressed to learn that Donald Gallup was the executor of T.S.Eliot's literary materials just as Carlo was of Gertrude Stein's. And once invited to brunch with the literate and gay the best I can do is insult the ex-lover of Tennessee Williams holding his éclair aloft in the kitchen.

What is it about me? I seem so often to burn a bridge before even crossing it. I add this latest to my shame bath where I soaked daily. All this self-destruct just to keep Mama happy?

How tiresome.

On the Road down the Aisle

Sunday afternoon at Mama Baraldi's.

Anne is lovely on the day bed, drawing in her pad. I turn from my small writing table and slide to the floor. She's used to my craziness and doesn't look up. I crawl to her. Now she looks up. We make love.

In the monosyllable of Hemingway it is good. In my not quite monosyllable it is intense.

I have the sudden conviction that at last I have it all. I am in New York in the footsteps of all the writers of the century I admire, serving my apprenticeship. I have Anne and her lovely boyish body to meld into. Is this some form of androgyny? I don't stop to think. I even have a perverse pride of holding out for my art, working in a zipper factory. And when the steaming sidewalks of New York overwhelm me, I hop on the F train. Forest Hills and its green are a half hour off.

Suddenly it seems I have more than it all. Anne is pregnant.

We should have expected it. That Sunday afternoon, no precautions taken, not when love had taken us. Whatever was incubating in Anne, it was conceived in passion.

I wanted stability and at 21 was not about to make a decision on my own. So we said to each other, "Why not?"

Flippant and perhaps cavalier (we were both 21) we say, "We're both part of it. We were both there when it happened. Why not get married?

It was a life saver for both Anne and me. I was the only one who could crack her free of that Swedish winter that was her mother. The woman laughed at anything I said, laughter not being her custom. She gave the impression that Anne should be grateful to have found me.

Her elfin scholar father adored me. And Anne adored him but was disappointed that he lived under the heavy thumb of his Swedish wife. Most important, Anne and I had an agreement so tacit I don't think either of us were aware we had made: we would neither point out the other's insanity.

The two of us sit in heavy silence in her parent's living room. Her thin Swedish mother strokes her hair with an open palm, looking down at the floor.

"What do you plan to do, Ger?" her father asks. This is the 50s. You asked the guy.

"Well Anne says, why not? Let's get married."

Her mother looks up and the Swedish winter melts from her face. "Did you Anne?"

Anne looks at her father. "It's what I want."

"Me too," I say. "I get a vote. Why not? I was there. I was part of it."

Her mother stands. "Frank, set the table. It's time for tea." She walks out of the room.

Frank Bartlett pushes out of his lounger. He comes to us. He puts a hand on Anne's shoulder. He pats my shoulder with the other. Anne looks near to tears.

I give Frank's hand a pat. He goes off to set the table. His wife hurries in to wordlessly correct what he is doing, aligning the knives and spoons with greater accuracy.

My buddy Alan McCarthur comes back from his parent's house in Minneapolis to be best man at our wedding. He's dropped out of Yale and is about to spread wings and take off for San Francisco. Meanwhile he's come to Forest Hills to give us, the uninitiated, advice on putting together a wedding.

Since guests have come from all over and are put up in neighbors' bedrooms, Alan and I find ourselves in cots in a basement next door to my soon-to-be in-laws. I sensed in the dark of that fateful night that Alan was having one of his neurosis problems. I reached across the space between cots. I took his hand. He was fearful. I expressed no fear. He joined me in my cot.

In the morning there was much guilt from Alan. I didn't understand. We're buddies, buddies do such things. Bachelor parties. Besides, he had already recognized he was homosexual.

For me, I couldn't be homosexual. I was about to get married. I gave him a few morning martinis and we set off to the church for a noontime wedding.

Clichés have their purpose since they come from collective truths, as I was told by one professor at Yale, so it is appropriate I say that our marriage in a small brick church held up by ivy in the garden community of Forest Hills was "story book." The picture that appeared in the local paper showed Anne and me heading down the steps, smiling and waving as though we'd just won an election and looking, well, young. And quite attractive.

My parents had driven up from Jacksonville. Dad is ramrod straight in his navy whites and hat with scrambled eggs on the bill. My mother gives a brave impression of enjoyment standing in the front garden of the Bartlett house for the reception. She's taller than anyone, it seems, and has a hat so wide that the small Frank Bartlett sidles up under its shade and gives her a smile. She looks down, returns an uncertain smile of her own, not certain whether she is being mocked.

My friend Ron Moore, the boy who played the lead in my first play produced at Yale comes and brings with him his stunningly handsome lover, Sam Wagstaff. Not only is Sam dramatically blond he has the sharp features of a ski instructor. He speaks with aristocratic confidence, his voice resonating over the crowd. His laugh is like a gathering storm. I know he's in advertising but that he's really interested in art, to what degree I did not know at the time.

After the reception, after the relief of seeing my parents leave who seemed painfully out of place, I start some serious drinking. Anne and I change into our civvies and head off to a Connecticut lake resort. Hard to judge whether Anne was drunk, but I certainly was. I was jolted to find myself on the wrong side of the twisting country road, dark as it is in the country. A car beam comes right at us. I swerve off, bumping to a stop in the roadside ditch. This marriage almost ended early.

The resort is familiar to us. It was rustic, appealing to New York middle-class intellectuals who were amused by its lack of pretense. They bird watched in the surrounding woods and gathered for afternoon cocktails in the aging barn. Some played horse shoes in the yard, mixing the clanging of iron with soft voices.

The dining hall was in old Chautauqua décor, picnic tables and checkered table cloths. The sons and daughters of the guests, happy for summer work, served the food. They were hired as waiters. Anne worked there one summer.

But this is late September. The owners of the resort have kept it open only to give us a place to come on our honeymoon. We are the only two guests. Trees are losing their leaves. Cold is coming in.

I miss seeing the bird watchers, the old lefties, the teachers, those who like sitting in the aging barn and reading the tattered books left on a shelf that is called the library. We are alone.

We unpack our few things in the drab and chilly cabin, asking the electric floor heater to do more than it was capable of. The whole day has been exhausting for the two of us. Anne is four months pregnant and probably needs her rest. I have to calm down after the near death drunken experience on the road. These are the lies we tell ourselves. At least, I told myself. Anne never told me hers. But it was obvious it was awkward to find ourselves in this ill-lit cabin on a night in which affections and their display were expected. We discover well-worn decks of cards in a drawer. I sit on the floor in a corner of the cabin and play solitaire. Anne deals out the cards in the opposite corner. She plays solitaire.

Anne and I stay out with the Bartletts while we look for an apartment in Manhattan. I leave Mama Baraldi's and schlep my few belongings out on the F train. To reach the Bartletts, I walk down the quaint village street of Forest Hills. In the book store window is an item the New York Times tells me is hot. On the Road by Jack Kerouac.

I step in, read a few pages, don't know what the fuss is about. Sounds like someone I know. I put it down.

When I finally got around to reading the book it had a different impact on me.

Period of Adjustment

Our first rental was up near Columbia, a five story walk-up which Anne now visibly pregnant had to waddle to climb up to. It was a single room. The kitchen was a converted closet with a hand basin for a sink.

We wisely moved out to her folks in Forest Hills for the birth of our son and then were luckier in our next try at renting an apartment. We found a one bedroom, one flight up, on Greenwich Street in the west Village. It was next door to El Faro an unassuming Spanish restaurant with terrific food which we discovered all the hip people went to assuming it was unassuming. We could take an empty pot down to its kitchen and get a take out of clams in garlic egg sauce. And paella. Heaven.

In the Village we found our people; those crazed on a daily basis, meeting at the San Remo bar, crazed on art and sex, the two motives for living, crazed on ideals. It made sense I was working for Zabin zippers. What I was really doing was writing. That was the given. Working in zippers only made it more romantic.

Who were the other patrons that filter through my memory? The sallow fellow in the corner had just written Zoo Story, Edward Albee, a play that started his way to fame. The lanky brunette, a beauty so cold you were surprised she wasn't blonde, that was Susan Sontag and her lover, a Cuban girl named Irene Fornes was a playwright. Sontag had a child by a one-time marriage but now had a lady lover. This was the Village.

My people.

My son Christopher was born in a Queens hospital near the Bartlett home where we stayed during those early days of diapering. This was March 1958. I was one month into being 22. Anne was three months shy of 22.

I was scared. I wondered whether I was up to the job, the father thing. I bought a bottle and took it to the Bartlett's basement and waited for a thought to bob to the surface. Self-pity won the day as it always will when a bottle is in the game.

I didn't really have a mother, I reflected, and tears of self-pity came up. I had hoped Anne would mother me. Now she has a baby with a more legitimate claim on her time.

What I couldn't admit is that no amount of leafing through Dr.Spock's book gave me confidence. I didn't know nothing about birthing (or raising) babies. Was I to become like my raging father? That was truly scary.

After we move to Greenwich Street, I often write and, let's be honest, often drink late then creep like a burglar into the small bedroom we share with our boy. I stare down at him in his crib. He is always beautiful. I am fascinated. He seems to live in another dimension, eyes closed, his hands moving in the air above him as though driving a truck. I grow weepy and sentimental which for the Irish is default setting.

Those were the pioneer days when you married young and didn't make such a difficult study of child raising. Less expensive too were the five-and-dime canvas strollers you could fold under an arm and toss the infant over a shoulder and take subways up and down Manhattan and assume the child was having a good time so long as the adults were. The emphasis was on the adults.

In the 50s we came to New York to be adults. We didn't want torn jeans and aviator jackets. We wanted to wear coats and ties and drink in the Oak Bar at the Plaza. And share witticisms with brainy folk like my buddy Cade Ware who was now working at a small publishing house.

While I wrote short stories which the magazines were polite enough to return with handwritten notes and occupied myself writing 18th century poems, I finally got around to reading Kerouac. <u>On the Road</u>.

It was not just that Kerouac, as reported in the Sunday papers, was the voice of a generation called "beat" and with the word came spiritual overtones of things being "beatific" whose rituals of drugs and sex were our "beatitudes." I was a little under-wowed that he gave his work epic resonance by identifying so many things, it seemed almost everything, as quintessentially American, such as "the American night" as though to remind us we are not traveling down just any road at night. This had meaning.

As I drove down Kerouac's road with him, hoping at some point to encounter a narrative, I began to notice how he described the girls he and his prankster buddy hotly pursued. The adjectives thrown the girls' way were appropriate but seemed perfunctory. When it came to describing his pal or any number of other men who cross his pages, Kerouac heats up. His prose becomes lavish in its adjectives. Seems almost erotic.

And he was just like me. A heterosexual.

Perhaps the short busy finger of fate was prodding me to a recognition that I had more than a circling interest in matters gay. There was the evidence of making love to my best man on the eve of my wedding even though I waved it off as an alternate form of a bachelor party.

There was the fateful (speaking of fate) drive across country with Dr.Rose, the gatekeeper who opened to me a glimpse of a new world. Then the seductive painter in New Haven who after I paid my sexual dues sent me on to meet Carl Van Vechten. Then my hurried pull-out from that dive into highborn homosexuality and into marriage. I didn't know what to think. Or even whether to think.

Until along came Eddie Bear.

Along Came Eddie Bear

There was always for Anne and me a small pesky problem of intimacy. For me at least. I can't speak for Annie but I believe she feared I didn't love her enough and blamed herself. Her stern Swedish mother had never given her much hope of her own beauty. Her mama was wrong. She was a distinct beauty.

For my part I feared I didn't love her enough and blamed myself. It had nothing to do with Anne's appeal. It had all to do with that dripping garden of my mind where I walked daily, boys and girls together having green thoughts in a green shade. I needed more.

As Jean Cocteau said, "A little bit more is enough for me."

Fate soon changed all that sticking his finger into my life again. I ran into Eddie Bear on the street.

Eddie Bear was not his real name, but that is what my toddler son came to call him. He was a class ahead of me at Yale and had become a sometime pal. He had been in a sweat over an oral exam he had before graduation on the metaphysical poets and was sent to me. I told him what I knew but truly felt he could find someone better.

I remember Eddie taking me into the vast common room of St.Elmo's not-too-secret society where he was a member. It was afternoon and the hall empty except for Eddie in plaid Bermuda shorts and a phonograph player turned to full volume. Opera. La Boheme. I had never listened to opera. This one was narcotic.

Eddie paced the room, eyes closed, conducting an imaginary orchestra, then putting one hand to his chest and extending the other to the balcony as he sang along with the tenor. Eddie was fleshy and roughly featured, he could have driven a truck but for that afternoon he was Prometheus, driving a chariot with the sun at his feet.

I brought Eddie home to introduce him to Anne. They hit it off. He came by the next night and brought food. He kept on coming nightly, bringing a pound of hamburger and a quart of beer. He was full of theatrical grandness and like many heavy people put his fingers together in delicate ways to express himself.

For what had to be more than a year he dropped in, cooked his burgers and built his showbiz castles in the air. He became the third member of our family. We needed that. I may have had what decades later were called issues (like seeking lost boys) and Anne may have had that Scandinavian gene that made her suspicious of human pleasure causing winter to arrive more often than expected. Whatever the causes, we needed a third. Eddie became like a girlfriend to Anne. My little rug rat, the beautiful Christopher, put a hand to Eddie Bear's knee and made a shaky attempt to stand. One of his first. Eddie enjoyed taking him out in his stroller, stopping he told us at a club where he sat the toddler on the bar while the afternoon drinkers toasted him.

The San Remo was our favorite bar. It was walking distance from the zipper factory or our pad on Greenwich. In those pre-psychedelic days when booze and a little weed were the only fuels, the wannabees of art gathered to shout their ideas over the noise of the crowd, steal each other's wives or claim to have.

Here were "my people" such as Ondine, one of Warhol's super stars. He could sing Puccini in falsetto so piercingly it stopped the drinkers with their noses in the foam. I grew to love him.

When I got a few writing jobs, Big Mike at the zipper factory between bites lets me go and is happy to hire me back when the jobs run their course.

Which writing jobs?

Hold a minute.

Gravelswitch

On a village street I ran into Joe Bob, the deservedly unknown author of a Broadway musical that closed not out of town but in rehearsal.

He offered me my first job in the theatre which was, like all things theatrical, an illusion. I had met Joe Bob briefly at Yale. He had been a lighting and tech major at the Drama School. A Southern boy with an accent like poured sorghum. I barely knew him. But he remembered me and wanted to know what I was up to. Writing, I said, more or less, when not working in a zipper factory. Joe Bob gave me a sly sideward look (he had no direct looks) and in a voice suggesting he wanted to sell me a stolen watch, told me he might have work for me.

He told me he had written a musical and that a Broadway producer was financing its development. He wondered whether I wanted to help him polish the next draft. For money! Sixty bucks a week.

I ran back and took leave of the zipper factory. At least for the moment.

The musical was called <u>Gravelswitch</u>, the name of a small town in Kentucky. It told the story of a rough but charming railroad boss and the gal with a loose rein on her virtue he falls in love with. The year is 1910. The laying of railroad track, the loose woman and throw in the sunflower ingénue he forgets in his rush to sin, and you have the story.

I read the draft and saw no reason to point out its similarities to <u>Carousel</u>. More than a few. Especially the score with such numbers as <u>It's June, June, June in Kentucky</u>.

I reported to work at the producer's apartment. I was impressed.

Its bay windows looked down at the MoMa garden across the street. I was impressed in a different way to discover that Joe Bob had talked his way into living in the producer's apartment and running up bills at the cleaners and the local Gristedes. And hold on, also living in the apartment's many rooms were the producer's Wall Street- wealthy parents.

The producer had not actually produced anything. Not yet. He had tapped into his parent's money to invest in a few shows but none that put any posters on his wall. But he knew how to access any theatre by the stage door, not given a hard time as were Ruby Keeler and Dick Powell those showbiz hopefuls in the old movie musicals.

First day I sat at the ready behind a small typing table on wheels. I had brought my portable Olivetti because it was friendly to my fingers. I rolled in a clean sheet of paper. Actually, a yellow sheet of paper since all struggling writers typed on rough yellow second sheets.

Joe Bob explained that he wanted to start with the local preacher warning his parishioners about railroad men and the platoons of loose women who follow them as they lay track across our country.

He could see I was giving this serious thought. He enlarged on his needs, "Make it charming."

Okay. Charming. Preacher haranguing. Backwoods Kentucky. 1910. I started by typing the character's name in the center of the page: PREACHER. That was a start.

Joe Bob poured a drink. He headed for the door then stopped. "If you need me I'll be in the next room." He turned then stopped a second time to add, "Thinking." He took his glass and left.

If the script failed to enthrall me, the discovery that Elaine Stritch lived in the next apartment did. She was a friend of the producer and seemed close to his father. What a rocket she was coming through the apartment: kiss-kiss for the hapless producer then run over and touch my typewriter.

"I love to be near the seat of creativity," she would say, adding, "Whatever the fuck that means." I was dazzled.

Two things of note happened during that job. For one, a fire broke out in the Museum of Modern Art and we looked down at the staff carrying Picassos through the smoke into the garden.

The other noteworthy moment was a shocker. Joe Bob exercised his co-writing privileges and chose to write the one page that mattered to him: the title page. It listed only one author: Joe Bob. I questioned this. His face went all squinchy as it did when he was simulating sincerity and he told me it was something between him and the producer, don't worry. He'd work it out.

"What does Larry think I'm doing here?" I asked.

Joe Bob had to close his eyes to get this one out. "Typist."

I wondered whether Joe Bob and the producer were lovers but I abandoned that. For one, Joe Bob seemed schoolyard pre-pubescent, a sly boy who would peek under the little girls' skirts. The composer of the musical, a member of the Julliard faculty, once told me that the producer, the sad son of the Daddy Warbucks father was incapable of erection, though God knows how he knew that.

A further deterrence to any on-site hanky panky were the august parents living in a wing of the apartment. When they wandered in we felt the impulse to stand at attention.

As I took my sixty dollar check for the week, I demanded Joe Bob let me know how he was going to work it out as he promised.

He slithered in late the next day, poured himself a drink which he only sipped (like Sidney Greenstreet, I distrust men who only sip) and pointed out that he had done his best in getting me my first job but to do so had told the producer I was his typist.

But now..

The producer had read the draft and found it better (could it have been worse?) and wanted another polish. Knowing I was about to walk – or as <u>Variety</u> would say "ankle the prod" - he confessed that Gerry had in the course of typing proven helpful with the dialogue. He suggested I share credit on the next draft.

I got a raise. Ninety bucks a week. I also was given Joe Bob's lawyer from the highly prestigious law firm of Paul and Weiss and Rifkin and so forth who wrote up my contract. The lawyer told me I had to join the Dramatist Guild.

I was thrilled. A member of the dramatist union at 22. An insider almost, at least inside enough to have watched a performance of Pajama Game from the wings.

There was suddenly concrete reason to question Joe Bob's sexuality. He casually mentioned one afternoon after an intense morning of thinking that he was having an affair. What? With an international figure. Who! He couldn't really say but this attractive young artist had recently won plaudits in Moscow. That could only be Van Cliburn, I said.

Joe Bob placed a crooked smile on his face and refused to say more.

Had he shown as much invention in the creation of his script – well, he hadn't. But we did get away one evening to Times Square to see the opening week of Some Like it Hot. No struggling writer should see that film. It puts all writers, struggling or successful, to shame. It is a perfect film. Bless you Billy Wilder.

As we filed out with the crowd at the end of the show, passing the folks coming in, what do my wondering eyes behold among them? Mr. Van Cliburn. Bush-topped, serious, handsome. I put an elbow in Joe Bob's ribs.

"You gonna speak to him?" I ask.

"Please," he answers. "We musn't."

"Oh."

As we pass the famous man, Joe Bob glances furtively, blushes and looks away. Van Cliburn doesn't give him a look. He's here to see a film and it is obvious he doesn't know or care who the fuck the creator of Gravelswitch is.

We hear no more of the affair.

Shopping for Angels

One of the perks of playing at being a producer is that you get to play at being a producer.

For Joe Bob that included interviewing prospective cast members on the co-producer's tab at the Plaza and other candle-lit rooms.

He dragged me along, of course, for background color: I at least remembered what the story was.

We met with Art Lund, a Broadway musical star, who said he'd be interested in reading our script when it is ready. We met with Kaye Ballard who frantically entertained us, never sitting, though I'm not sure she knew why she was being interviewed.

The most impressive interview was with Margaret Hamilton, who in green face paint and a crooked finger had threatened Dorothy, the wicked witch of all wicked witches.

In Joe Bob's apartment, she was amiable and down to business. Her business was to act. She was looking for her next job. No cute stuff about it.

Joe Bob was soon crowing that we had agreements from all three of these actors to appear in Gravelswitch. At least he had talked to Lund and Ballard and Hamilton. He had never even talked to Van Cliburn but that didn't stop him from his initial crowing.

There was a painful dinner with Jane Powell at the Plaza. She was not hitting it big in Hollywood any more and her agent sent her to meet Joe Bob who apparently was Broadway bound.

I couldn't take my eyes off this sweet lady, the chirping song bird of my younger movie days. Joe Bob told her our story, using salt and pepper shakers to represent the good and the bad of our story. When the butter knife and dinner roll got into the presentation, all was lost.

I hopped in and tried to reduce it to boy meets/loses/regains girl. Bad girl in between. She got that. She also realized she was dealing with amateurs but was too much a lady to do more than rise, tucking her hanky into her purse, thanking us graciously for dinner and beating a path to the elevator.

A few nights later, we went shopping for angels. A backers' audition. This one was on the Connecticut shore of the Long Island sound. We traveled up on a Friday night, three cars of Joe Bob, singers, me, and a glorious man I was meeting for the first time, Jay Thompson. He was the pianist.

The house was Yankee lavish, which is to say nothing was new or ostentatious and nothing was in bad taste. Chairs were set in an oval in the library. I stood with script in hand, a lanky Ivy League boy with a strained winning smile, and told in brief the story. My narrative was interrupted at various points by singers jumping to their feet and performing a song.

One of the singers later made a name for himself in the original cast of A Funny Thing Happened on the Way to the Forum playing Zero Mostel's son. Brian Davies.

I couldn't help but notice that Jay Thompson, at the piano, filled in the spaces with a sea of music. There was an orchestra in his fingers. The composer surprised him by unfolding a score sheet on the piano rack, a song hot from his head that day. New to the singers also, but too good not to be illustrated.

Jay leaned in to give the score a quick scan. He pulled out a pencil and made a correction. The composer got huffy. Jay merely smiled and said, "F seven." Of course," replied the composer, "isn't that what I wrote down?"

Jay caught me watching this exchange from the end of the baby grand. Our eyes connected. Jay's eyes rolled. I couldn't resist a smile. We both knew this was crap. From that first eye semaphore, we became friends for life.

Jay was just building his career. He had written much special material for the Julius Monk review, Upstairs at the Downstairs. He was without question the wittiest man I had met and the material he did for Jane Connell (later Miss Gooch in <u>Mame</u>) or Jack Fletcher or Dorothy Loudon (house mother in <u>Annie</u>), was distinguished by wit and intellect. He was fast on the climb.

Within a year of playing backers auditions for Joe Bob, Jay was part of the creative team that brought Carole Burnet to fame with their musical, <u>Once Upon a Mattress</u>.

Joe Bob told the gathered prospects in the Connecticut parlor that Miss Jane Powell had just consented to take a breather from Hollywood and star in our musical. There was polite applause, but I didn't see anyone reach for his check book.

Jay looked at me. My eyes told him this was a lie.

As the singers sat down after a rousing rip-off of <u>Carousel</u> extolling the virtues of June and while Jay mopped his hands with a cloth as if to cleanse himself of any guilt, I stood and told the story.

In the front row of chairs a slim elegant woman straightened her spine as I spoke, leaned forward so as not to miss a word and opened her deep eyes to me as a gift. What a gift. I found sympathy. Support. Maybe even attraction in them. I found myself telling the story mostly to her.

At the end of the evening, I was introduced to her. Margaret Sullavan. I knew her name more than her films but I soon made a point to see <u>Little Shop Around the Corner</u>, a film that Jacques Demy and I often dreamed of doing again. Later, much later.

She took one of my hands in two of hers. She thanked me though I wasn't sure for what. I watched her walk off. Her eyes remained with me.

Within a year she was dead. In a hotel in New Haven where she was reluctantly appearing in a play bound for Broadway. She overdosed.

Her daughter Brooke Hayward wrote a book, <u>Haywire</u>, about life with an amazingly charismatic actress mother who hated her life, hated to act since it made her seem unreal. Her neurosis was so difficult that her three children left her to return to their father. When that happened, it is said her wailing could be heard from in the closet and under the bed. She was advised to get back to work. She took the lead in a play. It never got past New Haven.

She was married to such strong men as Henry Fonda, William Wyler and finally her agent, Leyland Heyward. She built so strong a protective wall that even the king of marauders in Hollywood, MGM chief Louis B.Mayer himself said he hated to meet with her. She gave him the willies.

That night she was my north star. I took my bearings from her. She was nuts. I was nuts. She killed herself within the year.

I had less talent and less grit so I fumbled on, reluctantly agreeing to live.

Thank you Miss Sullavan for that night almost together.

A Married Man

I'm not certain my anxiety storms let me sit still long enough to appreciate it, but I was a married man. I had a beautiful baby son. I was living in the Village, sharing life with a woman who got the drill, starve for your art if necessary but make sure it is art.

She, of course, had a solid academic background and therefore higher standards. She applied these standards to all comers. Even, uncomfortably, to me when a little lie of encouragement would have been helpful.

Something like a year into marriage I woke at three in the morning with the jitters. I never asked for pills since pills were the fetish of my mother and I feared if I got hooked on them I'd be as crippled (and epileptic) as she. I stuck with booze. It seemed more innocent.

There was no booze in the apartment that morning I woke at three. I opened every cabinet door, looked under furniture. I certainly wasn't drinking alcoholically at that time but I also was never without the protection of a bottle. Except for this night.

My panic was so great I feared I lost the ability to breathe until, at last, the liquor store opened at seven a.m. I remember with fondness Knickerbockers rye that came in fifths with a fake cut glass pattern. A bottle was in my hand by 7:05 a.m.

I promised my bottle never to neglect it again. I would be always faithful to it. A vow I kept even when I played loose with other vows. Like the marriage vow.

Painful to admit without giving you some medical excuse but I needed marriage, to be attached, needed someone to breathe next to me through the nights. Especially to be there between two and three when, as I thought, the earth stops for an instant on its axis. All breath stops. All life. The earth then turns on for another day. Living restarts.

I believe this is called delusional thinking.

I always considered marriage base camp from which I could scale the peaks of adultery around me.

Annie and I did many wonderful things early along. Like going up to a high school on Fifth Avenue so far north it was almost in Harlem. It was the Heckshire Auditorium, where we saw the first two productions of a man just starting his company, Joe Papp. I'm not certain whether the company was called The Public Theatre then, but it became iconic later under that name.

The two productions deserved all good adjectives you could throw at them. In <u>As You Like It</u>, Rosalind was played by a luminous young actress named Nancy Wickwire. Sadly, she was to die early of cancer. She would have been a major Broadway star.

<u>As You Like It</u> was the first screwball comedy, in my screwball opinion. Never had put-down wit flown like arrows between two young lovers in a way that seemed as natural as conversation but still truly art.

As a counter to these lovers squaring off is a melancholy chap who sees good in nothing. Jacques. He is so loveable being morose that you would join his troop if only he could bear having enough people near him to form a troop.

The role was played by a newcomer, a man just out of the marines, George C. Scott. Think of those eyebrows, think of that turned down mouth, of those eyes astonished that you would even say such a thing, and you have an idea of what Scott did with his performance.

A rare moment.

The next night we went up north again to see Mr. Papp's second production, <u>Richard III</u>. It is an easy guess who played Richard. Mr. Scott himself.

As the evil Richard, he gave the impression that he licked Shakespeare's poetry more than acted it. Licked it, relished it, spit it back at us.

Is it possible for something to be more rare than rare? This was it, the rarest of moments in the theatre.

Only in New York.

We also went to the Village Gate on Sunday afternoons when it was cheaper and saw Dinah Washington and Nina Simone and Anita O'Day.

As said before, only in New York.

Our intimacy buffer, Eddie Bear, came by as he did so often. He had news. He had a gig. As a performer. As with all things showbiz this promised more hope than cash.

He was to perform on off nights at the shabby Duplex club on Sheridan Square. He was sharing the bill with a worn version of Anne Miller who liked to peel off her elbow-length gloves and grind through the lyrics of —

"Days may be cloudy or sunny, you're in or out of the money.."

He asked me to write some material for him. I did, a monologue of a comic Eleanor Roosevelt which he performed in a crushed hat. No false modesty to say it was dreadful but Eddie didn't seem to know and continued to recite it to the few paying customers who went on with their conversations.

He asked that I attend early rehearsals (which turned out to be the only performances) at the Duplex to give him notes. I attended but had no notes.

After each of these nights, I accompanied Eddie across the Square and down a flight of stairs to what was of course a bar but which was for me another life.

Lenny's Hideaway.

And Slow Curtain

My theatrical career had not quite made its last bump to a dull end. I heard that with our revised draft of <u>Gravelswitch</u> we had received a nod from Art Lund. Joe Bob went shopping for an ingénue. Meanwhile he had secured interest from Carol Haney to choreograph the show. At least he said he had.

We had a few meetings with the young choreographer and she was a no bullshit creative talent. Starting as a choreographic assistant to Gene Kelly in some of his famous films, she ended up with a stand-out stage role in <u>Pajama Game</u>. At the time we met her she was about to climb into a major career as a stage choreographer. She died at age 39 just as her production of <u>Funny Girl</u> was opening. Cause of death: pneumonia and alcohol. Cause of death: life consuming talent.

I admired the woman.

Most important, we had a director. A cultured, warm man he had one Broadway credit as director, a drama not a musical. A well-received one. His name was Robert Douglas and the credit that so impressed was <u>The Loud Red Patrick</u>. He sat with us a few January afternoons of 1959 and gave us suggestions that were, at last, rational and creative. He was the real item.

A date was set for first rehearsal. I shouldn't have believed in my good luck since it had just run out. Mr.Douglas got on a plane and didn't come back. He must have sniffed the faint aroma of amateurism. We never heard from him again.

The zipper factory was happy to see me back.

Then there was of course one last whack at live entertainment and it whacked back. The ill-fated review with Eddie Bear. And the walk across Sheridan Square to Lenny's Hideaway. Also ill-fated?

You'll have to judge.

Lenny's Hideaway was a gay bar. I admit an excitement going down its narrow stairs to what seemed a secret and forbidden place. I remember a crowd of young men, some who were daring enough in that Eisenhower era of the 50s to wear fish net t-shirts. Eddie would buy a beer and station himself behind the jukebox, a blazing Wurlitzer with a rainbow display of colors radiating from its face. Eddie liked being behind the large machine for it in part hid his not too thin body and for another, I believe, as he leaned against the machine it put a vibration into his groin as the Everly Brothers sang, "Dream, dream, dream.. all you have to do is drea-ea-eam."

One night Ed and I sat at a wobbly cocktail table against the wall. A waiter named Scottie, a slip of a boy in tight black pants and a narrow nose to go with his very white narrow face, scooted into a chair next to me. I was startled. I thought he should be working. What was he doing at our table?

He looked closely at me and asked, "Are you gay?"

I immediately went on the defense. "Why do you ask?" I said, I said sternly. I didn't want to be thrown out of the place.

"Because you're beautiful," Scottie said.

I felt a knife to my heart. Or maybe I felt blood rush to my head. Maybe both. The word struck me because, well, as was obvious men were not called "beautiful." Certainly no one had ever called me beautiful, certainly not mother or wife. How inappropriate. I'm not even certain mother or wife ever mentioned my looks.

Equally disturbing, this narrow-faced boy whose large eyes were turned to me, suddenly seemed beautiful himself. I wasn't equipped for the effect that had on me.

Scottie was. He jumped to his feet, went back to serving customers, flashing me a smile as he whizzed past. Eddie eventually had to go. I remained, playing with my beer.

At closing, Scottie came to my table and said, "You ready?"

"Yeah, sure," I mumbled. Why not, after what he had said? I followed him up the stairs and to a small apartment not many blocks away. It was by then heading for dawn.

The slim boy took off his clothes, then took off mine and our two bodies did some sort of horizontal choreography on his bed. I don't remember the mechanics. I do remember that we kissed.

We kissed. I had never kissed a boy, not like this, rolling over each other, reaching the back of each other's throats.

Never.

I made it home before the sun did. I slipped in bed next to my wife. She woke.

"Eddie wouldn't let me go," I explained. She nodded, put an arm over my chest and went back to sleep.

I watched the ceiling. I remembered kisses. I closed my eyes. More kisses.

The next night after the Duplex Eddie and I again went down the stairs into the lower depths of Lenny's Hideaway. I had given much thought to what had happened. I had kissed Jeanie in high school. I had kissed the girl from Smith whom I married. In both cases, it was because we were in love. So it must follow this had to be love.

I followed Eddie to the same table as the night before. Scottie was busy. He whisked past. I gave him a nod. He seemed not to notice. On his next flight past, I gave him a small salute, "Hi, Scottie." He nodded and rushed on.

Maybe it was too dark in there. Maybe he was a mental defective. As he came near again, I stood so I could say into his ear, "It's Gerry, right. You remember?"

He seemed irritated. "Yeah, sure." I mean why wouldn't he remember? He rushed on. What he didn't remember was the important part, the part that had weaseled into my brain: he had taken me to his bed because he loved me.

I don't know when or how Scottie left that night, maybe out another door. But there wasn't another door.

The next night he redeemed himself by saying those magic words, "You ready?" He took me home. There was some sexual boogaloo but not much kissing. He told me he needed sleep. He turned to face the wall. I went home.

After that, Scottie took to ignoring Eddie and me. I confessed to Eddie my confusion. Eddied asked, "Have you ever heard of tricking?"

There was a last night. Scottie was headed out the door with a thrift-shop lamp in hand. He let me carry it to his door. There he took the lamp and said, "You want to see me, lunch tomorrow at Figaro's. Two o'clock."

He went in and closed the door. I walked home under a moonless sky.

I got to the Figaro coffee shop early, McDougal and Bleecker, kitty-corner across from the San Remo bar. I didn't know what to do with my strong feelings and thought maybe a few coffees would give me clarity. A few coffees in fact made me jumpy as chickens in a church yard.

Scottie slid into the chair opposite. He did what many gay men do, he arched his back and leaned his body forward to touch the table but his head was held back, blowing smoke into the atmosphere. He spoke.

"I don't date married men."

Another knife to my heart. I sipped my coffee. There was more.

"You want to see me you got to get rid of the fish." Fish? What did that mean? He read my confusion.

"The woman," he said.

"You mean Anne? Why, what did she do?"

He left without lunch. He was not a nice man.

I bought a quart of vodka and took it to my apartment, my married home, and drank compulsively. I told Anne that we needed to give a party. When? Tonight.

I took my bottle to my bed (just like Mama) and called some of the people I had met on my Gravelswitch work. My voice grew hoarse as I explained on phone call after phone call this was an impromptu celebration of the winter solstice, a month off.

Anne put together some hors d'oeuvres. By the time guests arrived at the small apartment, I was shit-faced. My voice had taken on a Tallulah gravelly quality.

I moved among the guests and drunkenly explained I was in love with a boy named Scottie and he doesn't want me.

I didn't seem to register that Anne may have heard some of this. Or concern about how my new-made friends in the theatre might react.

This was my first heavy dive into booze. In its black space I was able to humiliate my wife, alienate my friends and melt into a puddle of self-pity. Not bad for an amateur.

Eddie left town for a year. He came back and invited himself to tea. As Anne poured, Eddie turned to me and asked, "You remember Scottie?"

I tried to be dumber than dumb-struck and asked which Scottie? "The waiter at the bar we went to."

"Oh yeah, I remember. The skinny guy."

"He was waiting tables at Cherry Grove this last summer. The Yacht Club."

"I didn't know they had a Yacht Club." I was trying to keep things light.

"Yeah, he committed suicide."

I scratched my chin, not knowing what else to do. Anne with cold Scandinavian control, lowered her cup slowly to its saucer.

"I'm happy," she said.

I later learned that Eddie, as Anne's best girlfriend had paid her a visit when the heat was on and told her to hold on to her man, he was straying with a waiter.

It was Anne's habit to hold things in. Hold things in long enough and you get to say, "I'm happy."

A Howl of my Own

I did not consider myself gay when I married Anne in September, 1957. I was free form.

I certainly could not be gay since I had just married at the age of 21 and then proved myself a father just a month into 22 when my son Christopher arrived.

Still, just beyond those facts I sensed a circling fascination with things gay or at least with friends who were gay. My two friends at Yale, Cade Ware and Alan McArthur, turned out to be gay. Then there was that little do-si-do with the good doctor from Harlem but that happened in dream time and wasn't real.

Now this psychic blip with Scottie the seducer but that was sometime out of the past too, a swell rising from killer mother or dead brother, you know, one of those things. I was swept up with no will to resist.

So I told myself.

Allen Ginsberg put it right, the best minds of our generation all had to go a little bat shit crazy and Scottie was my turn. Not that I considered myself the best of any generation but then I wasn't locked up and plugged into the wall socket either.

Shaky but confident, my facts aligned, I went with Anne the day after my black out party to the Village Gate. Sunday afternoon and the drinks were cheaper. Who sang that day? Was it Dinah Washington with the chilling fortune-cookie warning of what a difference a day can make. Anita O'Day? Nina Simone?

I was surly (okay, hung over) as I walked the outer room at the

167

break. I looked up from the comforting floor and saw Miles Davis heading towards me. He was here to listen obviously. Since I had no business to disturb him with my slavish devotion, I chose instead confrontation.

"Why don't you ever play at the Five Spot?" I asked. He turned on me. I don't think he was too fond of tall white college boys with snotty attitudes and he took my head off. He said something to the effect that he had once played there, I think, and who the fuck was asking my advice anyway?

I was humiliated but rewarded. Miles Davis had talked to me.

Shame and pride were the mix I chewed as I walked out one night through Washington Square Park later that week. I lied to my Annie, telling her I had one last performance with Eddie. Eddie had had his last performance.

I felt on the hunt, a hunger in my loins, white bwana in the jungle stalking something unseen in the shadows. The hunger had to be fed. My steps turned to Sheridan Square. I stopped at the door leading down to Lenny's Hideaway. I had never gone down those steps alone. Could I do it?

Hunger won out and I fell like Alice down her rabbit hole.

I stood clutching a bottle of beer in the press of young men shouting over each others' heads. Using the excuse that I was lifting the bottle to sip I allowed my eyes to do a quick survey. What was I looking for? I didn't know. Until I did.

A boy approached through the crowd, stroking his bangs forward with one hand. Pale. Slim. Someone out of the ether. I thought immediately of Rimbaud. I found myself with sudden courage. I grabbed his arm.

"What do you do?" I demanded.

"I'm a poet," he replied.

Rimbaud it was.

He had to repeat his name a number of times before I got it. It was Soren Agenoux. And though in the privacy of his 10th Street parlor floor apartment he may have scribbled his verse, it turned out he had a day job too. He operated the teletype machine at the famous ad agency McCann-Erickson.

In this dark club, he was shy, diffident as all lost boys who later enchained me were until, of course, I enchained them, then it was the devil's own job for either to break out.

He asked where I was headed. Headed? He meant at the moment. Putting him and me both straight, I said I had to get home to my wife and child. This seemed to interest him. He smiled sweetly.

Fear caused me to overshoot the mark that courage could have taken me and I said almost at a shout to be heard in this loud basement bar, "Can you think of one good reason I shouldn't go home with you?".

He put his eyes directly into mine. "If you come with me, I will possess you."

This was ridiculous. I laughed. He didn't. Though I laughed, his threat excited me. He could turn out to be really nuts.

That's always exciting. Isn't it?

I should have recalled how the beautiful and seemingly shy Arthur Rimbaud was when he knocked on the door of the very much married Paul Verlaine and before that psycho love affair ended the older man had shot the younger, ending up in jail and the younger gave up poetry, Paris and celebrity to head for Africa to become a gun runner. And he was just coming up on 20.

These lost boys have incredible resources.

I entered Soren's 10th Street apartment and thus stepped into the dimensions of the second half of the century, though I hardly knew it at the time. It was to me a new if not necessarily brave new world. He had made a collage of an entire wall: paste-ups of the Everly Brothers, a sinister Jean Genet behind bars, Suzy Parker at seaside, Billie Holliday tilting to camera under a huge gardenia, Donald Duck on a bicycle that glowed in the dark, many cut outs from posing magazines, young men with arms flexed behind them to better thrust forward the cottony pouches of their jock straps. Over these pouches Soren who never favored restraint had drawn and then overdrawn giant spurting cocks.

I was Alice and this was all new to me. I had been raised on Navy bases.

As I went off to the john to get rid of a number of beers, Soren put on Beethoven's Razumovsky as played by the Budapest Quartet. He was on the edge of his bed, face in hands, as I returned. I sat next to him.

"It's like a message being sent by trans-Atlantic cable. Static. You have to listen. It comes through." He looked up at me. "Cancer is the sign underwater there."

"My moon is in cancer."

"Is it. Really?" He studied me as though absorbing this fact. He looked back at the floor. "Moon lit. Listen." He lowered his head toward the music.

"What do you want me to hear?"

He looked up and for that moment his eyes too seemed moonlit. "Like a transatlantic call that you can barely make out but you know from the few words you get that it would decide what we would do tomorrow and the next day and the next and perhaps, portendingly, forever after that."

I closed my eyes, trying to hear those words through the crackling undersea. He gently pushed me back on his bed. He started to undress me. I wanted to help but he wouldn't permit it. I was at last naked, looking up at him as he took off shirt and pants. He stood over me. He was wearing white jockey shorts. With slight encouragement he made his dick grow inside the shorts. I reached up for it. He pushed my hand aside. This was his performance.

Before I left he handed me a Jean Genet book, some contraband copy brought from Paris. Genet was his hero. A prison poet who had turned gay sex into a sacrament, its communicants were cross-dressers, its holy of holies the pornography of violence and death.

I put on my jacket. I said to him, "Maybe we'll catch up, you know, Lenny's or somewhere."

He stretched back on his bed, put his hands behind his head.

"I'll have to get you the Razumovsky," he said.

"Well great. Nice meeting you."

I beat it out of there. This guy not only had a weird name but he was weird. But on the walk home, I put my palm to my nose and discovered him there, still there.

I slept late into the next day. The door to the bedroom opened. It was Anne. She had a phone in her hand.

"Do you know someone named Argonauts or something?"

"Huh?"

"He says he knows you."

I jumped out of bed and grabbed the phone. It was Soren. As though we were the oldest of friends he said he wanted to drop in that afternoon, he wanted me and my wife to meet some friends of his.

"How did you get this number?" I suddenly realized he must have checked my wallet when I was out peeing.

"You're 815 Greenwich?"

Defeated, I said, "Yep."

"This guy is Chinese, a painter. He's truly talented. He wants to meet you."

He hung up.

I walked naked into the living room to return the long-corded phone to the small sitting bar that divided the living room from the kitchen.

"It's some guy I met, he wants to come by. He wants us to meet a painter friend."

"What do they drink?"

"He says the guy's Chinese."

"Oh, I have Earl Grey."

"That's not Chinese."

"It's tea," Anne answered and busied about to prepare things.

What must have been going on in her mind?

The Man who Came and Came to Tea

That afternoon was the first of many visits from Soren bringing friends to tea.

His friends on this first visit were Dale Joe, the Chinese painter and his pale white-boy lover, Jack. Dale graciously received Anne's Earl Grey tea and as though he were continuing a conversation we all had been having earlier (when would that have been?) Dale described the trouble he had cleaning out his parrot cage.

"You have a parrot?" I asked, glancing at Anne to read her response to all this. She was calmly pouring tea.

"I had a parrot but we got rid of it," Dale answered softly since he never spoke but softly. "But we still have the cage. It was a mess."

"They had a duck for my birthday," Soren said as he leaned forward in his chair, spine erect, here for a proper tea.

"Oh not really," Dale demurred.

"A live duck," said Soren. "Everyone chased it around his loft."

"It's not really a loft, it's on the Bowery," Dale softly explained, "it's large but - "

"Everyone chased the thing, that honking beast around the loft - "

"It's not a loft," Dale insisted.

"Until Dale wrung its neck," Soren said perhaps with a flourish if I knew exactly how to recognize a flourish.

"Oh my God," said Anne, also softly.

Dale leaned forward, patted her hand reassuringly. "We couldn't roast it while it was still squawking."

"You roasted the duck?" I asked, though not quietly.

Dale smiled and said, "It was Soren's birthday."

That was the first afternoon. The next, Soren brought by the choreographer Jim Waring and a beautiful black dancer named Rufus Collins.

"Rufus has changed the face of ballet," Soren said.

"Oh yeah? How?" I asked.

"By laughing," Rufus answered and laughed.

What a beautiful man.

The unannounced tea guests arrived for what seemed months. One afternoon he brought over a magical Cuban named Carlos Clarens who was writing a history of the horror film long before anyone would have thought it necessary. A compulsively happy man with a wild afro who seemed to make everyone happy and everyone in turn sent him tickets to come visit – for example, Bertolucci for Carlos to come to Rome, Agnes Varda for him to come to Cannes.

During his visit, there was a knock. Soren opened the door to a poet named Gerard Malanga, poet and movie star handsome. Behind him was a man with an explosion of white hair holding a 16mm camera. I wondered how this guy got his hair to look that way: perhaps by pulling at it. They were headed out to Brooklyn to shoot something. Carlos and Soren threw on their coats to join them. Soren introduced the pair. The white haired man was Andy. We later learned he had a last name, Warhol. He said nothing but peered into the apartment, seeming to study me in case he had later to give testimony.

No plan had been made for me to meet up with Soren a second time but the bwana hunter in me took over and I marched out into the night to a jungle beat and finally – with one massive leap of metaphors - I slid down the rabbit hole to Lenny's Hideaway. Soren was impatient at the bar. It was as though he were expecting me.

"It's too loud in here," he said and headed for the stairs. He didn't look back. He assumed I'd be following. His assumption was correct.

There was no monologue this time. The door was in the swing of closing itself when it banged shut from the weight of two bodies falling against it, kissing men, undressing men.

I had known intensity I thought of as love but not until the danger of Soren and the incestual link that was to my brother that I felt out in Soren, did I at last know I had in my hands what had been always departing – out the door – to war – to a secret sexual life - my brother – now as flesh he wrestled into me as no girlfriend had. I had orgasms with girls – only two girls, in fact - at high school, in college – but nothing like what this two-backed beast Soren and I achieved on the parlor floor in the Village brownstone where somewhere between two and three in the morning, that death moment when the earth poises on its axis as though hesitant before deciding to spin on for another turn of day – at that still point of the no longer turning world – I Gerry – I merged with the brother in Soren. I flew through dimensions, escaping all in that trajectory, through all flights orgasmalerious and behold, death was not for that moment proud –

I was!

After one of those early tussles, I sat on the floor, leaned back against his wall, bare except for the sweat running down my body. Soren offered me a cigarette.

"I can't smoke. Makes me sick. Unless I'm drinking."

Soren found a water glass and walked naked to me. He filled the glass with Scotch. Johnnie Walker black label, a surprisingly pricey item for this humble poet.

With cigarette and uncut Scotch, I was able to assemble myself.

"How did you get to my house?"

"It's no big secret."

"That first time. How did you know where I lived."

"I thought you wanted to see me."

"Or who I was, for God's sake." "

"You asked me to come."

"Not how I remember."

"You don't understand."

"Let's see, Frankie Avalon was singing Venus Goddess of Love on the jukebox—"

"I don't like Frankie Avalon."

"— when you poetically wafted by and spotted me and said ah, there's a hot trick. Since meeting you I've learned all the language, a trick is a one night sleight of hand and trade, trade is not a fair exchange. "

Soren bowed his head. "You sound like every fucking fag dick-licker in this town." He looked up. "Have you ever had a lover?"

"I'm married," as though that meant anything. He studied me wondering if there were any comfort in this.

"You don't trust me," he said.

"We're even. I don't trust me."

He wanted none of it. He walked naked to his portable record player. Again, he put on the Rasumovsky.

"I trust you" he said, "and I'm going to watch you, watch you expand. That'll help you.. very much. I will."

That first night he had given me a copy of the Jean Genet book, <u>Our Lady of the Flowers</u>. I put it under my bedside table in the room where wife and child slept unaware the earth had stopped in that night.

"I loved him with my usual violence," Soren had underlined in the book. It proved a template for my long wrestle with Soren.

How necessary marriage seemed to me, strange as it may sound. How necessary Anne was, though I doubt she'd be flattered to hear why. I needed her stability as I raced out the door to chaos.

I may be crazy but not stupid so I knew well enough that this was not good behavior, why else would I so quickly learn to lie about it? However I felt in whatever was my core that it was justified. How so? Like my mother with her booze, I called it my medicine.

Self-serving, yes, but true.

Over Whitman's Bridge

Dale Joe invited me by to see his art. Soren was to meet me there in Dale's Bowery apartment. This was the late 50s and the Bowery was still the Bowery, a place for poverty and winos like logs to be stepped over in the street.

Soren wasn't there when I arrived. As I looked at Dale's serene collages, laid out in exquisite splodges like a Chinese poem, he complained it was so like Frank to be late. Frank? Oh, he corrected himself, Soren to be late.

I had learned from Mother Madeline to probe like a tongue in an empty socket for the truth. Dale with a few maidenly demurs spilled the beans. Or as one of my Southern maiden aunts who purposely mentioned the family secret about Uncle Lem, a custom down south called "dropping the bobbie pin," Dale dropped the bobbie pin on Soren.

Soren was not originally Soren Agenoux, how could anyone be? He was Frank Hansen, who left a vague pursuit of education at Berkeley to come across country to New York, perhaps passing Kerouac since this was about the time poet Jack was gathering notes on the road too.

Frank Hansen was slim and poetic, the type that can be persistent when they make up their minds and soon after his arrival in New York he won the affections of an emerging heavyweight artist, Cy Twombly. The artist who was known to be married (straight, like me) didn't like waking to discover Frank Hansen crouched on the fire escape staring through the window.

To rid himself of Frank, the artist simply knocked him flat

whenever he encountered him on the sidewalk or at an art opening or standing poetic and slim next to his mailbox when the artist came down for a saunter over to the Cedar Bar.

Frank revealed his bruises to his Chinese painter friend, Dale Joe, whom he had known at Berkeley. Frank said it was beyond endurance. He was leaving town and vowed never to return. Dale advised patience but Frank would hear none of it.

No Frank for a number of weeks. One day at Gristede's, Dale spotted him fingering the cantaloupes, probing their fontanels for ripeness.

"Frank," Dale called.

No reply.

"Are you deaf, man?"

Frank looked up at his old friend and introduced himself. He was now Soren Agenoux. Soren because of his affection for Kierkegaard, also a Soren. And Agenoux, not "ingénue" but "agenoux" as in "on your knees" because of things medieval and French and Catholic. Soren certainly was not an ingénue.

I once wrote a clerihew for Soren, a verse form I cribbed from Auden. Mine went:

'Remember Soren Agenoux,
That Greenwich Village raj your knew
Who never found this life appealing
Unless he happened to be kneeling.'

Annie and I were forced to leave our Greenwich Village digs, they were raising the rent from $90 to $110 a month. Soren had left McCann-Erickson and was now working for the avant garde theatre run by Judith Malina and Julian Beck. It is always referred to as "the legendary avant garde theatre." Its name was The Living Theatre.

He walked with Anne and me and baby in the stroller across the Brooklyn Bridge. A beautiful crossing on a sun-lit day and fraught with history as Soren reminded us that Walt Whitman watched this bridge being built and was among the first to walk across it. He wrote poems to it.

We discovered just a block below Brooklyn Heights a district called Cobble Hill. We rented an apartment there. Soren was a constant visitor. He was the Steppenwolf that Herman Hesse wrote about, the outsider sitting on the freshly polished stairs getting off on the fumes of bourgeois floor wax. He longed to be part of us. As pointed out, we seemed comfortable with the company of a third. Almost needed it.

In the evenings I ran to Soren as to familiar chaos, to embrace the forbidden, a flirtation with death. Short of that, an oblivion sliding to death. On Tenth Street.

Soren had everything I wanted. Chaos, insanity, intimidation, adoration, a door to the underground of forbidden but soon obsessive sex.

Who could ask for anything more? Excuse me, who but Gerry could ask for anything more?

I was soon able to buy a 1953 Plymouth that came with a repair book that permitted me to do such things as replace the carburetor myself. It had a hole in the floor. I could look down and see the road rush past between my feet.

It could often be seen parked late on 10th Street in front of Soren's place.

Soren Before Breathless

Sometime in the 50s, certainly before Jean Seberg appeared in Godard's <u>Breathless</u> selling Herald Tribunes on the streets of Paris, there was another American doing the same: Soren Agenoux, known then as Frank Hansen.

He was later to write to his friend Ray Johnson:

> Dear Ray –
>
> Do you still have that photo of me selling the Herald Tribune in front of Notre Dame?
>
> I'm going to be screen-tested for a part in Jean Seberg's next movie, "Lilith," and I want to show her that photo if I see her.
>
> We'd be playing inmates of the same insane asylum. She has to wear her hair exceedingly long and I'd have to have mine close-cropped.
>
> Soren

Soren was always ahead of his time. He was in fact the first of the public graffiti artists, though unsung.

He was threatened, he told us, by a transit officer in the Brooklyn City Hall subway stop where he had for many mornings corrected America's perceptions of itself by writing over its advertising boards. With Magic Marker.

Because of that and because of the small acclaim he won among us for standing up to the transit cops, our friend Dale Joe re-named him Little Miss Marker.

Little Miss Marker was a role played by little Miss Shirley Temple, the mention of whom was lingua franca among the slowly visible gays in the pre-Stonewall era.

I say he was the first because he marked up the subway station in 1959 as he was on his way to our Cobble Hill apartment where he breathlessly told us of the confrontation with the cops.

Cobble Hill in that era was Lebanese and not so real estate desirable but desirable to me since around the corner on Atlantic Avenue a Lebanese baker sold small tri-cornered pastries of lamb and pine nuts that, with a quart of Rheingold beer, could restore your navigating tools after a night of drink.

We lived in a brownstone which faced a line of brownstones opposite, creating a dun-colored canyon that amplified and volleyed back and forth the harmonies of a quartet of teenage boys who sang every night. Their hair slicked back in helmets that reflected the lamp light, they woo-wooed and whooped towards love and stardom, in Brooklyn though it had a flavor of New Jersey.

For a short while Soren moved in and lived with us where he shared family affections as though a visiting cousin, a generous one who surprised us with gifts, gifts such as a sun dress for Anne or a chocolate cake and my first LP of <u>Don Giovanni</u> and tickets for the early run of <u>Gypsy</u>. The real <u>Gypsy</u>. The one with Ethel Merman.

These gifts were made possible because of Soren's work at the Living Theatre, that historic avant garde theatre where Soren tended the box office for not much salary but there was the cash drawer where money was for the taking, at least for Soren's taking.

Christmas 1959 Anne and I hung our Christmas tree upside down from the ceiling because we had agreed without saying never to be ordinary. Having Soren in and out the door was not what you would call ordinary.

Among the tacit agreements Anne and I had was not to mention the other was insane Not insane as in frothing and convulsions but insane in the way that some have of taking their orders from invisible sources which they obey because, well, they fear reprisals and follow instructions even on matters so trivial as hanging a Christmas tree upside down from the ceiling.

It was occasionally too late for Soren to make his way back to the Village. He slept over. Sometimes Soren and I would go down a half-flight of stairs to a small room I rented for writing and there go at some sort of furtive love. I never knew what Anne thought — of Soren, of the time I spent with him. We never discussed it. I assumed that Annie assumed what I assumed: we were bohemians, now beginning to be called beatniks, free-thinkers, avant garde. It wasn't cool discussing things.

The only ornament hanging from the overhead Christmas tree was a collage sent us by Ray Johnson. It had a string attached for hanging. One side was a photo of the little princess herself, Shirley Temple. On the other – well, it would make no sense without knowing who Ray Johnson is first.

And then of course it makes no sense but it's okay because with Ray it makes sense if it makes no sense.

It Started With Lucky Lindy

Soren asked me to come to a coffee house to meet a friend, Ray Johnson. Ray's friend Richard Lippold joined us. Ray came in exhausted from creating a mural on the stairs leading up to the Living Theatre on Fourteenth Street. He colored the walls by running up and down, winged with crayolas, four hundred and sixty-four times. It was Soren who calculated the number.

Ray said he didn't like it and was going to paint over it. Pink. We laughed. Ray looked solemn, cutting his eyes around to count the laughs. He received laughs more often than he sent them. A man in his thirties, he was already bald and his glance was impish.

I learned from Soren that the other gentleman, Lippold was a famous sculptor. A wire sculptor. That is he created bursts of gold and platinum wires that represent the sun and the moon. MoMa had one. The Met another. And the glittering box kites over the bar in the newly opened Four Seasons was Lippold's work. Later, the gold planks hanging over the lobby of the Lincoln Center opera were the work of Lippold. He was married and he was Ray's lover. I see, like me, he was straight.

They had both attended the experimental (is that the word for it?) avant garde college in the South called Black Mountain.

I also learned from Soren that Ray lived in an inauspicious building just below the Brooklyn Bridge as it slopes down into Manhattan. Soren claimed that Ray's neighbors down the hall were Robert Rauschenberg and Jasper Johns. Perhaps the two didn't live there anymore since by that time I believe they had become major art world successes.

Soon after our move to Cobble Hill, I found myself stuck in a train in a tunnel under the river going out to Brooklyn. An old train with dim hellish light bulbs. The rain had been torrential as we left City Hall. The tunnel was flooded. The old train growled to a stop. The overhead lights flickered. I was crowded in with passengers in wet overcoats that started to steam as the heat rose. I knew at that moment I was to die. I tried to remember how to pray, the way I prayed as a teenager, promising God if he ever got me out of there I would never take a train under that river again. He heard my prayer and I lived up to my promise.

I walked to work daily over the Brooklyn bridge. I'd wave down to my new friend Ray Johnson in the building below in the shadow of that bridge. He'd stop his shaving and put a wet cloth on his head. It covered his bald head. Ray humor. I made up poems on the bridge, starting with haikus. It took about as much time as it took to cross the bridge to create one of the short Japanese poems –in English, of course.

Walking west at dawn
East at night – the winter bridge
Trembling at my feet.

Gold caterpillar
Alight on the black river –
Ferry in the night.

Ray was sending me odd humorous scraps of things, usually in an envelope with an envelope enclosed asking me to send the second envelope on to someone else, most often to a celebrity. Inside was some sly Dadaistic joke featuring, say, a plastic comb and a cut-out of the Bride of Frankenstein greatly in need of a comb.

He had made up something he called the New York Correspondence School of Art – the art being the correspondence he sent and having nothing to do with a school. I in return sent him some of my poems.

I often wondered whether Ray found inspiration – or at least a comrade in Robert Creeley, the poet who also attended Black Mountain. One of Creeley's poems seems almost a creed for Ray's work:

THE CONSPIRACY

You send me your poems,
I'll send you mine.

Things tend to awaken
even through random communication.

Let us suddenly
proclaim spring. And jeer

at the others,
all the others.

I will send a picture too
if you will send me one of you.

Since I wanted to be an essayist on the jumping jack art happening around me (I had no education in the field at all) I started writing critiques in the form of poems, figuring the soft focus of poetry would cover my lack of real knowledge.

I sent Ray long poems, more or less about his work. One was about Lucky Lindy, that is Lindbergh. Ray smoked Lucky Strikes. He surprised me by sending back a collage of Lindbergh by his plane, a Lucky Strike emblem to either side of it. The collage was about the size of the business envelope into which it was squeezed.

That started it.

For the few years to follow I received collages with two Lucky Strike targets cut from a cigarette pack glued to them, examples not only of Ray's humor but brilliance..

Thus it started, a long generous flow of Lucky Strike collages, witty, humorous, gorgeous, which I pinned to my cork board not realizing they formed an accidental narrative of my friendship with Ray.

Each of the collages referred to some incident out of our shared lives. For instance, he sent the ornament for our upside down Christmas tree. Because of Soren, he included a reference to Little Miss Marker, Shirley Temple.

Verso, that is to say the flip side of the collage, shows a news photo of an arrested child killer being hustled off to jail. On top of that a clipping from God knows what book, a small moral tale:

"Although this happened a good twenty years ago, that small boy is not only still bald but the most careful and extreme caution must be exercised in choosing maids of a particular type whose only duty is to sit very quietly on his head at night."

As if this isn't enough to chew on, Ray added in a child's scrawl a quote from a stutter record. You have every reason to wonder what that might be.

Ray found on the street, spilling from a turned-over trash bin (why do I think it was on Canal Street, a street of so many bins) vinyl records being thrown out by a stutter remedial school. The school must have recorded their students as they started training, stuttering painfully, then again as they improved, but hardly that much.

I wrote a series of Stutter Poems and sent them to Ray. Stuttering love poems. I'll spare you those.

In 1964 I moved on to Hollywood. The collages had stopped coming by then. I took them off my work board, all of them with holes from being tacked up, put them in a box where they stayed in a closet for decades.

In 1991 the Lannan Foundation expressed an interest in what was in my closet. I spread the works on a table, more than fifty, and sent a photo thru a friend to Ray. On March 7, 1991, I came in and heard Ray's voice on my answering machine:

"I have just looked at the color photos of the Lucky Strike collages that Janice brought back. I'm gasping here at their beauty and their quantity.. dot dot dot."

The patriarch of the foundation died, the curator the glamorous

Lisa Lyons moved on, interest was lost.

Ray was hugely disappointed. He sent me a white on black ink drawing that said "UCK YOU."

Then another which said simply "THE END." Ray may have sent this last drawing to many different friends all with different meanings between them. For me, it was the last mailing I received.

Within a time, I can't remember how much time, Ray checked into a motel in Oyster Bay and in full suit of clothes, swam out to his death. The end.

Like everything in his life, it was without reason except the reasons that exploded in his private universe, giving it light.

Last Stand on Minetta Lane

Soren introduced Anne and me to a lady who lived on Minetta Lane. Though you entered her apartment from a pavestone patio, once in you had the impression you were in a basement. The window out to the main street was at sidewalk level, feet passing.

We thought of Franny Witlin as a latter-day Gertrude Stein. She was not lesbian but she had an entourage of what seemed exclusively homosexual boys. Like Gertrude, she was writing an IMPORTANT AMERICAN NOVEL (all caps) but unlike Gertrude she did not publish. She had written something like 2,000 pages, none of which we saw.

Gertrude on the other hand set her flag in new territory with The Making of Americans. When I arrived in Manhattan and took a room at Mama Baraldi's I crossed the island to the Strand where I found a worn copy of Lectures in America by Gertrude Stein. I took it back to my small room with its Edward Hopper loneliness and read the text aloud. I became intoxicated on the rhythms, as one would later with a Philip Glass score. Not always certain of the meaning I was taken by the long breath, by the dynamite power of the repeated word.

To be honest what attracted us also in those pre-Beatnik days was Stein's social skills. An orca-shaped woman whose wife had the face of a miner's skillet, she was nonetheless the center of all things artistic and ex-pat in Paris, her Buddha presence in a salon of painters and writers and poets and such. They all seemed flattered to be invited and saved their sarcasm until back out on the street. Or in the case of that peevish gossip Hemingway who saved his snipes at Gertrude Stein for a posthumous memoir of his Paris days. All she ever did for him was teach him long sentences with short words which is one of the first things you think of when thinking of Hemingway, unless it is the macho posing he did for any lens pointed his way.

Though Franny may have resembled Gertrude, she in fact had a hunky boyfriend, a radical who initiated a walk across country as protest against nuclear armaments. A small pack of believers trudged the distance with him. We met a few of them, bearded and dusty and cheerful.

Franny was always home on Minetta Lane on Sundays for her informal salon, receiving the gay boys, slim as letter openers. Weekdays she was devout over her typewriter writing her important novel she never described and perhaps never finished. With careful step for she was a large woman under her full gypsy skirts, she moved about her small quarters, stroking back wisps of hair that wouldn't behave, preparing to feed us as she spoke softly of matters literary or perhaps her new interest in Indian vocal music which sounded like groaning. She laid her table with the most elaborate synthesis of the random and the selected. She would instruct John Daley – a beautiful Irish boy who resembled a sly raven - to set this dish here and Dale Joe to lay that loaf wherever he was inspired to. Above all do not brush the cat off the table, this is his home too and he is privileged to step among the plates. A pineapple stood proud in the center, unsliced, Franny's slicing to follow, a casual ritual, a quartering, then a cutting into eighths, a carving around the rind, a severing of the topnotch, placing the pieces at the center of a rosette of naked cheeses, all the while Franny reminding us that all motions on earth, including the sectioning of this innocent pineapple, were mere copies of motions happening elsewhere.

She also had what they call a day job, though not one that required regular hours. She did piece work at home. She wrote synopses for Columbia Pictures. She was a "reader." Columbia's New York Story Department assigned her and a few other lifetime (but not successful) writers books to be read overnight. The books were often in galley form, sometimes manuscripts. The readers were expected to bring in a two page single-spaced "report" the next day. Unless they deemed the book important and then a "long report" was done, double-spaced, five to ten pages long.

For the two page report, the pay was $19.00. Extra length books brought a bonus of $1.00 for every hundred pages over 300. The long report was $25.00 plus $1.50 for each double-spaced page.

Since the reader was given on average three books a week, he/she could make almost a hundred bucks a week. This was the late fifties when a quart of beer cost 35 cents, Rheingold the local favorite. So were the Rheingold mermaids who enticed you on early black and white TV with their incessant under-the-skin song about Rheingold being the one beer. Times were more subtly sexy then.

Franny like many soft-spoken intellectuals of the early union movements in Manhattan, was fearless. She once bit a hole in the boot of a horse-mounted cop. It was a labor protest. She was also tough.

Anne and I and baby makes three came in from Brooklyn to Franny's salon to hear, say, a poet who loved his poetry so much he could barely share it with us his voice was so muffled. We came also to hear the most important Indian vocalist (Franny said) of the time who sat squat in the corner and sang his woes in three tones, head, chest and bowel.

Because I was a wise ass, when Franny asked me what I thought, I answered I liked best the last movement. What was that? The bowel movement.

Back in those pre-psychedelic days of crowded bars and drunken affairs with other people's wives and heated positions shouted over the heads of others, long before acid and related mental retardants kept the young behind the scarred doors of their naked bulb apartments from which they emerged long after dark wearing shades to go to Max's or a disco, anywhere that blasting vibrations could buoy them through to dawn without the effort of word since words like rabbits were always a hop or two beyond the stoned mind's pursuit –

take a breath, Gerry –

in those days there was always the sibylline Franny to visit. Annie and I were happy to be included in this latter-day rue de Fleurus, I perhaps happy to be among so many pretty boys. But then perhaps Anne was too.

At Soren's insistence I read aloud from Robert Creeley. Soren said I sounded like Burton, which I did not. Creeley was my new discovery, his poems were small and took short Creeley steps like early poems of W.C.Williams but combined with them pop-culture, nursery rhyme, even comic book reference.

To my amazement, Anne listened without reaction as I read aloud Creeley's Ballad of the Despairing Husband:

> My wife and I lived all alone,
> contention was our only bone.
> I fought with her, she fought with me,
> And things went on right merrily...
>
> Oh come home soon, I write to her,
> Go screw yourself is her answer.
> Now what is that for Christian word?
> I hope she feeds on dried goose turd.

The poem is a mix of longing and anger, the poet missing his tough lady but fearing if she returned she would not listen. It ends:

> Oh lady, grant me time,
> please, to finish my rhyme.

After the rape, Franny's place went dark. It was a black man who broke in, a giant of a man, she told the cops. They informed her she had just described thousands of men in Manhattan. Franny had never trusted cops. They instructed her to go to Bellvue to confirm the forced entry – into Franny, not the window. Franny lay there, knees up, holding above her the long sheets of a galley she had to read before the next day. She suffered the probing of an inept intern just enough then put a foot to his chest and sent him flying across the examining room.

She knew from her reading that rapists return for a second assault. She laid a trap. She devised a Rube Goldberg network of ropes and pulleys, which if pulled would lock the doors of the living room. Her plan was to sit in the kitchen with the help of her slim gay boys (this was pre-Stonewall, they suddenly realized how tough they could be) and left a light on in her sleeping nook, and sat the long hours of the night in the small kitchen, ready to pull the ropes. The plan was to lock the rapist in while the cops were called. Her boyfriend pointed out if the man were as large as she said, he could crash through the door and out. Franny, the biter of cops' boots, was not deterred.

Franny and her fragile corps, they sat there night after night. They spoke in whispers.

The rapist did not return. Vengeance was never served.

Sam Meets the Mysterious Podber

After a long absence, Ron Moore appeared again in Manhattan, that beautiful young guy who had played the lead in my first produced play at Yale. He was living in a single room in Hell's Kitchen. The character he played for me was an escaped lunatic lost in the delusion he was Julius Caesar and equally lost in poetic musings.

Obviously the work of an undergraduate.

The Hell's Kitchen room was spare, having only a huge Persian rug that was left him by a grandmother and a 19th century horse hair sofa which was worth a lot of loot but a torture to sit on. I remember Ron saying to Anne right after our wedding that she must begin her jewelry collection with simple gold pieces. Never buy paste. Never buy cheap. In truth, we were lucky to buy simple groceries at the time.

Ron was furnishing his Hell's Kitchen digs with only quality pieces. Two is all he had at the time. He enjoyed walking Fifth Avenue on a Sunday. He would head out in suit and waistcoat from Tenth Avenue and walk east. Once past Sixth, he felt safe to put on his gray chamois gloves. It seemed appropriate for Fifth Avenue of a Sunday. I reflected that I first saw Ron the poetic lunatic as my creation. His current delusion and distracted air were his own creation.

Ron took me by Sam Wagstaff's apartment on the upper east side. Sam was born to money and to art. He collected and was a museum curator a few times. I was impressed to see the objects that filled the glass shelves in his apartment. Here were terra cotta and bronze figures of antiquity that I actually permitted myself to pick up and hold. They didn't let you do that at the Met. All of them seemed erotic, not just the melon like buttocks of heroes or even the priapic rods of the satyrs, but even the miniature vessels seemed molded with sensuous touch.

Sam came in and I jumped back from the glass shelves. He didn't seem to mind.

"Yes, Gerry, how is married life?" he said and shook my hand.

"It's making me feel sort of married, tell you the truth."

Sam bellowed a laugh. Apparently he found more humor in that than I did.

"Tell me more about Ray Johnson," Sam ordered.

"You've heard of him?" I said

"Bits from Ron. Tell me more."

"Well he was, you know, at Black Mountain college, I guess he studied with Albers. Cage was there. He became buddies with Johns and Rauschenberg."

"I don't need a history, what does he do?"

"Collages. I think he's really hung up on Josef Cornell. He's like a sort of Dadaist or something, clips out everything and glues it together. And when he grows bored with what he's done, he cuts it up in pieces and makes new collages."

"Tell him I want to see his works."

His works. For Ray, this smacked of high seriousness and he smirked. But he agreed to have me bring Sam by. The setting was familiar. Dark stairs and walls of failing paint in a building on the lower east side.

Ray answered my knock and with a sweep of an arm invited us in. He told Sam to sit down. Sam looked around. There was no place to sit down. Sam was impeccable in expensive tailoring and tie.

Ray's place was stripped bare except for a mattress on the floor, covered by a crisply laundered white sheet. The walls were gray, the floors also painted gray. A bathtub sat in the end of the room that was meant to be the kitchen.

Sam was hardly shy. He calmly sat on the mattress and tucked his glowing shoes under his knees like a yogi.

Ray went to a closet with double doors.

"My work," he said and swung open the two doors of his closet. Out walked his scary surreal friend Dorothy Podber, hair of Brillo, eyes black as buttons on an executioner's coat. She was later to describe herself as "witch and famous." She took slow motion steps into the room. In her two hands she carried a tea cup with a glove hanging from it, fingers down. Sam watched the show with a hardly sincere smile.

Dorothy slow stepped into the kitchen, pretended to be drinking from the empty cup and watched. Ray reached into the closet and pulled out a cardboard box. We got a glimpse of other boxes stacked in the closet.

Ray placed the box on the floor, pried open its flaps. It was stuffed with "his works" which at the time were all about the side of the cardboard that came back in your shirts from the laundry. The box was crammed to the gunnel with these uniform-sized collages.

Ray's finger went to a collage, though hardly an informed choice since all he could see of the piece is its top edge since it was packed in with its fellows. He pulled out a collage. He stepped over and placed the collage on the floor by the base board letting it lean back against the wall.

Sam gave it a squinting appraisal. "Nice," he said.

Ray dragged out another box, opened it. Again at random he pulled out a collage and placed it on the floor and let it lean back on the wall next to its brother.

This time Sam responded with a hum. A sort of considered yummy hum.

This went on. After a row of collages occupied the floor base, Ray propped more on top of them, as in a house of cards, carefully placing each so that it didn't topple the whole structure. The dreaded Dorothy watched from her perch on the edge of the bathtub. It took time but at last Ray covered most of the wall with his art. It was also an art to stack them so they didn't fall.

"May I see the third over there, on the second row? The one with the mouse ears."

"The mouse ears," Ray responded, repeating it until it became a nursery song. "The mouse ears.. the mouse ears.."

He handed the collage to Sam. Sam gave it a close look, put it in his lap and instructed Ray to pass him a few others. Ray did as instructed.

Sam stood. He had four collages in hand.

"I'll take these." His voice took on the low foot-pedal notes of an organ as it did when he made pronouncements. "They're sensational, you know that."

Ray admitted to nothing. He picked up a pile of collages, slow stepped to Podber. She received them with ritual solemnity.

"Well, you should," said Sam. He motioned for me. I gave Ray a little wave, ignored Dorothy for fear of contamination and followed Sam out the door.

Bill Wilson, closest longtime friend of Ray, his archivist and now his executor, said of Podber, "She was this marvelous, evil woman. You didn't accept candy from Dorothy."

I remember her and her twin evil sister, Malka Safro at gatherings that Soren took me to. Knowing that they had spiked the sugar at the Automat with acid, I stayed clear and never accepted a drink from them. I feared insanity and believed psychedelics a quick fall into insanity. I saw Dorothy and Malka as two heads of a female Cerberus, two bitch dogs at the doors to eternal insanity.

Here's how Joy Bergmann writes about Podber –

"'Dorothy was dangerous,' said Billy Name (Linich), Andy Warhol's collaborator. 'She terrified Andy.' Linich remembers the autumn day in 1964 when Podber showed up to be part of a Factory shoot, one she intended to direct, unbeknownst to onlookers. Podber arrived wearing a black leather outfit and lady-like gloves, toting a little purse and her Great Dane, Ivan de Carlo. Warhol was busy working. Podber grew impatient; she wanted to shoot a picture.

"'There was a stack of Marilyn Monroe silkscreens against the wall,' says Linich. 'She pulled out a pistol and shot Marilyn right between the eyes. After she left, Andy came over to me and said, 'Please make sure Dorothy doesn't come over here anymore. She's too scary.'"

The Marilyn with the gun shot in it became an expensive auction item in the decades to follow.

Who knows how it influenced Valerie Solanas, feminist nut case and creator of The SCUM Manifesto who four years later came into the Factory and shot Andy himself.

A few days after our visit to Ray, I got a call from Sam. He was irritated. "What are we going to do about your friend Johnson."

It had never occurred to me we could do anything.

"What's the problem?" I asked.

"I called him and asked what he wanted for the four collages. You know what he said?

"Nope."

"Surprise me."

I knew that Ray didn't want to be seen as a serious contender in the art market for fear others wouldn't see him as a serious contender, better to make a joke of things. I also guessed he hoped the rich Mr.Wagstaff would write out a large check, no questions asked.

"I have an idea," I said to Sam. "Send him a check for fifty bucks and ask him to bill you for the balance."

Sam thought. "Good idea," he said and hung up.

Ray was angry with me, though it would be a betrayal of his Dadaist nihilism to show it, so he instead showed nothing. For some time, he only smiled at me. Didn't say a word.

I'm certain he never replied to Sam's letter.

Franny Taskmaster

Annie and I became additional satellites in Frannie's wide circling course through literature, music and thin gay boys. We had asked her to teach us to write synopses. We hoped to become free-lance readers for one of the four film companies who still hired readers in New York. Zipper factory and occasional writing jobs were not paying the rent.

Franny gave us what turned out to be a six week course. She was an exacting taskmaster. It did not occur to us until much later that she had standards and rules for writing synopses that were shared by no one else. Yet she made us believe we had to pass with her approval before we could be sent out to knock on story department doors.

Among her rules:

1. Start your hero in motion toward his first significant action, even if it appears long into the novel. "As John walked from the commuter station to his too expensive home up the Hudson, he was alarmed to see the front door open, swinging in the winter wind."

2. Give him a short appellation that will identify him when he later appears in the short two-page text so the reader won't have to check back to figure out who is who. For example, "John, the red-headed stock broker.." will always be so identified.

3. Do not cut from his point of view. He discovers his dead wife on the floor; he calls the police. But when information comes

he couldn't have observed, we still keep him center to our narrative. "Only later does he learn that his sister-in-law had been over for coffee that afternoon and they had discussed divorce.."

4. The first time a character is seen, and only then, his name is printed in bold type. That way, a glance thru the synopses can establish the main cast of characters.

5. In the case of a murder mystery, start with the second murder. That's when the action usually gets started.

6. In the case of gigantic historical novels (seems Doubleday had many of them) read all the dialogue and only the first sentence of each paragraph. Enough can be learned about a 600 page book to speak with two-page authority by morning. Forgive me, Nabokov, but I had to sit in a publisher office and read Ada in an afternoon, dialogue and first sentence of each paragraph. I recommended against it as a film. The Columbia v.p. Leo Jaffe, not a man of literature himself, had sat next to agent Swifty Lazar on a plane and was persuaded to buy the rights nonetheless, not having read a bit of the book or asked for opinions from his story department. He bought it for a lot. It was never made into a film. However, Lolita which I read for pleasure was licked, chewed and swallowed by me more than once.

7. Having summarized the novel in two single-spaced pages, you were to fill in a small box at the top marked "Theme". Which had little to do with theme but was meant to be a three sentence reduction of the book. "A fashionable New York journalist goes to Kansas to investigate the killers held for trial in the murder of a middle-class family." You get the idea.

8. And if that is not reduction enough, at the top of the printed form for these synopses you were to write title, publisher, pages, pub date. And then a curious entry: "Type" followed by a full colon. Here you were meant to describe the book in a word, maybe two.

"Comedy" or "drama" were simple enough. Requiring more thought were, for instance, Jean Kerr: "Suburban comedy." Joseph Wambaugh: "Police procedure." Richard Drury: "Political expose."

I was once corrected by Franny when I identified a book as a drama. She said it was instead a melodrama. What's the difference? In a melodrama, the heroine dies in the end. She was patient with me.

Decades later, I was in a healing group for HIV men run by new age guru, Louise Hay. A group of thirty young men sat cross-legged on the floor of her Santa Monica apartment, sang songs about healing skies and overhead bluebirds and passed among them a healing pillow with a crimson heart embroidered onto it.

Ms.Hay grew tired of hearing me drone on about my various woes (strangely, I had just gotten started) and told me to pipe down and that I was a drama queen. I corrected her. I was a melodrama queen. The difference?

"In a melodrama the heroine dies in the end."

Because of Franny we were able, Annie and I, to be hired by Columbia Pictures. While I went to other offices, Annie went to 711 Fifth Avenue to the sixteenth floor where they kept the readers and writers safely tucked away out of sight. As that fate that seems always to confuse me with the deserving, it decreed that in the outer office was my Yale classmate, Larry Kramer. He was about to leave to London to work for Columbia's European head of production. Mike Frankovich. By some process unknown to me, Larry ended up writing the screenplay for Women in Love, brilliantly so, for director Ken Russell.

The finger of fate proved even longer. Working as the Assistant Story Editor was a cheery chatty woman Anne and I knew well: she lived next door to us down on Greenwich Street. We never knew what she did.

"Annie, I didn't know you and Gerry were readers," she said with what seemed unusual delight.

"Well, not recently," Annie lied, "we were working at RKO for Archie." It was a familiar obstacle to employment, you had to have experience. Franny told us to lie about RKO and the Archie we never met since the office had closed down and Archie had left town.

"I love Archie!" said our neighbor lady. Larry came to the office door and added he knew Anne's husband, they'd been at Yale together. That sealed it. We were both hired. Anne was immediately handed two massive galley proofs and the tissue-thin forms on which we were expected to write synopses with six carbon copies.

By tomorrow.

Piece of cake. Especially if you soak it or you in enough vodka.

Franny had unintentionally done me an additional favor. She prepared me for film writing. Her rules for breaking down, simplifying, giving a spine to a narrative is what film writers do all the time – or used to.

What makes a screenplay is essentially reducing the action along the lines she laid down. Hero in motion towards the first significant event. Two or three word appellation that will stay with him in the text. Maintain his POV. If action happens out of his view, make certain he learns of it so we can keep easy track of the narrative.

Old rules, old Hollywood, yes, but a Hollywood that captured the world with unintentional art before intentional art came along and muddied up the waters.

SNEEZES

In 1878, the internet tells me, Walt Whitman returned to New York and saw the nearly complete Brooklyn Bridge. The sight of it was "the best, most effective medicine my soul has yet partaken - the grandest physical habitat and surroundings of land and water the globe affords - namely, Manhattan island and Brooklyn, which the future shall join in one city - city of superb democracy, amid superb surroundings."

As though Anne and I had graduated cum laude from her private courses, Franny invited us along to celebrate bridge day, that special day each year that she organized her troops to walk across the Brooklyn Bridge. Perhaps with memories of Whitman's praise, perhaps because of its beauty, especially on a bright glistening fall day as this was.

Franny's hunky boyfriend had returned from his march across the continent to protest nuclear arms. With him, his band of bearded and shaggy and enthusiastic boys and girls who sang as we marched across the bridge, not a 'we shall overcome' song but a drill master's song of 'I had a good wife but I left, right, left..'

Franny insisted we cross from City Hall towards Brooklyn. Her reasons had something to do with magnetic truth and it was the only way to cross. She also instructed us to search the small City Hall park for rocks, small rocks, pebbles even, and to carry one with us.

Soren, considering himself senior staff, walked next to her. Behind him, the slim Chinese painter, Dale Joe, took fast scissor steps to keep up. His lover, Jack, kept pausing to click off a picture of the river and Dale had to wait impatiently for him, causing an even more rapid scissoring of steps to catch up.

Franny let go an unending flow of opinions and instructions. She was obviously the nucleus of the group, bobbing a turbaned head above them all, wind-catching cape fluttering dramatically, she seemed a stiff-necked crane lifting arguments from the group and tossing them aside with an angry shake of her head.

She was particularly proud to introduce us all to a thin stick of a woman, close-cropped hair, never without a cigarette in her mouth which may have explained the erosions to her face. She wore pants and combat boots.

"You all must meet my oldest chum, Bambi, we go back to the dark and dangerous forests of political protest. We were Bleecker Street revolutionaries together. In fact, we met in jail, how classic is that? She was in for crocheting fuses – me, for biting a mounted policeman on the leg. Put a hole in his boot as I recall."

"I do!" Bambi said and cackled.

Franny peered over her shoulder at me.

"Gerry, you have met Dale Joe? Of course you have, Soren has introduced you surely. He always puts together the attractive people so long as he extracts his commission." She lowered her voice as if imparting secrets of state. "Dale is marvelous with a thin oil. As a Chinese-American he combines the best of the oriental and the occidental. That is, he paints majestically but on a small scale."

To Dale she added, 'I don't know whether you've read them, but Gerry is a poet, without maturity and therefore without funds."

"But I have a drawer full of contributor's copies," I said in my own defense.

Anne and I were pushing our son Christopher in a small collapsible canvas stroller. It may have cost twenty bucks. It was inconceivable for young marrieds of the time to buy a gleaming Mercedes-resembling craft for the status conscious parent since certainly the baby was aware of no other status than hunger and soaking diapers. What made it even more unimaginable is that such sidewalk yachts didn't exist and more important, no one we knew could have afforded one. We pushed on, secure in the knowledge that when it came time to return to Franny's we had only to fold the stroller under one arm, hold on to Christopher with the other and jump on a subway.

Mid-point on the bridge stood a handsome (in a sort of sinister way) man, a man who resembled the French actor, Charles Aznavour. He was leaning on the railing with his back to the river. He was smoking. As he exhaled, he lowered the cigarette and he smiled in a crooked way as we came towards him.

Franny didn't know or notice him. She stopped the group. She instructed us to face the water. "What a marvelous day for a crossing. It's not April sunsets that move us old broads, it's this!" She spread her arms to include the entire river.

She instructed us to raise our stones, poise to throw them, and then in unison to sneeze. Sneeze? Yes, a sneeze is the involuntary hosanna our electric systems make to the universe, an explosive act of praise. And like life itself, intense and soon gone.

Once we had sneezed, we were to launch the stones in as great an arc as we could create and then trace them with our eyes as they fell to the water. Their flight was like life itself, intense and soon gone.

Sneezes came but not in unison. Stones flew but not with particularly notable arcs. One hit a bridge cable and bounced back at the thrower. She smiled sheepishly, grabbed the stone and said to Frannie, "Like life itself," and gave the stone a mighty heave.

I noticed the slim man laughing now, watching us, leaning back like a sly lizard against the rail.

I was next to him. I said, "You didn't sneeze."

"I fully intend to, but I'll wait until you're gone. It's like sex, something best to do in private."

"Oh really, I always do it in public," I said with forced humor.

The man half closed his eyes until only his pupils were given an opening to the world. "You'll have to let me know." He smiled and it was hard to say whether he was enjoying the joke or smirking or, always this, being seductive.

Soren rushed up, not too pleased to see me in conversation with this man. "Oh hi, Dennis," he said and didn't wait for a response. He turned to me. "Franny said to hurry it up. Big lunch at her place."

"Yeah, I'm coming," I answered.

I nodded at the man. He extended his hand. "Dennis Selby," he said. I shook his hand.

"Gerry," I answered.

"Come on," said Soren and ran off.

"Gerry Ayres," I said to Dennis.

"Is that Welsh or Scots?"

"Not sure. I'm a Celtic mongrel – Irish, Welsh and Scottish. And you?"

"Welsh. As from Wales Welsh."

"Not much sun bathing in Wales, huh?" I said because his look was making me nervous. But not for long. Soren rushed back and grabbed my arm.

Franny was waiting.

Among the Walking Laundry

On October 1959 Anne and I started work as readers for Columbia Pictures. Its East Coast Story Department was in Columbia's home office at 711 Fifth Avenue. It occupied three rooms on the top floor of the beaux arts building in that swank strip of Fifth Avenue. The top, that is, sixteenth floor was a collection of after-thought departments, a place to keep matters artistic or too egg-headed out of sight.

Most especially keep out of sight the freelance "readers" (story analysts) who left their desolate home typewriters where epic novels were gestating undelivered for years and brought in their synopses and got paid. Writers, in other words. Baggy, like walking laundry. Not only could they resemble Communist agitators but some in fact were just that. Or had been.

My growing uneasiness with subways meant that I was to be a stay at home papa while Anne took our work uptown and got paid. In untraceable cash, like drug sales or other such transactions. Soon Larry Kramer disappeared for better position: he moved on to London as assistant to Mike Frankovich, the head of Columbia's European operations.

As for our neighbor lady who, on the occasions I delivered the synopses, seemed compelled to pull back her skirt to check her hose, extending a shapely leg by resting her heel on an open desk drawer. She quickly stroked her nylons smooth as if surprised to see me standing there. She also disappeared, though I have no idea where she went.

This gesture was seen on film, Prick Up Your Ears, the flawless Vanessa Redgrave did something similar when her client came to the office.

I don't know who it was, but someone of the brass on the Eleventh (executive) Floor brought in a new man from Hollywood to be Story Editor. I thought at first he was a joke. Well, for one, he was so California and how would that go over with the snooty publisher types he would soon be taking to lunch?

He came from behind his desk in casual Hawaiian shirts and high-hitched gabardine slacks and shook the hands of us readers and gave us cheery smiles of encouragement. The readers were by class a cynical breed and all they wanted was to pocket their cash and get back to the unfinished Russian novel they were writing.

He asked one of these troopers, a snappish old fellow, whether the book he had just covered was "a good yarn."

"Not as tightly knit as Crime and Punishment," the old guy mumbled. His new boss laughed heartily and shook the man's shoulder. "Keep it up," he said.

The new Story Editor was named Erwin Gelsey.

I had written a short report on a galley proof I had just read, Catch-22. I told Mr.Gelsey that this was a humdinger. He agreed and sent me back to write a long form (twenty-five double spaced pages) on Catch-22. He wanted the Hollywood studio to buy the rights on the basis of his recommendation.

One problem: he knew, he said, the tastes of the studio and they would not cotton to the character of Milo Minderbinder. Minderbinder was the second most important character in the book, certainly one of the most antic and surreal. I balked. He told me to go to work. I redid my twenty-five pages, minus-Minderbinder. Thank God only the studio execs would ever read it. Perhaps Gelsey understood that the thin-skinned studio execs would think they were being satirized by the Minderbinder character, a man of their stripe: amoral, greedy capitalist, the prophet of profit, whose only sincerity was what he happened to be saying at the moment, forgotten soon. Hollywood exactly.

The next time I came into the office, Gelsey came out with a toothsome smile and said there was someone in his office he wanted me to meet. Joseph Heller himself. The soon to be famous author of

<u>Catch-22</u>. I walked into the office as one would climb the scaffolding to the guillotine. Heller stood and shook my hand and thanked me for my enthusiasm. He had in hand a copy of my long report.

"I told him you were a bright lad and you loved it," Gelsey said. "He hasn't read your report yet, but wait till he does."

Thank God, I thought, there's time to get out of here, maybe he won't remember what I look like. Before I could reach the door, Heller waved my report at me and said, "I can use a little joggling of my memory. I forgot what the book is about."

Gelsey guffawed. I turned softly red as a lobster in steam. I smiled at Mr.Heller and ran for the elevator.

Now for you students of another century, I have to describe what trouble it was for folks film-addicted in the late 50s. The best source for seeing old movies was the Museum of Modern Art. There were only a few cinemas, revival houses as they were called, that showed old movies. If you ran you could catch 30s classics and develop that lifetime addiction to director Busby Berkeley and Fred and Ginger and Ruby Keeler, all active operatives in the cineaste's mind. There were no video tapes at that time, no discs, no cable stations dishing out old treats. By treats I'm thinking mostly of the screwball confections of Sturgess and Lubitch and Cukor and Hawkes and the list goes on. Nor did you get a glimpse of the ass that changed Hollywood, or at least, caused Hollywood to start censoring itself. Jean Harlow in clinging white satin, obviously having forgotten her knickers, undulating away from camera with that free-flowing buttocks like a exhortation of a Taoist – go with the flow.

There were two classes of movie goers, those who wanted Harlow and those who wanted to be Harlow. That is, men and women. Gay men, well, I guess they wanted both.

Her incendiary sexuality caused such a fuss among the good Christians of our country (the same good Christians who got us Prohibition and thus created the Mafia as an enduring American fixture) so ranted on about the luscious Harlow that a production code came in and films had to slow down – but only slightly.

They still dished out sex and zany humor at a time when the

country was by and large out of work. But not out of films which arrived at a rate, as I'm told, of about three a week at the local house.

Which brings me back to Erwin Gelsey, the man I thought of as a joke. As my education in films grew, Gelsey became a hero and I am pleased to have worked for him. He was vintage screenwriter and a solid story creator.

Like so many who worked in Hollywood in the 30s and 40s, writers were accustomed to the factory ethic. If you're a writer, you get some of your stuff in, the other guy gets some of his. Sometimes the scripts came out like a game of fold-and-pass, the exquisite corpse, in which its three parts were done by separate hands, none knowing what the other had done.

I learned from one of the old writers of that era there was something called a Hungarian script. Legend was that Hungarians signed on one of their family as a writer but split up the acts among family members all of whom, it was rumored, moved in and lived in their studio offices. Thus any script in which the parts don't seem to fit together, was called a Hungarian script.

Part of being on the assembly line of a factory in which product is churned out is that the status of the writer was about as low as you could get.

There's an old joke: did you hear about the Polish starlet who came to Hollywood and slept with a writer?

Richard Dreyfuss once told me that the four brightest people he knew in Hollywood were the four dumbest. Graciously, he included me among the dumb.

"You guys think what you do is going to end up on the screen," Richard said. "There are eight egos between you and the screen. You don't have a chance."

In the late 70s I lived in an apartment in West Hollywood a half-block down from the famous Schwab's Drug Store, famous in large part because it was claimed Lana Turner was discovered having a malt at the soda fountain counter.

What I remember most is that if you got there early enough, Schwab's had behind the cigar counter a few copies of the New York

Times that had been airmailed in. If I could grab one, I would sit in the coffee shop corner of the huge pharmacy where I was surrounded by cigar smoking, dyspeptic, complaining writers.

"The dumb cock sucker, the director," one would say at the next table as I was trying to get into a Reston editorial, "he was told by Mayer the thing had to be shorter so when his hatchet man came on the set, that dumb cocksucker ripped three pages out of my script and shoved them at the little mouse and said, 'Tell Mr.Mayer we ain't shooting these.'"

Screen writers are known by the vintage of their whines. Those who were fucked over by some of the old and great legends had reason to be proud. It was like earning Purple Hearts.

Another trait of those brought up in the film factory system, none of them, thank God, thought of themselves as an artist. Few of them would ever brag about their credits. Only a chump would brag.

Which brings me back to Erwin Gelsey.

Though he never mentioned it, he had shared screenplay and/or story credit on 24 films between the years 1932 and 1947. It was 1958 when he came to work as Columbia's East Coast Story Editor. Someone on the executive floor must have remembered him.

And what there is to remember: some of my favorite films, many of them classics. To name a few:

> 1933 Gold Diggers of 1933
> 1933 Flying Down to Rio
> 1935 We're in the Money
> 1936 Swing Time
> 1936 The Big Broadcast of 1937
> 1944 Cover Girl

Gelsey was smiling as always and seemed mighty proud to see me. We all embraced. I said, "Erwin, you never told me about the pictures you wrote."

He laughed, hitched up his pants, "How about the pictures you been making?"

"Can't compare."

"Oh, shut up," his wife said and gave me a buss on the cheek.

I later learned this little lady was the widow of one of the Epstein twins. Ring a bell? Among other credits, they are credited, along with Howard Koch, for the screenplay of <u>Casablanca</u>.

I love the inter-linking of Old Hollywood.

Postscript: the surviving twin was asked to speak to a class at USC. He was asked how he plotted his films. He answered in the first act you run your hero up a tree, in the second act you throw rocks at him, in the last act you let him down.

Maybe what I love is the no-bullshit let's make the fucking picture attitude of the old greats. That's the Old Hollywood I love.

And miss.

The Speeding Soren

The play, <u>The Connection</u> by Jack Gelber, opened in 1958 at the Living Theatre on 14th Street and Sixth Avenue. The play was directed by Judith Malina, wife of the co-founder of this landmark (should I say, justifiably famous) avant garde theatre. Anne and I were given tickets early along. Because Soren was working in the box office and like all conmen, could not let money slip through his fingers without some sticking, Anne and I were also lavished with gifts: Anne with dresses and cake, me the Siepe/Josef Krips recording of <u>Don Giovanni</u>, followed by being taken to see Mr.Siepe himself perform the role at the Met, the old Met as it is called, before it moved into Lincoln Center.

Soren kept me very busy and for that matter, Anne too. Soren was addicted to amphetamines. It was a full-time job keeping up. What he laid on me was a course in music, art, theatre, gay life, and the arcane (at least for me) shadowy corners of sex. From the moment I walked into Soren's 10th Street apartment and was faced with a wall of collage ranging from Lady Day to Donald Duck on a bike to young men in bulging posing straps, I was falling down Alice's hole to a new and unexpected dimension. Fancifully, I later liked to say it was my door into the aesthetics of the second half of the 20th Century.

What do I owe Soren and his insane obsession with me: so much. At Yale, the Drama School was doing Commedia delle'Arte. At the Living Theatre they were doing <u>The Connection</u>. As part of my free tutorial from Soren, I was reading about Stanislavski and Artaud, learning of the theatre of cruelty and of the Moscow theatre's method of acting and its group-probing for truths.

The Connection was a power blast, like opening the door to the furnace. It fascinated and frightened me. I was easily frightened by madness. Here was a group of junkies who to all appearances lived on the small stage at the Living Theatre. As we took our seats, they were lounging about on the ripped furniture, wiping their drug-runny noses, exchanging mumbles that weren't meant to be understood. There was a piano. At it sat Freddie Redd, the man who wrote the music for the production. He started to play, a light riff over the mountain tops. The soulful Jackie MacLane stood behind him with his sax and wove melodies around Freddie's. There were more in the combo. I can't remember how many. I do remember it caused the audience to settle and after the music faded, to listen to what seemed authentic bitching from authentic junkies growing impatient as they wait for their connection to show up.

The audience felt they had truly dropped in on a junkie's pad, one that fortunately had such an exceptional jazz combo in residence.

At the intermission, the cast wandered out in the lobby and accosted us, panhandling, needing money for their drugs. We all dug into our pockets: in my case, shallow pockets.

The connection at last arrives. In a searing performance, Warren Finnerty fixes up, injects in front of us squeamish souls, od's and dies. The pad rather quickly clears out. No one wants to deal with the dead junkie's body.

That play changed my perceptions of what theatre could be. It made me dizzy with delight and anxiety. Where was Soren leading me? Into insanity? He knew I feared insanity. I didn't want to be that much like my mother.

Good news. Dale Joe's paintings were included in an exhibition of Sixteen Americans at the Whitney Museum when it was still an outbuilding in MOMA's garden on 54t Street. Anne and I had just purchased our first painting, one of Dale's, which looked like an aerial photograph of desert terrain and crooked ravines. It cost $250. He let us pay for it on time. It took almost two years to pay our last.

So of course we followed Soren's smoking tracks up to the

Whitney. The exhibition also included the action painter, Alfred Leslie.

I recall falling in love with the image of Alfred Leslie. His paintings yes, but also the photo of the painter standing in his studio, legs apart as though bracing for action, a broad paint brush held down to his side, now limp but still dripping from the orgasmic action that spatters the surrounding canvasses. His hair was an act of action also, going where whim would take it: dark, unsettled as were his dark eyes, a romantic figure if by that I'm thinking Byronic and such. Overalls caked with past ejaculations of art.

The paintings were kinetic, as often said. Even mounted on the wall they seemed still to be moving as though the artist were at work, his broad splattering brush still slapping the face of the canvas. I sensed him handsome, romantic, errant, aggressive, leaving so much to chance for in the interstices of chance the life-propulsive is lived. In those spaces the body speaks to mind and their meeting up is called art.

I love the Marshall McLuhan quote: Art is whatever you can get away with.

I remember standing in front of Leslie's paintings as my muted critic and wife, Anne, Swedish, careful when arriving at anything, puts a finger to her pursed lips, considering. I am beside her, beside myself waiting for her to point out where flesh meets thought, soul body, it's Action as in Orgasmic art.

"Very good," she said and moved on.

Leslie did not climb as high in his career as others in the exhibition. But then, things that flash upon the night are often not there the next. But I can look at the paintings today and I am again back in that night, burning.

Thank you, God, for art. And while I'm at it, thank you for a heart that still burns.

Soren came back to Cobble Hill where we had recently moved with son Christopher. We splurged and bought those tri-cornered lamb pastries from the Lebanese bakery around the corner on Atlantic Avenue. With extra coins (Soren so often had them) we bought two quart bottles of Rheingold beer.

We ate and drank into the night and I without much prompting read aloud to Anne and Soren. Probably the poetry of Cavafy. What I loved so about Cavafy is not only his lack of poetic devices, but his assumption even when young of the voice of an old man. I loved the idea of being an old man. Somehow, I felt, that would be the answer. To what? The current daily storms of anxiety.

Annie lay down on our bed seen through an alcove. The day had done her in. While Soren watched, I walked over and lay beside her. She was vaguely aware of me; she sighed and put an arm over me. I caught Soren's eye. I motioned him to join us.

Soren lay on the other side of Anne. Her eyes opened, she turned, saw Soren looking at her.

"Hello," Anne said.

"Hello," Soren replied.

Soren tentatively kissed her. That amused Anne. She made the kiss more engaging.

"Hey," I said, "what about me?"

Anne turned and kissed me. Soren leaned over her and his lips joined ours. We made love to Anne..

The three of us slept in that bed together that night. Soren never came back to our bed. It never seemed important.

But a fire had been lit in me. An image of Anne and me in bed with another man, the three of us making love.

It came close to consuming me.

Boy Story Editor

I made a friend on the Eleventh (executive) Floor at 711 Fifth. Stanley Schneider. Stanley had some sort of vice president title, but his executive weight came in part from being the son of Abe Schneider. Mr.Schneider senior was chairman of the board and president of the company.

I don't know at what point I saw Bobby Morse on Broadway doing How to Succeed in Business without Really Trying, but honest injun, I had no interest in business. I considered my work for Columbia day work while I went home to Brooklyn nightly and wrote and dreamed of becoming a playwright.

We ended up moving into a floor of a brownstone in Cobble Hill. There was a cubby hole a half flight down where I could put my Olivetti portable on a table facing the unfinished wall and write and write.

Abe Schneider was a man for whom I had much respect. He had the calm of an old Indian chief, listening long before speaking, then like Solomon himself, would rest his hands on the table, one on top of the other and make wise decisions that saved the baby from dissection. He even resembled an Indian chief, dark skinned perhaps from golf who knows? A nose that was long and had a small crook in it, like a plain's Indian. He had served long in New York in sales and distribution while Columbia's true founder and gangster madman, Harry Cohn, supplied the product. That is to say, the films.

Harry Cohn had cobbled together a number of small independent studios that clustered around the intersection of Sunset Boulevard and Gower Street. It was known as Gower Gulch. Harry bought up one of these independents after the other and created Columbia Pictures. Its staple was B pictures, especially those with recurring heroes.

An order would come out from New York to the Studio saying we need for this year two Boston Blackies, one Blondie, two Randolph Scott westerns – or some such.

Harry also let it be known that Columbia was open to films that the big studios had trouble with. There were so often one or two floating around and Harry would give them harbor. It Happened One Night was one such picture. It set Frank Capra on the road to fame and also started a long relationship between the garbage-mouthed Harry and the gentlemanly Italian, Mr.Capra.

Claudette Colbert had an old grudge against Capra, their first film was a flop. She demanded her salary be doubled and her commitment be no more than four weeks so she could go on vacation. It was said that her co-star, Clark Gable, lightened her spirits somewhat and they played practical jokes on each other during production.

Gable was another problem. He was being "punished" by being sent over to work for Harry Cohn. He had refused a role MGM assigned him and they took the lash to him.

In all, the two actors didn't do bad by the film. They both won Oscars. In fact, It Happened One Night was the first picture ever to win all five major Oscars for the year: Best Picture, Director, Actor, Actress and Screenplay. It took about forty years for another picture, One Flew Over the Cuckoo's Nest, to match it.

My dream was to work in the theatre. I was a child of my time and films were considered trash art. There were no film schools. Only my friend, Carlos Clarens, took film seriously enough to write books about them, one on crime films, one on horror films.

Through me, this madcap Cuban was introduced to the quiet functionary who ran the East Coast stills department. He seemed to have few demands on his services. He mailed out stills from the latest releases, as ordered, but that was about it.

Then in walked the Cuban with the wild Afro hairdo and the flashing black eyes and an exuberant habit of saying "Carumba!" or in moments of disgust, "Quelle horreur!" The gentleman in the stills department had a new friend in Carlos who visited him, pulled stills out from decades of files, oohed and ahhed over them and since the man offered no resistance, slipped them into his case.

Later, Carlos started a film stills archival business.

Stanley Schneider was a guy only a few years older than I. He enjoyed having me come down to his office and we'd have long chats. He was as mild on the surface as his father but seemed always alert to who was saying what and when. As though he was keeping notes. He had plans.

He laughed at my jokes and seemed to value my opinions on stories and our friendship grew. When Erwin Gelsey moved along (was let go?), I was appointed East Coast Story Editor. I believe I was twenty-four. I also believe that Stanley had something to do with my sudden rise in the ranks.

As Story Editor I was given the opportunity to hire some of my writer (that is, out-of-work) friends as readers. I was told, as I was about to hire the first, that I must talk first to Leo Jaffe's secretary.

From my view, down and looking up, Leo Jaffe was the bad apple in Columbia's hierarchy. In titles and power he was right behind Abe Schneider. Over the years, his conservative (that is, predictable) tastes and his general disliking for me, cost me a lot.

I think I started off badly with him. He was a short man and when introduced to him, I stood up and shook his hand. I am six three. It is always best to shake hands with a short man while I remain seated.

I reported, as told, to his secretary. I told her I was about to hire a reader and gave her his name. She asked me to hold on a minute. She opened a lower drawer, pulled out a stapled sheaf of papers and scanned it, looking for the name I gave her.

"What is that?" I asked. She didn't answer. She put the papers back in her drawer.

"No problem," she said and answered a phone.

I later learned that she still had a copy of the black list of suspected-communist writers that was established during the notorious House on Un-American Activities days, the days of that megalomaniac drunk, Sen.Joe McCarthy.

Apparently Jaffe was the only one in the organization who continued to hold on to such a list, or so the usually reliable network of secretary gossip let me know. I found this difficult to square with the fact he was on the board of Brandeis University, a group I thought of as actively liberal. But what did I know? All I know is his secretary still had a list.

I never ran a name by her again.

It was Leo Jaffe who hired Bosley Crowther as a creative consultant after the New York Times fired him or let him go, or some other term more kind for being put to pasture. This alliance between Leo and Crowther later caused me trouble.

I imagine it was also Leo who hired Max Gordon to scout scripts for the Story Department. For that I am grateful. I got to meet Max Gordon.

One day the door opened and a gentleman stepped out of a time machine and into our offices. He was wearing a dark cut-away suit, wing-collars ready for flight, black tie and as memory serves, spats. He had a venerable briefcase of floppy leather which he opened. He pulled out a few scripts and flopped them onto the table in our center office.

I introduced myself and he shook my hand with a brief, "Max Gordon" for a reply.

"Get onto these. They're hot as the depot stove, glow ruby red in the dark."

"Okay and what are these?"

"Leo didn't tell you I'd be scouting scripts? Get on to these."

He gave me a half bow, shook my hand and went out the door.

Who in God's name was Max Gordon?

Who better to ask than my expert in all things, the mardi gras Cuban, Carlos Clarens?

Gordon was a gentleman now coming up on 70 who had started back in vaudeville and rose to be one of the most successful Broadway producers during the Great Depression.

For one, he produced <u>The Jazz Singer,</u> a hit on Broadway which later became the first talkie musical with Al Jolson singing about his "mammy."

For another, he produced <u>Born Yesterday</u> for which he discovered Judy Holliday. It later became a smash picture again with Judy Holliday.

His stage hits included <u>My Sister Eileen,</u> <u>The Solid Gold Cadillac,</u> and a 1936 version of <u>Dodsworth.</u>

He was so famous in the 30s that Cole Porter included his name in one of the verses of his song "Anything Goes."

And now, dignity and wardrobe intact, he was schlepping scripts for Leo Jaffe. I sensed it was more than a little humbling to be tossing scripts on the table for a boy story editor, but I never failed to thank him with a solemn gratitude. He gave me a fishy glance and went out the door.

Since I was among the egg-heads on the Sixteenth Floor I was asked on occasion to lunch with the famous but fading. For instance, Rouben Mamoulian, who was sent on to me by Jaffe's office. Here indeed, across the lunch table at the St.Regis, was film history. Mr.Mamoulian told me of the challenge it was to his cinematographer to change focus for the last shot of <u>Queen Christina</u>. The camera on a crane was to start some distance out from the ship on whose back deck sat the abdicating queen, Greta Garbo. The camera is to end up close on her face and the drama to end on that image. But they did not have lenses geared to change focal length rapidly back then.

The day of shooting, the cinematographer came in with a long strip of glass on which he had the camera shop grind different magnifications. The glass was moved slowly, by hand, across the lens by an assistant. It took a few tries but the result was, well, film history.

It was gracious of men like Max Gordon and Rouben Mamoulian not to indicate they were having lunch with a twenty-something who knew little about film.

They made gentleman back then.

With the notable exception of Brendan Behan who became a drinking pal. One of his plays was on Broadway and he was receiving press for shouting insults down on the actors from the balcony. He took a shine to me and gave me a copy of his book <u>Brendan Behan's Island An Irish Sketch-book</u>. He inscribed something to me in the fly, in Gaelic, which someday I will have to find a sober Irishman and ask him to decipher.

In my mid-twenties I found myself dining with Ed Doctorow, Isaac Asimov, Robert Gottlieb as well as those mentioned above. Though I did dine with Brendan Behan what we did mostly was get piss-eyed drunk at lunch and I had to go back to my office and lie down behind my desk.

Columbia had promoted ultra-ambitious Joyce Selznick beyond her skills to be a casting consultant. A bullish lesbian with a snarling Edward G.Robinson manner and more than ample breasts, she falsely claimed to be related to giant, David Selznick. Seeing her in her office, I led Brendan in to introduce him. In a blur, the Irishman jumped over her desk onto mannish Joyce and kneaded her left breast all the while singing "I was Lady Chatterly's Lover." With a sharp push, she sent him sprawling.

I have never gotten close, really close, to anyone who isn't crazy.

Drink took the man early. It almost took me too, but that for later.

Home Fires

While Anne and I counted our coins and wrote synopses for Columbia Pictures, we followed Soren's many suggestions and kept up with the scenes, art, poetry readings in bars, you name it. It kept us moving around the twin boroughs, Manhattan and Brooklyn, our Uncle Whitman's old stomping grounds.

For one, Soren sometimes babysat for his friend Diane di Prima, the only woman poet in the entire men's club of the Beat Poets. She was living with the playwright and terrifying force then named LeRoi Jones. He later became Amiri Baraka. From reading them, we were led on to the San Francisco City Lights group, most especially Lawrence Ferlinghetti whom I adored for his more mature wit and grace. I also got goofy over Gregory Corso but not for his maturity. He was young and cute and shot from the hip. His poems were small but well-tuned aggressions.

There was another woman poet allowed into the Cassady-Kerouac kingdom of cool, and her name I believe was Barbara Guest. All I remember clearly is her line, "take your cut throat off my knife."

I should confess that I took Soren's opinions as gospel. How was I to know any different? When he told me he was responsible for the first two editions of Warhol's Interview hip tabloid, I took him at his word. As I did when I was told that Andy had unfairly let him go.

I took as gospel also that Andy Warhol was the great P.T.Barnum of our age, a superb showman who assembled other people's ideas and with great cunning marketed them. For instance, Tullie Kupferberg, according to Soren, was influential in Andy's graphics, especially drawn words.

More close to home, Soren told us that Ray Johnson was the first to appropriate Elvis Presley and James Dean in his collages and Andy followed his example, creating an industry of celebrity art. It was also Ray Johnson who went to sinister images, accident victims, child murderers being hauled off to jail, transcriptions of pathologic stutterers. All with humor, of course, which was the default setting of camp.

It never occurred to me that Soren didn't speak with authority. Also, it was easier to accept than doing research on my own. I was too busy writing, drinking and sexing, like all good boys of the early 60s.

Soren showed me a copy of a mimeographed deeply underground publication being churned out by Diane di Prima. It was called The Floating Bear" (remember Winnie-the-Pooh afloat on a jar?) and Soren was an important part of it. Until he wasn't, reasons obscure.

So he started mimeographing his own underground tabloid, calling it <u>The Sinking Bear</u>. In it he included pages of quotes of those deep in the underground, especially the boys (and very few girls) over at Warhol's Factory. He even included a poem he credited to me, a bad little piece that I don't think I wrote. Perhaps Soren wanted to do me a favor. It wasn't appreciated.

He was the first to alert me to Rauchenberg and Johns and to say they were onetime lovers and lived under the bridge in the same building as Ray Johnson. I believed him. He also told us that they had landed with the powerful debonair art dealer, Leo Castelli. A show of Rauschenbergs was going on at the Castelli gallery on the upper east side. Anne zipped our son up in his snow suit and we took a subway uptown to have a look

Leo Castelli's was at 4 East Seventy-seventh Street, a place my favorite critic Peter Shjeldahl called "ground zero for the explosion of Pop Art and minimalism." An elegant townhouse just off Fifth Avenue, within smelling distance of the trees of Central Park.

Wife Anne, always a little vague in a Swedish way, came in with our two year-old. It was snowing out. Chris was in a heavily zipped snow suit. As I got on to the important business of being knocked over by the art of Rauchenberg, Anne set our son on a wooden chair and went about unzipping his suit.

The highly tailored Mr.Castelli came running from his back office. Waving hands in the air. "No, no, Madame, that is a painting."

Anne hadn't noticed that the wood chair was attached to a Rauschenberg painting and its feet were not touching the floor. Anne mumbled an embarrassed apology and took our son off the seat of major art.

Among others who migrated north to visit the Castelli
shrine: Johns, Twombly, Warhol, Lichtenstein, Oldenburg,
Rosenquist, Judd, Flavin, Morris, Stella, Nauman, Serra.

Years later, after Mr.Castelli had moved down to Broadway across from the Public Theatre, I dropped in to interview him for an original script I was writing about a painter, Dangerous Angel, a script that was later written about in the Warhol's Diaries.

Castelli and I were surprised by the arrival of the ever charming and affable Bob Rauchenberg. He seemed always to be running for mayor of a small town and he certainly would have had my vote. I got him to sign a poster for his latest show at Castelli, something he didn't apparently do but I was younger then and flirtatious and he was always generous. Generosity, yes, that is his most appealing trait. He gives, all, whatever, under the instinctive eye of the accomplished artist, yes, but he is generous. He lets us in. I loved the man.

Anne's combination of Swedish blood and Gemini sun made for a maddening vagueness, a language that required more twists to include the absolute truth than I was willing to make. And often, she appeared mean as lizard spit.

I decided one gloomy winter afternoon because I was young and drunk to have an impromptu picnic in our small Greenwich Street apartment. After all, our carpet was some sort of cheap woven grass which bravely gave refuge to the dirt of many seasons. Sitting on it would be almost like a picnic, right?

Not many came. Among them was my classmate from Yale, Larry Kramer who had been helpful in landing us our reading jobs at Columbia. Anne and I uncharitably concluded Larry had gone out and bought a new pair of Levis as proper wear for coming to the hip Village. The new jeans were as stiff as he.

He lay on the floor where the picnic was laid out, drank a lot and was soon laid out himself. He got piss-eyed drunk. He looked up at the girl sitting next to him, my wife Anne who was, as in all social occasions, Sphinx-like in her reserve (read: fear).

He asked in what seemed near to tears, "Anne, why don't people like me?"

Anne gave it short thought and Sybil-like intoned, "Because you are incredibly square, Larry."

I always wondered why I never got along too well with Larry.

Anne's vagueness at times had bizarre consequences. As you will see.

Richard's Egg

In the late 50s Anne and I and Soren would meet on the stone plaza outside the now famous Seagram Building, the most successful of Meis van der Rohe's buildings, tricked out inside by Philip Johnson. We felt we were seated in a place of true proportion, the actual sitting made us part of the vast creativity of the building. And then, when coins were saved, we could go into the building to the Four Seasons for an expensive single drink and ogle the wire sculpture over the bar done by Richard Lippold.

Richard not only had wire sculptures in MOMA and the Met, but was a married man and father and beyond that the lover of Ray Johnson. He was at the coffee shop with Ray when Soren introduced us all.

Richard started to drop in on us. We were still in our small apartment on Greenwich Street. Living room with Pullman kitchen, bath and small bedroom. My son's crib was in the bedroom next to the bed Anne and I shared.

Richard had come on the idea that I reminded him of the beautiful creature he was when he was my age (he was only 44 at the time). Nothing turns on a narcissist more than such reminders. He was so moved by his mirror image in me that he once drove in from the island with a large branch of dogwood sticking up from the back seat to present to me. Of course for Anne too.

He came bearing more gifts. In a self-impressed voice he let us know that Baron Rothschild was a friend, that he had spent time at his chateau in the Bordeaux countryside, that he and the baron had wandered the vineyards together. All this conveyed as he uncorked a bottle while standing at our narrow eating bar. He encouraged us to taste the sun, even the rain that had fallen on the responsive grapes that grew in dreamy Bordeaux. The earth too, we should be able to taste the earth, roll it around on our tongues.

He created a truly beautiful (now lost) wire sculpture of a platinum wire egg with a gold star burst inside. It was a few inches high and stood on a marble base. He gave it to us with a drawing that described its inspiration: it was meant to show Anne's and my lips coming together in a kiss.

I apparently failed to give Richard any assurances that I found him as compelling as he did me, so he stood outside our door one morning, perhaps half way up a flight of stairs to conceal himself. I was, as often happened, hung over and sleeping in as Anne let herself out, leaving me gasping through sleep and our son snoozing in his crib next to me. Being Anne, she wasn't mindful of locks and such. She left the door unlocked.

I woke out of a boozy haze to realize that a naked Richard Lippold was embracing me from behind. In my bed. Should I add, uninvited? Oh well, he was a guest in my house. I couldn't rebuff him.

I closed my eyes. I came. He went.

You see, people were crazy too in those days before heavy drugs.

Soren My Socrates

One of the challenges of writing about New York in the late 50s is making the contemporary reader understand that it was long ago and in another country.

It was before the Beatles, for one. Before psychedelics, for another. A time when the bohemians were just starting to be defined beatniks.

Before that, young hopeful artists came to New York from campuses all over the US to be grown ups. Adults. This pre-dates the take-over of the US by kiddie culture.

The ideal was to meet a publisher at the Oak Bar at the Plaza to discuss your manuscript he was considering and drink tall stemmed martinis. He would be in business suit and tie. The writer type would be in crumpled Harris tweed jacket and an oxford button down shirt, but had purposely forgotten his tie.

To get this picture, look at <u>North by Northwest</u>. There is no kiddie culture in the entire movie.

Of course I had my private tutor, my own Socrates, to lead me through the doors from the academy to camp. I had Soren. I credit him with so much of what I was or came to think I was and rightly so. Yes, opera. Yes, new art. Yes, electronic music. Or just as bad, dissonant modern music even if modern meant composers dead now for decades.

Most important, I musn't forget he introduced Anne and me to Franny and she set us upon the yellow brick road to Hollywood.

I should give credit – or even a medal – for his introducing me to sex, not the mechanics of sex that has more variations than sand, no,

I mean the sex that was the twisted and personal and totally enthralling sex of little Gerry at last in his playroom with the other children inventing sex, slurping inventions.

Is this insane? I hope. Only those who learn to be insane escape fear. Desire is insanity.

"Sooner murder an infant in its cradle than
nurse unacted desires." — William Blake

Soren got two tickets in the upper ring of the old Met to hear and partly see <u>Wozzeck</u>. We were seated close under the roof of that vast space at an angle the ticket warned us was 'obstructed view' and Soren was up and down from his seat, running to the railing to see the stage at the bottom of that chasm. I joined him, eager to find the excitement in this screaming score and the nightmare tale of how the low bulbs in this life are eventually crushed. I hated innocent victims since I found comfort in thinking of myself as one. I particularly understood young men made weak-kneed by the bullies, the real men who take your wives.

We visited a composer who made electronic music. He lived not far from Carnegie Hall itself, a small apartment as cluttered with snips and pieces of wires and devices as a repair shop. He played for us a piece he was working on, called Cough Music. He had put together ten minutes of audience coughing, snipped from live performances. His name was Richard. Like so many serious artist who seek new ways to unsettle us, he looked undernourished and depressed. Not as undernourished and depressed as Peter Hujar, the photographer I was later to meet, but Peter perfected those traits.

The reward at the end of the day was a quick call to Anne to see if there is anything I could pick up at the store and promise to be home early, which I never was, because I went to the children's room, to Soren's, to the stunning poke and prod and daring of kids who got away with things when the parents were out.

Paradise enough.

Soren took me now and then to Warhol's Factory, perhaps to

impress me though Andy had not yet become the massive celeb he later did. I found him and his hangers-on creepy. Andy would see me arrive and turn to whisper to someone near him, nodding his head in my direction. I assumed I was good gossip, a married man having an affair with their Soren. I also thought they found me odd since I was given to riffing on 18th Century poetry and depending on the amount drunk, reciting it by the yard.

I was puzzled by Andy. I knew he was changing the definitions of art, but he sounded like a breathless high school girl who drew unicorns in the back of her books.

Only later, years later when a documentary maker was doing a film on Ray Johnson, did I have another thought. The film maker, John Walter, was interviewing Billy Name whom we knew as Billy Linich. He was part of the Factory history: after Andy was shot he went into a back room for a year (two years?) and did not come out. But of course he did come out. I was at the Factory one night, God knows why, Andy of course had gone uptown to his mother, and Billy came out of a narrow door. It seemed cut into a dry wall. Unlike the David Crosby-walrus he has become (and is still adorable), at that time he was thin and dark and because I knew his story, he seemed dangerous and dangerous is always attractive.

I can't remember whether we said a word. He led me through that narrow door into a room that seemed (speak, memory) a pie sliver between dry walls, and we made love. Speak again, memory, the love went on for some time, perhaps till light was coming into the streets but never, of course, into the factory.

Billy was asked by the documentary maker his impression of me. "He was the most beautiful guy in New York."

Far from bothering to believe this or be flattered, I complained, "Why didn't anyone tell me?"

While at the Factory, I saw a book on a table. It was written by the man Dennis Selby I met on the bridge. This Aznavour look-alike fascinated me all the more. This stranger with the crooked mouth and deceitful eyes who salivated on his cigarettes, he had actually published a book. It was called <u>There's No Such Thing as a Naked Sailor</u>, and in it was the first mention ever of Scientology, which got Andy's attention. Andy always had his ear to the rails and knew what was coming.

He was Celtic like me, this Selby. He came from a land of cold rocks and merciless seas.

I climbed the six flights up to his apartment on Sullivan Street, across from the forever <u>Fantastiks</u>. How did this come about? Who remembers, except to say that lust finds a way.

I was in awe of a man who had published. And who looked authentic, though authentic what, I'm not entirely certain. He seemed pleased to see me and rolled a joint and did some major saliva work on it. He smiled.

Being nervous and hoping for approval I turned to the one thing I felt would give me a purchase on his attention. I went into his toilet. Within moments, I walked out totally naked. His crooked lips pursed in what I presumed was a smile. He took his eyes off me only long enough to stub out his cigarette. Wordless he rose, stood beside me, put his face against mine and caused me by some act of magic to float back on his day bed.

Was it he who introduced me to Cavafy's poems? I do know he gave me the Rae Dalven collection for my birthday,

Feb 3, 1962 which had recently been published. Still my favorite translation. In the fly he wrote, "To Gerry with nervousness and calm. Dennis Feb 3 '62" I fell under the spell of Cavafy. He and Robert Creeley were my heroes in those days.

It came to pass in this fairy tale that was our Village Days that Anne became attracted to Dennis. I had brought him out to Brooklyn to dinner and the two of them fell into the same space, seemed to laugh at the same instant. They seemed to be laughing at me. They were the wizards and I the hapless bumpkin.

Dennis is one of the few friends from that period still on the right side of turf. I wrote to him recently wanting to know whether he and Anne were mocking me.

His reply:

"Strikes me that a great deal of your success came from your being an initiator. U say u didn't know u were stunning, but u behaved like a bulldozer. Where'd you get that self-confidence. If not from your looks? Oh yes, your charm! U could charm a lamppost if u found it sexy. What a combination! No wonder u went, as they say, far."

What appears as self-confidence, Dennis, is fear. It was a gear I could shift into when the panic of the moment was about to make me crash. That's how I went, as they say, far.

In the same email, Dennis includes a recollection that stirs my viscera even after all these years.

"It was a hot summer afternoon, Anne and I were slow dancing in the living room. U came up behind Anne and pulled down her shorts and panties, and she kept on dancing as though oblivious. Then u came up behind me and pulled my pants down. I danced on as though oblivious. then u led us into the bedroom."

Thus Dennis ended up with Anne and me in bed. And I suspect with Anne when I wasn't around. His cool lack of easy emotion appealed to her Nordic soul. She told me once she fell in love with him.

She also told me that an image that remains for her is her coming out of sleep at dawn to see Dennis and me at the foot of the bed, naked, silently pulling our pants on, back lit by the tall townhouse window. She said it was the most beautiful of images for her.

And she became an art curator.

I do know that the images of Dennis making love to Anne while I pull in close to absorb their heat, yes, that was beautiful for me too.

Soren got wind of this, perhaps from Anne, and he called Dennis, telling him to keep his hands off me or he would kill him. Or beat him up? Dennis laughed in his face.. well, into the phone.

This was the beginning of the sixties. I was an Aquarian. It was the dawning of my age. Time to wake up.

To what?

I often wonder whether such a ménage could survive for long no matter how much it might excite me. All those egos battling for their own little reasons to be?

Not likely.

All I come up with is the astonishing conclusion that everyone is sexually bizarre.

Desire makes us all strangers to ourselves. And of course, to others.

An Orange Light in Union Square

Anne was large with our second child, soon to be an astonishing girl baby named Elizabeth. We had our two year-old Christopher in his canvas sling of a stroller and hurried in the fall cold over to Union Square. We wanted to see John Kennedy. He was campaigning to become president.

We fell instantly in love with him.

I leave it to my betters to describe charisma. What won our hearts was a man who spoke our language, alternately lofty followed by a home truth that he delivered like a finger poking at your chest. Then there was his academic wit. Anne and I would deny it, but we were snobs. We preferred wit, especially seasoned with sarcasm.

As I once tried to explain to a Hollywood star lady, when she questioned what did I mean by irony, I said it was not something you brought in with the laundry. It was the ability to say something that had simultaneously two meanings. One meaning didn't negate the other. The art of living was to live with the co-existing opposites.

I said all that to an actress? I am truly naïve.

What I remember looking up at this flat-voweled Bostonian is that he appeared orange. His skin seemed tinted by a light brushing of water color. I associated this with aristocratic genes (forgetting for the moment his father was a gangster) and imagined that I remembered other aristocrats who from a distance appeared orange.

He was our light, orange though it seemed, who glowed from Union Square and he took to the White House all of us, young and hungry for a young president who knew to laugh at himself as a way of criticizing you, who had a lady with him who made expensive

233

fashions seem so appropriate they were almost modest. A man who invited Pablo Casals to the White House and with him came Bach played, as by a Spaniard, soulfully.

It was years later I heard that John Kennedy had a blood tincture, some disease that caused his pigment to appear orange.

Yes, he took us with him to the White House and when he was taken away, we had nowhere to go. We were left in the dark ages of grief and distrust of all things promised by men. When he was joined in death by Martin Luther King and Bobby Kennedy and even, for some of us, Jimmy Hendrix and even Mama Cass, the grief became even darker and the cynicism deeper.

On December 7, 1960, there was a large snow storm in New York. I can attest to the snow in Brooklyn since it was the evening of December 6 that I bundled Anne up and walked her the two short blocks to the Long Island University Hospital. After midnight, only 19 years after the attack on Pearl Harbor, Elizabeth Anne Ayres was born.

It was still snowing badly when I came to walk mother and child the few short blocks to our Pacific Street apartment. The clerk who checked us out told us we must exit the hospital by the front door which would put us a block further south than Pacific. I asked why? There was an emergency exit just down the hall that would let us out onto Pacific Street, only a block and a half from home.

It was against hospital policy. If anything were to happen to the infant before it left the hospital property, their insurance would have to carry it.

I was young and hot on that cold day and suggested that he best call his insurance carrier in a hurry since we're going out the back door.

I took the blanket with infant wrapped in what the Bible would call swaddling clothes and motioned to Anne, who quietly followed. I got to the emergency door, kicked its handle bar and it flew open. I led child and wife into the snow.

We were home in three minutes.

My little girl, Liz, has grown up to be a very head-strong young lady. I have to wonder if this early experience influenced her unduly. Or is it just being a girl. Aren't they always being, well, head-strong?

Especially when they were beauties like my Liz.

Lady Bird

In my writer's cubby hole in Cobble Hill, I set to work on a small jazz opera, <u>Lady Bird</u>, aimed at the Living Theatre where I had connections through Soren. This was perhaps before he stole their adding machine and was arrested. But that later.

My opera was modern dress, set in a Village garden, a retelling of the myth of Phaedra and her itch for her stepson, Hippolytus.

My Hippolytus, stripped to his bikini (these were pre-Speedo days) was sunning in his garden and plotting a trip with a hippie buddy who was black and beautiful. They were going on Kerouac's road. Phaedra, for reasons well-established in the myth, didn't want him to leave, using the excuse he must wait around for his military father's return from war. Also to give her more time to plant her claws in his luscious flesh.

Not surprising, like my own mother, Phaedra had grown up in the San Joaquin Valley and has delusional musing about her perfect past. And the military father, you don't have to guess, yes, is my Navy officer father, that

can-do, ship-shape man fueled by rages.

I did a few versions of the libretto and asked Freddie Redd, the composer of The Living Theatre's <u>The Connection</u>, to write the music. He was also on stage, performing in the Judith Malina production, both as musician and actor.

I remember the times we spent together Freddie was never without his plastic sax. He was fearful someone would steal it. He even brought it out on the beach at Rhys park where Anne and kids and I had taken him for a picnic. I have an image of Freddie sitting on the sand, wearing shoes and socks and bathing suit, never going near the water but coaxing mellow thoughts from his sax.

Freddie was a sweetheart, always with a smile, nodding to himself even when a question hadn't been asked. He was attractive in an impish way, a black man with a hue near to dark plum. Quite appealing. He was straight and I was closeted so there was no thought of my motives other than to be the first to do a jazz opera with just four singers and the combo on stage.

He seemed to agree to all my suggestions as I babbled on. Then he went home and improvised on his piano, recording while he played. Only problem is none of this fit with the libretto I had written. We'd cloud the room with cannabis and I'd rightly praise what I was hearing, but I'd ask how this was to fit the words. Freddie played on. We continued to suck our weed.

I realize how stupid of me. I was young, inexperienced, if that's any excuse, which it isn't. I wanted a three piece combo on stage and in view while my actors performed/sang down front. A chamber opera.

It never occurred to me what is now obvious: Freddie's music was wonderful. Put him on stage with the combo and let him perform while the actors spoke the libretto, a sort of rhythmic sprechstimme (if I could possibly know how to spell that) a sort of spoken non-musical singing. The rehearsals would be to time the pulses between music and dialogue, sometimes one taking over the other, but nowhere was there a need for Verdi or Pucinni or formal arias.

Could have been, but.. the libretto wasn't that great. There are a few patches of passable stuff, but was not that great. But I never went beyond first draft, still trying to figure how to blend the music and words. What a mistake. Its great value to me looking back is that it made an aria of my longing to run out of the shadow of parents and/or wife and go on the road, any road, with my sexy hippie buddy for life. I did so, but it had to wait until March 1971. But the hippie wasn't black. Oh well. You can't stage manage all of life.

All this became soon academic. The IRS would lock the Living Theatre's doors for failure to pay entertainment taxes. Judith Malina and husband Julian Beck were anarchists and disagreed with taxes. They would move their astonishing avant garde company to Europe where the IRS could not reach out a punitive hand.

The Magic of a Magic Realist

How in God's name did Soren find us at the White Horse tavern? There he was, at the window, staring in at us.

And how in God's name did I end up there? My Bleecker Street hipness made me superior to the White Horse, a place I felt was too much a stage set waiting for another Dylan Thomas to stagger in and do last damage to his liver.

But I was with my friend Harold Stevenson who was most theatrical and loved a set on which to perform. He was always sleigh bells to me, jingling and merry and whenever I needed a moment outside myself, I dropped in on Harold. For a confirmed narcissist such as I to take time outside of self was tantamount to a prison break. Soren was crowding me, I felt. He seemed to have woven himself into every fabric of my life. I needed Harold to make me laugh at my ridiculous self.

When I got to Harold's, he was throwing on his raccoon coat.

"Thank God you're here. Let's go out."

"Trouble?"

"Pressure-cooker Tennessee Williams. They're in the second act. I don't want to stick around for the third."

He jerked a thumb in the direction of the window. I looked down the two stories at the small garden behind this row house on Bank Street. I saw Athan, a young man of Homeric beauty, someone you would sack a small town to keep happy. Athan was at this moment standing on the ancient wall that closed in a fish pond. In the pond itself was a naked boy, Johnnie, son of an Italian laborer who lived near the river. He loved to swim in the fish pond though it was cold.

He loved to keep an eye on Athan because Athan seemed to like him and you could never tell what crazy thing Athan would do next. You see, Athan was a failed actor, which apparently explained everything.

At the moment, Athan had a crowbar in hand and was prying loose the stones of the old wall. He was angered. The naked ten year-old had to jump aside as one after another stone fell into the pool.

Harold rented, or was given free rent to, the top floor where he slept and created his art. He was a painter. The house was owned by Cecile. She lived on the garden level. She had given the second floor to Athan who took his dark moods with him to retreat for days at a time.

Cecile was pale as pastry dough, a college professor whose husband had died a few years back and left her with money that so bewildered her she seldom went near it. She gave the impression she had just recovered from tears or was about to break into them.

She had met Athan one night when she was walking her black poodle near what was then her house on the upper east side. A light rain. A mysterious stranger (there should be eerie background music at this point) appeared out of the mist and started talking to Popo, Popo of course being Popo the Poodle. Athan stooped down. As Cecile stood motionless, this mysterious and beautiful (more music) stranger spoke to Popo and the dog put a paw on the boy's knee and frantically licked his face.

Athan didn't say a word to Cecile but his conversation with Popo was intense. Athan stood, looked down at the dog that was now scratching at the legs of his worn Levis.

"Sure, pup, if you want. Lead on."

Cecile started home. Athan fell in with them, making small snick-snick noises at the dog as they walked. Cecile stopped at the entrance to her townhouse. She was hoping this stranger would look up. She wanted to see his eyes.

"His name is Popo," she said. At last he looked up, his eyes at last, a dangerous gift.

"I know. He told me."

Cecile opened the door and went into her house. Athan followed them. She went into the kitchen and poured water for Popo.

"I'm cooking," she said.

Athan found that agreeable. He nodded and sat at the kitchen table. Cecile put fresh shrimp into a braising pan.

"Did you tell Popo what your name is?" she asked.

"Athan."

"Oh, good." Cecile sliced three shallots into the pan. They sizzled and gave off smoke.

"Cecile," she said to the boy.

"That's you?"

Athan ate dinner with Cecile and Popo. Cecile got from him information that he had been an actor but had given it up.

"I'm sorry," Cecile said, saddened to hear of any misfortune befalling such a beautiful young man.

"Don't be. It soulless."

"Is it?"

"Takes it right away. Your soul, I mean."

"Oh, that's not good." Cecile had looked up from stirring her shrimp and now they started to smoke. She went back to her wooden spoon.

"I understand it's a cruel profession," Cecile said and set a plate in front of him. She put a plate opposite and sat herself.

"Depends on the producer," Athan said.

"All about getting a good one."

"All about getting one that keeps their hands out of your pants."

"Oh, dear," said Cecile and put a shrimp in her mouth.

"Sounds awful."

"Depends."

"On what?"

"The producer."

Athan busied himself with dinner. Cecile studied him. "You mean, these were men, right, men producers? Or maybe there were lady producers."

"Doesn't matter," Athan said.

"Doesn't it?" Cecile asks.

"Should it?"

Cecile shook her head slowly and carried her plate over to the sink.

That night, Athan slept in the guest room. He wasn't invited nor did he ask. He just seemed to end up there. Within the week he came over with what looked like a sailor's sea bag containing his earthly possessions, or so he said. Cecile was pleased but tried not to show it.

Cecile stood at the door of the guest room, not that night but soon after and watched him sleeping. Without opening his eyes, he said, "I'm sleeping."

She felt foolish and exposed. Tears came up, but silent of course. "Don't be rude," she said, speaking more strongly than she ever had.

She took Popo to bed, held him in the dark. Her door opened. Athan came in. He sat on her bed. His face was difficult to read in the dark. He put his hand on her back.

"Okay?" he asked.

"Me? Oh yes, I'm okay."

Athan pulled back her covers and crawled in beside her. With rapid motions that terrified her, he pulled his shorts down his legs and threw them to the floor. He put his hand on her arm. She froze. He turned her to face him. The gesture seemed ineffably gentle.

He stroked her hair. "I'm not rude," he said and he entered her.

That was three years ago. Athan hated the upper east side so Cecile bought the house on Bank Street. He requisitioned the second floor where he could be contemplative though what he was contemplating he never said. Some afternoons he climbed to the top floor to visit Harold Stevenson. Cecile suggested that Harold paint Athan. Harold didn't do commissions. Besides, he felt Athan had been over-painted too many times. But he painted him.

Harold was never certain how often Athan went in to lie with Cecile because he had been rude. Or whether he ever did. But he did know she disapproved of the neighborhood boy swimming in their fish pond.

The evening I went out with Harold to the White Horse had followed a tense day. Cecile was concerned that little Johnnie's parents might call the police.

"For what? I haven't done anything."

"For disturbing the fish," Cecile actually yelled at him.

Athan was furious the she might think he had molested the boy. He liked Johnnie because the kid worshipped him. Cecile demanded the boy not come back. Like Achilles with his anger, Athan retaliated. He tore down the ancient wall of Bank Street. Cecile couldn't watch. She sat at the kitchen table, her face in her hands.

Athan climbed the stone wall and pried its stones from their lodgings then raised his arms in triumph as each one tumbled into the pond. Very Homeric.

This was the story that Harold told me in the White Horse tavern. It distressed him. Me, I wanted to make a movie of it. Or a book. No, wait, it had elements of my opera. Older woman, younger man, worshipper on the side. It was literature.

Harold preferred painting. He was a magic realist though he never explained what that was nor claimed to be one. But it had said so in the Times.

He did large paintings in which the figures seem recognizable which is to say humans looked human and cows were cows. But they floated in dream-like space, strangely nudging each other's separate worlds.

I was haunted by a floating figure that seemed taken from my own memory: an old woman whose features were blurred as though she were a negative. I thought I recognized my Auntie. Way across the painting, a boy also with indefinite features was looking over at her. That of course was me. But I didn't tell Harold.

I so admired the two small studies he had done of each of these figures before incorporating them into the large painting. I carried on so about them that he ended up giving them to me. They hang today on either side of my bed, that sad boy looking across at his fading auntie.

Harold was short which may explain why he had to wave his arms in the air when speaking. He was from the south, from Oklahoma if that is south, from a town that also suggested sleigh bells. Idabel, in Oklahoma.

Harold wore only spattered work clothes but when he went out for the evening he threw on a raccoon coat that reached all the way to his ankles. It wasn't much of a reach. When he told his stories, raising his arms theatrically above him, turning his palms to the heavens, then laughter came like sudden rain.

Oklahoma had given him a syrupy accent that made you wonder whether he was speaking truth or whether these stories were front-line coverage from his very mendacious interior. It wasn't that he lied so much as that he set the truth to music.

I looked up and saw Soren out on the walk, staring in through the window at us. The music stopped.

"Oh, it's Soren," Harold said brightly.

Out on the walk Harold stopped to shower Soren with some southern charm. Soren wasn't charmed. He was eyeing me as I stood by keeping up with traffic. Soren spoke to me.

"I'd like to take your nuts and squeeze them till you shoot off sparks."

Harold laughed. "Oh my dear, we're all good Christian boys and unless you want Nana to wash your mouth out - "

"Fuck you," Soren said.

Harold laughed again. "Now that's exactly what I'm talking about."

I turned to Harold. "I'll take it from here."

"Well, boys, I'm off to create a little trouble, if I'm lucky maybe big trouble – "And then in a Delta blues voice, "Big and bad. I mean, I have a foot of dick and a bucket of balls and if that ain't trouble, tell me Mary what is."

He leaned forward and kissed Soren's cheek. He kissed my lips. He aired out his fingers in the way of a bye-bye and went off up the walk, his raccoon swirling about him.

I told Soren I left my '53 Plymouth over at Harold's. I could drive him home, being a good Christian boy.

"I thought this was our night. You told me to keep Wednesday open."

I started walking. "You mean before you tried to kidnap my son?"

Soren rushed to keep even. "Maybe you don't understand."

"You got that."

"I was walking Christopher across the park."

"Christopher was in his carriage and you were running off because I told you -"

"I know what you told me."

"To stop calling my friends —"

"Bull shit I did."

"And threatening them, intimidating them. And you ran off with my baby."

It turned out Soren wanted me to drop him at Franny's. This was an evening he was to be on rape patrol. I pulled to a stop on Minetta Lane. Soren didn't get out. Okay, I'll match him with silence. I turned off the ignition.

He finally broke the silence. "You don't understand."

"Very good chance of that."

"I'm from California." There was a pause. I wondered whether there was more to understand. "Where I grew up we had a front lawn, a large one. I had five sisters. Sort of."

"Sort of five sisters?"

"Sisters and brothers. I never see them anymore."

"Maybe because you live in New York."

"I've been here two years. But I have been patient."

"What are you waiting for?"

"I thought I had found it.. a couple of times."

"Ah the lover, here in the promised land."

Soren didn't care for my sarcasm. He looked down sadly. "Someone.. someone who cared. It's the greatest thing in the world, to care."

"Let's say I'm working on it."

"Do you love me?"

"Oooh," I said and added, "well." And then, "I can't get away from you, if that's any comfort."

That seemed to cheer him up, I don't know why. Now he looked up at me. "I met a painter once who cared," he said. "He made me write poetry."

"That's a neat trick. What'd he do, wind you up?"

"But it didn't matter that he cared. He wasn't there, he just wasn't there."

"Let me guess, he was what you'd call a slut?"

"He didn't know what it meant to go out into the streets, to walk in them. And that's where people in this city live, where they have their real lives, in the streets. I couldn't touch him, touch his living. It didn't matter. He was minor."

"You want me to get serious?" He gave me a fishy look. "I mean shouldn't I give it one try."

"Whatever you say to me it doesn't matter. You're an artist, an important artist."

"Then you better wind me up."

"You will be and that's so much more important than whatever you say, or whatever I feel."

"You didn't like the poem I sent you," I let him know.

"I never said that."

"You never said nuttin."

"You need me.. very much."

"That's sweet of you, but —"

"You're wrong about Anne."

"Anne? How'd she get in this?"

"I love Anne."

"I'll tell her."

"It's boys that will ruin you."

"You're a boy."

"I'm the fire you jump to."

I hooted. "From the frying pan?"

"From boredom," he answered.

There are many things I could feel being with Soren but boredom wasn't one of them.

"They will ruin you," Soren said.

"I like to make friends."

"You have to sleep with every friend you have?" Suddenly he seemed to be shouting.

"That's it!"

I jumped out of the car. I walked around it and opened Soren's door. I motioned. He didn't move.

"What about drugs?" I asked. I was angry.

"Why do you ask? You want some?"

"Don't twist my words. I'm asking, you still using amphetamines?"

"You talk about drugs, ridiculous, it sounds phony in your mouth."

"Are you?"

He jumped out of the car. He ran to Franny's wrought-iron gate and pushed it open. He hurried down the three steps to the pavestone patio.

"You're already losing your teeth," I shouted at him.

"Fucker!"

"The hair goes next."

He gave out a banshee cry and ran up the steps, flailing his arms at me. I stepped back. He kept flailing. I kicked him in the chest. He sprawled back in the patio.

A window opened in an apartment above. A woman leaned out. "You're no kind of good," she said, strangely.

Soren was in a heap on the ground. I came up to him, leaned down. He was crying. I put an arm around him.

"Soren," I said. He kept on crying.

I stood. I looked up at the woman in her window.

"You're right," I said and headed for my Plymouth. I had to get home to my family.

How many times did I drive that Plymouth over the Brooklyn Bridge as the sun was threatening dawn, catching the highest cables with first light. All that early world seemed bleary and flat to me, washed by guilt and fear.

What was I doing? Driving this bridge after a night of Soren. Creeping into bed beside my sleeping wife who turns and lays an arm across my chest.

How did I describe this to myself? Oh yes.

Free form.

Why Not, Young Man, Go West

Stanley Schneider asked me down to his office on the 11th floor. He told me to cancel my lunch plans. He'd have sandwiches sent in.

This was new. Coffee was usually all he could squeeze in between important large-table meetings where Stanley sat, waiting his time, watching his Indian chief father, calculating how much longer Leo Jaffe would muck things up, looking around at our baggy-suited heads of publicity and sales and wondering why we were not as hip as, say, the Mirish Brothers, or United Artist.

Stanley was on the phone as I came in. He waved at me to sit. The secretary came in with box lunches. She put one on the coffee table before me, the other on Stanley's desk. While yammering on the phone, he gestured for me to go ahead and start.

The phone conversation went on. Stanley gave me a guilty look. He lifted an African primitive statuette from his desk, over a foot tall, a man's figure carved out of a dark hard wood. From a distance you didn't see the man. It looked like a phallus, the man's head the head of a penis. Impatient with the call which I could tell from clues was London calling, Stanley placed the base of the statuette on his fly. With an impish look at me, he started stroking the phallus. Jerking it off. He thought it was cute.

I went into panic mode. Had someone leaked that I was a closeted gay married man? Or worse, had someone leaked that information and Stanley was flirting with me? Impossible.

He at last hung up. He opened his lunch box and made some joke about the deli not having mayonnaise and baloney for a big shaggitz like me.

"Forget it," I assured him. "I'm converted to pastrami."

Stanley laughed. "Leo tells me he's thinking about making you an honorary Jew."

"I'll have to thank him."

Stanley ignored that. He leaned his elbows on his desk and gave me a serious look. "You know Frankovich."

"You mean Mike Frankovich?"

"What the fuck Frankovich do I know, yes, yes, M.J.Frankovich."

"Well, I saw him at the opening here of Lawrence and we shook hands but everyone was talking, who knows?"

"Frankovich the head of our European operation. Soon not to be."

I sat up straight. "He's being fired?"

"He's taking over the Studio out in Hollywood."

"When's this?"

"First day of next year, 1964, January 2 or whatever the first day is."

"That's great. You like him don't you?"

"Yes, I like him don't I," Stanley said flatly. He sounded ironic, unusual for Stanley. "Oh well," he said and swiveled in his chair to look across at the St.Regis Hotel. He picked up the statuette and fiddled with it.

"You ever been to California?" he asked.

"I guess you'd say. I was born there."

"Ah," said Stanley as though this was important.

"Can't say I really lived there much, Dad was Navy and we were always being transferred to a new Navy base. They tend to look alike."

Stanley swiveled back to look at me.

"How'd you like to go to California?"

"For what?"

"I know you're smarter than that, go to work for Frankovich."

"I don't know, leave New York?"

"What's so fucking great about New York."

I took a toothpick to some pastrami in my teeth. It gave me time to think. "Actually, New York is getting sort of heavy at the moment."

"Mike asked Leo for a suggestion and Leo of course asked me and I said I had the answer in my back pocket. Gerry Ayres."

"I never realized that, I'm in your back pocket."

"Mike's gonna need an executive assistant."

"Am I qualified?"

"Sure, you seen the idiots running the place now? Think about it."

I nodded vigorously. I stood. I turned for the door and as in every movie I ever saw, I turned back for an extra line as I reached the door.

"Is there anything special I need to know?"

Stanley smiled like a cat with bird in mouth. "Yeah, don't forget your old pals."

I got the message; I think I got the message. I was Stanley's man. He would have his own man in the studio. No more going through the suits at the long table.

I went into the stairwell since of course the Columbia elevators were too small for me. I climbed a few flights and then stopped. A thought blocked my way.

Stanley stroking that phallus, he was secretly gay. It wasn't about my qualifications because I didn't have any. Stanley was in love with me.

Wrong, wrong and wrong. But the alternative was to think I deserved the promotion.

Madeline wouldn't like that.

Crosstown Mail

Dear Gerry,

What a man you are, the way you resist me! I'd like to take your nuts in one hand and squeeze and watch the sparks fly. That's what I do when I rush after you and shovel words out of your mouth. My hand-wringing desperate sentimentality! But I know its exact value whether you do or not – you wouldn't know what a man is if one dropped his pants right in front of you on the street.

You have treated me like this before – the only difference is that "master race" bit with the car – slamming up and flying away leaving your witless defiler flung on the pavement. I'm pretty ferocious when I get like that. Deny me the small comfort of sitting next to you in your marvelous machine and I see red. Maybe I should get one, too, and push you over an embankment. But forget it – I know what you're doing. I know now what I must do.

Soren

Dearest Lunatic,

I run to you always as to familiar chaos, the embrace of insanity, the flirtation with death.. But now it's time I sit. Find some light. Burn in that light.

Gerry

Gerry –

Since you threw acid in my face I've been able to live on my new face alone. My life, the movie version of your passion, is on its third reel.

You've given me the pitch, now give me a revival. Let's forget my old face, my lovely rival. My mask changes with the cue of your passions. So you see you disfigured a chameleon.

Soren

Soren, before you paste on a new face, here's what I think about the old one:

    my kiss is blue
    my passions without color, love,
    my thoughts a blank sheet
    on which, as metaphor would have it,
    you could inscribe your fancy -
    but I fool myself.
    too quickly that sheet fills up
    with fancies quite my own:
    your hips in quarter turn,
    your waist thickly between my hands,
    the gentle trace
    from kneecap to thigh -
    these and more
    undo my metaphor
    and I am held
    where fancies wage chromatic argument
    where colors blaze together,
    garish
    seared
    and most unblue.

    Gerry

G -

When I enter the San Remo and you tuck tail and run out the back door that is acid and my face melts. If you go places where I go, I will speak to you.

I write to you from a prison... my only escape from this prison is death... both our deaths.. fantasy has failed, madness has failed, love has failed... I didn't know these before they failed any more than I know death now. Innocence was like another heart, it was born with me and the one that pumps blood, but it failed. I would like to transform this despair, make it mine, make you despair on my account.

Soren

Okay,

no more letters, not for now, I don't like pushing you back into a crowd of gawkers at the Bleecker Tavern and see you sprawl among them with girlish screams - it caused that heart you don't think exists to break - I don't want to waken you and have you sail your poems like paper gliders over my wall. They go so much higher than mine and brand me again your inferior.

Your humble inferior
Gerry

Don't tell me please what you were doing down on your heathen knees at that bar? Groveling? Hoping those airy sylphs would pop their glove-tight pants with excitement of you? No, don't tell me.

Soren

Dear Soren nee Frank,

If you had taken a moment before your mouth blew out those bad head winds and obscured your view, you would have seen why I was on my knees. I was showing off my new toy - a metal whale out of whose opened mouth you pull a small fish and since it is attached to the whale by a string even when you place it far away the whale will race after it and swallow it whole. You know about swallowing whole. You have tried it on me.

Your humble victim,
Geraldo

I told you keep the tabloid blather to yourself. To me you are a stranger I love a magnificent physical stranger like a body of water I cannot cross, like roots growing deep and to the surface of the ground that I trip over running or kick in preoccupation or sit on never sensing if it moves or whether it is dry as it seems, or whether it's diseased in any way or whether it's got to go down again sometime to do its work, never caring because never knowing, or a digging dog moving, moving in my tempo, with different senses, different reasons, valueless and contemplative, moving and breathing with lungs and a tail moving and twitching eyes always looking very close to the ground and a prick that comes out of fur red as freshly killed meat and moist and throbbing with its own intentions.

the name is Soren

You should call yourself Soren Name like Billy Linich calling himself Billy Name, with the same degree of authenticity. I'm back to writing the poetry you hate and the wife you claim to love, whatever that means.

G.

Dear Gerry, I never hate your poetry. I love supporting your work – safe in the knowledge how much of you is created by my need. I have created you but you cannot protect me – but if I am not your wife, I am certainly your child. Until you push me out. Then I'm an orphan, ever a man alone lovelorn and lost in all the ways men can be by women or other men – but I'm your child and I cannot grow without you. What if you were lost by accident? The only way you could be you or be me is to do away with myself or hurt you so terribly you wouldn't know who we were (and that's possible).

Okay, time out. No more threats. Scare me enough and Anne will call the police. She can always tell when I am scared. This is a serious threat from my side.

    G.

Change, darling boy, or change me. Make me grow up in your affections or kill me. Pound yourself out of me. Be fire. Burn me. Burn after that in little ways all the rest of my life – on candles and matches and in fits of anguished nostalgia in street fires, put out after a few hours of fighting with ladders & axes. You could burn me for good. Now you just consume me as fuel and I'm split down the middle.

    Soren

I have changed enough, at least for this season and if you want thanks for the job, then consider it sent. But work is done. Crews have been sent home. Stop the letters. They are overheating my box as in mail box. Please.

Gerry

Darling boy, I call you darling boy again. I have taken the drug you despise for four days now and suffer from the most terrible inertia. I have had my coat on ready to go out a few times then have had to hear the last movement of the C# Min Quartet over & over again sometimes putting the needle on the movement before last sometimes just before the coda. As if it were telling me a story over a transatlantic call that I could barely make out but knew from the few words I got that it would decide what I would do tomorrow and the next day and perhaps portendingly, forever after that.

What would happen if I could lace magic into your food, would that defeat Anne's pragmatism? Would it at last send you into freedom over the cliff you fear. Any magic outside the life you two live would be improvement. What if I gave this drug to G to take, would Anne take some too, and then they'd relate to each other in some proper way – which seems not to be in any way imaginable under the bonds of marriage.

There's more to life than producing children.

If I'm giving my life for love, I think sometimes I should take other lives to join me in the journey.

Soren

And then this from Soren. It did not come in the mail. It was written with what seemed the stub of a pencil and slipped under our door in Brooklyn.

alone you, come out
for yet I control you
as good at home but better still
outside the door
why such a fret you hiding
shamelessly
for your dumb, unblemished
hair.

somewhere a place for us
Sondheim, poet
a boy like that
he kill your brother
poet, Sondheim

As night came on and we looked out into the streets to see if Soren, as Sondheim had said, was down the street around the corner. We left dishes in the sink and bundled our children into the '52 Plymouth and sped down the coast to Florida to spend time with my parents. Even though it involved dreaded days of silent tensions of family, Anne and I thought it better to be there in a city where Soren wasn't.

Safer, certainly.

We had discovered he was insane, a tardy discovery perhaps since our standards were so soft. You had to be really nuts to qualify.

Soren was really nuts.

Escape from New York

"Actually, New York is getting sort of heavy at the moment," I had said to Stanley Schneider and didn't realize I meant it until I said it.

It wasn't just Soren and his psycho threats that made us get up and leave the wieners half-cooked on the stove, it was also my deepening intoxication with the Welsh wizard, Dennis Selby. I believe, but can't prove, that Dennis was part motive for me to leave New York in 1963.

Obviously, the greater motive was the offer to go to Hollywood and work for the new chief of Columbia Studios. Either way, I was ready to go.

I was surprised by two events – one a non-event – after I left the humid dream of Florida behind and returned to Brooklyn.

I was surprised to meet Mike Frankovich. I was surprised not to meet, so to speak, Soren.

First Soren.

Soren was in jail. As we might have known, he had come after us. Or at least tried to. I can only imagine how Bickings and Madeline would have responded answering the door to him.

Our departure kicked him a level higher on the loony scale and he stole an adding machine from the Living Theatre. The reason was obvious: he needed financing for his trip south. He took the machine to a pawn shop. The owner of the shop, a treacherous man according to Soren, told him to leave the machine and come back next day and he'd have a figure for him. A money figure.

Stupidly, Soren came back. A detective was waiting for him. He was arrested and put into the Tombs.

The police called Julian Beck, the founder and soul of the Living

Theatre, to tell him that they had recovered his machine. They had the thief incarcerated. The thief insists that he is a friend of Julian Beck's and begs that he come down and bail him out.

Who is this thief? Frank Hanson. Beck rightly said he'd never heard of him and is not about to come down and bail him out.

Another call came from the police. At the crazed insistence of the thief, they agreed to make one more call. He wanted Beck to be told that he knew him by his nick name, Serkin or something. Soren? Something like that.

Soren was jail wise enough to know that giving a false name could get him into serious trouble. How did he know that? Dale Joe had told me that he learned his ways from his papa who was a conman. Like father, our Soren.

Julian Beck came down to the jail house and informed the detectives that he was a pacifist and anarchist and was not about to press charges against his friend, Soren.

That presented a problem. The detectives told him if he, Beck, pressed charges, Hansen would be arrested for a misdemeanor. If Beck refused then the detective who made the arrest would press charges and the thieving Hansen would end with a felony indictment and much jail time.

This irritated Julian the true believer and he reprimanded the police. And refused. Only when he caught up with Soren himself and heard his pleas did he give in.

Against his religion, he pressed charges. But when called to appear in court where Soren's fate was to be decided, Beck in loose shirt and bald on top with a shaggy skirt of hippie hair surrounding it, stood tall which is difficult in sandals and lectured the court on the corruption of the American justice system.

Fortunately for Soren, the judge didn't have time for all this and gave Soren probation and a fine.

A fine in this case was not fine. Soren was out and his allies – or rather, those circling jackals who didn't want to miss out on an event to talk about – threw a bail raising party for Soren. The hostesses were the twin witches, Malko Safro and Dorothy Podber. They knew better than to invite me.

The cake event, so to speak, of the party was presenting Soren with a postal money order to cover his fine. He would soon be a free man to walk the streets, let the streets beware. He told Malka he was going to the post office himself and would do them a favor by mailing off the check.

Oh didn't they know our Soren? Or were they too drugged to think it through. Soren took the money order to the post office, claimed to be the buyer of the check and asked to cash it in. They complied.

The courts didn't get their money. But Soren got drugs. And some more jail time. I did not see Soren for some time.

A Bad Penny

Decades later, in the years of constant dying, the plague, my marriage long behind me, my lover recently dead of AIDS, I was startled to run into Soren outside LACMA, Los Angeles's attempt at having a first class museum.

The last I had seen of Soren was mid-seventies. He had popped up in Hollywood and dropped in on me and Anne with a loud young man appropriately named Lance Loud. They invited themselves to stay a few days until they got into tugging matches with my children over the cereal box. Or until Anne heard they were borrowing money from the kids.

Anne went to the door, held it open, and they got the idea. Lance wrapped himself in a table cloth he had just bought in a thrift shop and followed Soren out the door to that adventure called living on the fringe.

These many years later, on the cusp of the 90s, I was startled to see Soren coming up the walk. He seemed worn. He was toting a string bag through which I could see oranges and Kierkegaard and perhaps a sock or two.

He had dyed his hair orange.

He smiled and spoke as though we had been in the middle of a conversation.

"You still have all your teeth?"

I was taken back since I was only in my wee-fifties and prided myself in my yoga body and my periodontically up-to-date teeth. I cherished the friends who said how young I looked for my age and carefully acted as though I hadn't heard them.

Soren pulled back one cheek to reveal where a few teeth were being held in place with masking tape. The years of amphetamines had come to collect on their debt. The tape hung loose.

He told me he was a book seller. At a lunch later that week at the French Market, an amiable coffee house serving gay men and Jewish widows, I heard what he meant. He took a city bus which no one I knew ever did to a downtown used book store in which he had talent to spot a choice item. He bought it and spent the rest of the day taking a different series of buses down to Long Beach where a dealer would buy his find. He netted about fifty bucks a day. On that he ate and paid for the night in a hustler motel in West Hollywood run by a Japanese war bride and her cross-dressing son.

If he had a worry, he didn't express it. He was living among his people, the bus and street people, the young and bizarre who had devised their own presentations of what it meant to be young, bizarre and sexy. He had survived for decades as tutor to one bad boy after another.

One night the drag queens partied late and Soren called the police. By morning, Soren was asked to leave the motel. I had to go over, pay off his bill and gather his few items. A worn book or two, socks that should have been thrown out. The only title that comes to mind was The Heart is a Lonely Hunter.

I wondered for a flash whether Soren when I saw him was coming out of the hospital for himself, whether he was there for treatment of his own. He didn't say. He was in a hurry to catch a bus. I stuffed my number in his string bag.

Within a week I was in the AIDS ward at UCLA. Soren had left word on my morning machine that he was there. He said he'd leave me a number but this wasn't a hotel.

As I approached his bed, he was smiling, not shaken it seems by the death crawling over him. I asked him how long he had been there, occupying this bed in this long line of men lying in theirs.

He had a gift for me. He was Catholic (that came as news) and the hospital sent a nun to help him through God's door. One of the sisters pulled a long string from the terry cloth robe the hospital had provided. With it she macraméd a rosary, white string, tightly crafted, a remarkable piece.

It hangs now from the bulletin board above my work table. It is still remarkable.

I went back to my house in the hills. I pulled my hound George up on my lap and stroked his belly. He tolerated it briefly then jumped down to find his ball.

Soren was soon gone. He had lived a life of brilliant but never completed writing. He teased me with the information that he had an aunt out somewhere in the desert and he left with her a suitcase holding his life's story. He refused to tell me who she was or where she was. He had sacrificed his all for the pursuit and desire of bad boys, content as long as he had an orange and a book of Kierkegaard and a room for the night. This shriveled man was one of the heroes of my early years. And now about to become one of the truly unique and forgotten.

I received a form letter from the county coroner. I was surprised to learn Soren had listed me as next of kin. I was being asked to come take his ashes or he would be buried in potters' field.

That didn't take much thought. Soren would be mixed in with the common folk, the bizarre and yet original folk with whom he rode the bus, all of whom wore some improvised costume of love. Or was it sex?

His people.

The New Boss

I was to meet at last the powerhouse executive who ran our European operations, Michael J.Frankovich. While the Hollywood studio was churning out mostly low-voltage product since the death of the founder of Columbia, Harry Cohn, over in Europe Mike had just finished holding Sam Spiegel's hand and kissing David Lean's nether parts and overseeing the production of <u>Lawrence of Arabia</u>. That, students, was as near to a perfect over the center fence home run as any film can be.

What I loved most about it, if anyone is holding onto their breath to hear, is that it was not just an epic but it was motivated by the quirky pathology of a baffling and thrilling hero. A sort of insanity changed the course of history and that portrait of the man was as important as the guns and camels and warfare included in the film. Yes, Lean is what they do and should call a genius, but my vote always goes for the writer. In this case, Robert Bolt. It is his creation.

I was shown into an eleventh floor office where Mike Frankovich was involved in reading through papers that were obviously important because he held them up before his face and removed his English pipe and invisibly underlined important information with the stem of his pipe. He looked up at me, motioned for me to sit.

I did. And I watched him. I knew that he had been a football star at UCLA and had been all-league or all-star something. I knew also that he had married a woman a little older than he but way above him in celebrity, the English actress Binnie Barnes who is one of the many reasons I am an Anglophile. When they married, Mike was hustling to put together some small pictures in Europe. Binnie was starring in classics.

As a football star, he was a large man. He seemed to have a broken nose or maybe that was genetic, but it gave his long face a menacing look. Mike enjoyed menacing.

He threw the papers down on the desk. He put a thumb into his pipe to tamp down the tobacco.

"You're from Yale, is that right?"

"I went to Yale, yes," I replied. It was my well-rehearsed answer. I never claimed to have graduated. In the fifties and sixties, there were no Ivy Leaguers in Hollywood (now it is infested with them) so no one was likely to say oh what was your residential college or what was your secret society or did you know..?

I didn't get the idea until I actually arrived at Columbia's studios that it was run by many ex-cloak and suiters who were suspicious of bright college boys. Many of the backlot department heads reminded me of the salesmen at the zipper factory. Competent by all means, but not polished.

Mike re-lit his pipe, stood, showing off his smart English tailoring (Binnie had been a good influence) came to me and handed me a script.

"I'm going off to Bangkok to drop in on Richard Brooks."

"Yes, sir, I know, <u>Lord Jim</u>."

He looked at me with a small challenge of suspicion.

"You like it?"

"Yes, of course, it's a classic."

He wasn't sure that was what he wanted to hear. I put my hand out to take the script but he held onto his side of it.

"If Richard hears I gave it to you, he'll have both our nuts."

"Well, I value mine," I answered. He gave me another suspicious look. He didn't laugh. It was the first indication that Mike might not fit into the classification of Jewish uncles who ran Hollywood studios. Turns out he was not Jewish as so many thought. He was a Serbian. Which explains his lack of humor. He laughed only at his own jokes and none of them were funny. One of my Jewish uncles would have had a funny response to my admitting a closeness to my balls.

"Send me your read on this," he said and let go of the script.

"Where do I send it?"

Mike never answered questions he didn't ask. He sat back in his chair. He swiveled to look out the window. He spoke away from me.

"You have any questions?"

"I guess not, no sir, you know, I mean I guess you mean you want me to come out there?"

He swiveled around. He put his elbows on the desk, leaned forward and gave me one of his important looks.

"Stanley's handling everything," he answered.

He put the pipe back in his mouth and picked up another pile of papers. He shuffled through them. It took a few moments for me to realize our meeting was over. I stood.

"Thank you, sir."

He didn't look up. I left.

LADY DAY

There wasn't much for me to do in my office, waiting for Hollywood's siren call. I went home to Brooklyn where I could listen endlessly to Billie Holliday and drink, also endlessly. She was my greatest solace, the patron saint of self-pity. If I suffered so often for failure in love (I gave it a lot of tries) it was somehow justified by what Billie had to say. The blues are a failure of love. I remember her voice was gravelly with age. "I get along without you very well, of course I do, except when soft rains fall, and I recall the shelter of your arms.."

That's irony, right Lady? You can't get along without us, how were we to survive without you? Never.

I was in my office on the top floor of 711 Fifth. The radio was playing I Wanna Hold Your Hand by a new group from England. They were proving such a hit that word was they were heading for New York.

I was surprised to see Dennis Selby walk through the door. He was quiet, as was his habit. He sat and I chattered on about Soren and his jail house blues. I took another look at Dennis. He wasn't listening. He looked, as he later described it, that he had "gone green."

Dennis's lover had committed suicide. Dennis had just left his apartment where the police were taking the body off to the morgue.

As I got the story, Dennis had come in and discovered his dead lover the night before, his sliced wrist in a bucket of water to avoid coagulation. Dennis sat in the apartment for the night and much of the next day, smoking, contemplating the corpse on the floor, sorting his memories, before calling those who take away such things.

His lover was a hustler, drug partner of Dennis, with the nomme de guerre of Erik Bruhn, a name borrowed from the beautiful Danish ballet star who was a celebrity at the time, especially in the gay world. Dennis's Erik did not live to see his idol die young, age 57, in Toronto, of what was said to be lung cancer. That was 1986, a time when it was difficult to list AIDS as the cause of death.

He was buried in an unmarked grave near his hometown in Denmark.

Why compare a street hustler in New York, beauty though he was, to a man considered the greatest male dancer of his time? One died with his sliced wrist in a bucket. The other was put out of sight in an unmarked grave . Both died gay men under a cloud of shame.

Exuent All

There was a handicapped lady who worked in one of the offices in that warren on the top floor of 711 Fifth. As I went to my own office I often saw her making her difficult way on crutches from the elevator to her work. I smiled, hoping I wasn't seeming patronizing. She never smiled back, but nodded gravely.

On November 22, 1963, mid-afternoon, the door slammed open. I looked up. It was the handicapped lady, so distraught she had forgotten her crutches. She grabbed either jamb for support and screamed in at us.

"They shot the president."

Crazed as a Delphic oracle, she had visited us with tragic news. She disappeared from the door.

But not from memory.

New York had become a land of death for me. If this was reality, I needed out. I needed to go to a place where dreams were manufactured.

I walked into v.p. Stanley Schneider's office and said, "What should I do? This guy says he wants me to work for him but I can't get him on the phone."

"He's in Bangkok with Richard Brooks."

"I understand but he didn't say when he's —"

"You want my advice? Go on. Get out of here. Go to Hollywood."

I went to Hollywood.